Phantom Armies of the Night

"Claude Lecouteux marshals what must be a virtually complete recounting of stories from throughout Europe involving nocturnal sightings of the Army of the Dead, also known as the Wild Hunt, and traces their thematic origins from pre-Christian times through the filter of the medieval church. His primary sources are exhaustive, ranging from the medieval period to 20th-century accounts by various authors along with church records and folktales. His secondary sources draw extensively on scholarship, particularly from France and Germany. The connection of the figure now known as Harlequin and other figures to rites for the dead is particularly well presented. The Wild Hunt was clearly associated with the spirits of the dead but also with fertility, fecundity, and certain times of the year. Lecouteux explores these and many more aspects of a civilization that both lies behind us and is in faint form still present."

JAMES E. CATHEY,
PROFESSOR OF GERMAN AND SCANDINAVIAN STUDIES,
UNIVERSITY OF MASSACHUSETTS AT AMHERST

"One of the most frightening and persistent visions recorded throughout Indo-European history, legend, and folklore is the spectral array of the Wild Hunt. Claude Lecouteux's brilliant scholarly detective work results in the definitive study of these ghastly processions that have haunted the night skies of Europe for millennia. *Phantom Armies of the Night* is teeming with tales that will fascinate, delight, and terrify—often all at once.

MICHAEL MOYNIHAN,
AUTHOR OF *LORDS OF CHAOS:
THE BLOODY RISE OF THE SATANIC METAL UNDERGROUND*
AND TRANSLATOR OF *BARBARIAN RITES*

"This is an exciting and absorbing study of a form of folk mythology that has spanned Europe for more than a thousand years. Lecouteux provides both a mass of valuable information and a viable working hypothesis of explanation."

RONALD HUTTON,
PROFESSOR OF HISTORY,
UNIVERSITY OF BRISTOL, ENGLAND

Phantom Armies of the Night

The Wild Hunt and Ghostly Processions of the Undead

Claude Lecouteux

Translated by Jon E. Graham

Inner Traditions

Rochester, Vermont • Toronto, Canada

Inner Traditions
One Park Street
Rochester, Vermont 05767
www.InnerTraditions.com

SUSTAINABLE FORESTRY INITIATIVE
Certified Sourcing
www.sfiprogram.org
SFI-00854

Text stock is SFI certified

Originally published in French under the title *Chasses fantastiques et cohorts de la nuit au moyen age* by Éditions Imago, 25 rue Beaurepaire, 75010 Paris
First U.S. edition published in 2011 by Inner Traditions

Library of Congress Cataloging-in-Publication Data
Lecouteux, Claude.
 [Chasses fantastiques et cohortes de la nuit au Moyen Age. English]
 Phantom armies of the night : the wild hunt and the ghostly processions of the undead / Claude Lecouteux ; translated by Jon E. Graham.—1st U.S. ed.
  p. cm.
 Includes bibliographical references (p.   ) and index.
 ISBN 978-1-59477-436-2 (pbk.) — ISBN 978-1-59477-806-3 (ebook)
 1. Wild huntsman (Tale) I. Title.
 GR75.W55L4313 2011
 398.22—dc23

2011022863

Printed and bound in the United States by Lake Book Manufacturing
The text paper is SFI certified. The Sustainable Forestry Initiative® program promotes sustainable forest management.

10 9 8 7 6 5 4 3 2 1

Text design by Virginia Scott Bowman and layout by Priscilla Baker
This book was typeset in Garamond Premier Pro with Tagliente, Jenson Pro, and Franklin Gothic used as display typefaces

Inner Traditions wishes to express its appreciation for assistance given by the government of France through the National Book Office of the Ministère de la Culture in the preparation of this translation.

Nous tenons à exprimer nos plus vifs remerciements au gouvernement de la France et le ministère de la Culture, Centre National du Livre, pour leur concours dans le préparation de la traduction de cet ouvrage.

Contents

Acknowledgments

I begin by expressing my gratitude to all those who have helped me in this investigation by providing many hard-to-find documents: Virginie Amilien (Oslo), Anne-Hélène Delavigne (Copenhagen, Auffargis), Baukje Finet-Van der Schaaf (Metz), Diane Tridoux (Bibliothèque nationale de France), Jacques Berlioz (CNRS), François Delpech (CNRS), Leander Petzold (Innsbruck), Lutz Röhrich (Freiburg-im-Breisgau), Luciano Rossi (Zurich), and Herfried Vögel (Munich).

I also thank †Jean Carles (Clermont-Ferrand), Ronald Grambo (Konigsvinger), †Felix Karlinger (Kritzendorf), and Philippe Walter (Grenoble), with whom I have long discussed this matter and who also provided me with numerous bibliographical references.

Without this invaluable support, this investigation, which has lasted for time beyond measure, would not have been brought to a successful conclusion.

---

† indicates that the person is deceased.

Introduction

*[V]elim scire, esse phantasmata et habere propriam
figuram numenque aliquod putes.**

PLINY THE YOUNGER

Once upon a time there was a phenomenon that fueled local gossip
continuously: During the long winter nights a strange and unidentified
troop could be heard passing outside, over the land or through the air.
Anyone caught by surprise in the open fields or depths of the woods
saw a bizarre procession of foot soldiers and knights, some covered in
blood and others carrying their heads beneath their arms.... This was
the Wild or Infernal Hunt, the host of the damned, a theme that still
inspires poets, writers, and painters.[1]

This throng has been known for centuries, and the first accounts that
mention it have been lost in the depths of time. Myth or legend, it represents a belief that has deep roots in the mentality of Indo-European peoples; it has assumed a thousand and one forms, and the multiple nature
of its variations obviously indicates that it is not some fossilized fact but a
still-living tradition. Blending paganism and Christianity, the narratives
that have come down to us form an enormous body of knowledge that is
inextricably tangled and fraught with controversy. These stories are characterized by an advanced syncretism and the synthesis of information

---

*I am therefore desirous to know whether you believe in the existence of ghosts and if
they have any real form and supernatural power.

1

from a wide variety of traditions. Their opaque nature is so formidable that it has formed an obstacle to any satisfactory decoding by researchers up to the present. Tackling this complex of myths and legends means either running the risk of falling back into old errors or rushing headlong into the wall of received opinion, because everyone has his or her own opinion on the subject, even if he or she has not studied the Hunt's ramifications. For this reason no progress toward its understanding has been truly visible for the past fifty years. In short, we find ourselves confronted by the final equation of a problem whose wording must be recast.

After patiently gathering all the pieces of this case file, then analyzing and comparing them, I am now prepared to draw up a balance sheet. This book is motivated by one ambition: to present the facts and suggest an interpretation without seeking to conceal the exact portion of hypothesis upon which each of my findings is based. I therefore start with a simple definition that subsequently becomes more explicit: the Wild Hunt is a band of the dead whose passage over the earth* at certain times of the year is accompanied by diverse phenomena. Beyond these elements, all else varies: the makeup of the troop; the appearance of its members; the presence or absence of animals; noise or silence; the existence of a male or female leader who, depending on the country and the region, bears different names—the devil, Wode, Mother Hulda, Dame Holle, Percht, Hennequin, and more.

One of the difficulties of the investigation arises from the existence of numerous nightly hosts, which became confused in people's minds, merging before separating anew, and each time bequeathing one or more elements to the narratives to which they were temporarily connected. This confusion is due to the evident kinship shared by all the different bands, but it also results from the medieval church that hastily cast as anathema anything that gave off a whiff of paganism.

---

*Walter von Wartburg's definition—the Mesnie Hellequin is a "procession of wicked ghosts who fly through the air at night"—is wrong in two respects: the Hunt involves not incorporeal ghosts but revenants who possess actual bodies, and it travels more often over the ground than through the air. I must add that wickedness is not a pertinent criterion of identification.

The Wild Hunt falls under the heading of what we call folk mythology—that is, a wide array of beliefs much older than Christianity. These beliefs gave structure to daily life, possessed their own consistency, and formed an elaborate system for interpreting the world (*Weltanschauung*). Like all human creations, they have been so extensively subjected to the erosion of time and memory, to historical evolution, and to attacks from the true faith that today we find ourselves holding a palimpsest. The *interpretatio christiana* overlays all the ancient elements. It has rethought them, reorganized them, and integrated them, whenever possible, into the dogma of the dominant religion—and whenever it could not, it eliminated them. This is why the Wild Hunt's consistency has vanished. All we have are scattered fragments, actual puzzle pieces that we must put together with nothing to guide our efforts. We are confronted here with a fantastic and mysterious—and perplexing—world. We must try to gather the largest number of elements before trying to connect them. More important, we must refrain from throwing away those elements that are too disturbing—which, unfortunately, is an attitude that is far too frequent among many researchers who strive to make the texts say what these men and women already believe to be the truth.

Once we have set foot upon the shores of folk mythology, we must remain conscious that its banks are shifting and ever changing—and are deceptive, because the accounts are never firsthand. They usually have gone through three stages of transmission: first, the accounts are oral. Next, they are written down, at which point they find their way back into the oral tradition. The medieval church invented nothing. It picked up preexisting elements so that it could remodel them. It therefore created its own mythology from an older substratum, and this mythology soon fell into the public domain, where it continued to nourish beliefs and legends. These beliefs and legends either partially conserved the Christian message or dumped it in order to wrest back the original meaning. Furthermore, what might appear to be a folk belief could very well have emerged from scriptures, scholarly literature, and even sermons.

Here there exists an incontrovertible paradox: in order to destroy these beliefs, the church publicized them, mainly in sermons intended to instruct the faithful. In doing so, the church's indoctrination and preaching sometimes reactivated moribund elements by implanting others that were nonnative. This action helped to spread these elements and gave them a firm foothold in reality. As it happens, the bulk of the accounts at our disposal are from clerics. These narratives contain many distortions that veil the true nature of what was recorded. We must therefore set aside the interpretations suggested by the authors of these accounts and what they sought to impose upon their readers, and stick only to the facts—in short, we must accept nothing but that which has been verified and double-checked.

This book is the culmination of my research in the beliefs and legends connected to death, the afterlife, and that which, for the sake of

Oskoreia, engraving by Hans Gerhard Sörenson for T. A. Bringsværd's *Phantoms and Fairies from Norwegian Folk Lore* (Oslo: Johan Grundt, 1970)

convenience, we might call the soul. These legends and beliefs form an unrecognized and heterodox anthology, which made it necessary for me first to focus my study on phantoms and revenants. This allowed me to discover the existence of the Double (alter ego) and brings me here to the Wild Hunt. As in my earlier investigations, I strive to let our witnesses—the texts—speak for themselves, so that the reader may form his or her own opinion before becoming acquainted with my deductions.

We begin with a look at the various hosts that roam the night and what lies hidden beneath them. Next, we study the many facets and avatars of the Wild Hunt during the Middle Ages and pursue this research into more recent times. We will not discuss similar phenomena among peoples who are removed from Europe—the troop of dead warriors mentioned by Ueda Akinari (1734–1809) in Buppôsô, for example—because their cultures do not really fall into my area of expertise. Such study, I believe, would take us too far astray with adverse consequences for the clarity of this text.

PART ONE

The Hosts of the Night

1
The Good Women Who Roam the Night

Andad de día,
*que la noche es mia.**

Certain nights play host to the passage of all kinds of nocturnal troops. These legions were sometimes composed of the living, led by Diana[1] and Herodias,[2] Satia, and Dame Abonde,[3] or alleged witches whose Doubles had quit their sleeping bodies. Sometimes they gathered the dead,[4] revenants, or damned souls who could find no rest (the Mesnie Hellequin, Oskoreia, Asgardsreia). Finally, demons or the devil in person or his minions could be seen walking or riding in the darkness. On every occasion these figures were associated with a specific kind of activity, and it is worth examining the accounts in detail if we want to avoid the erroneous combinations and confusion that make it so difficult for us to understand these nocturnal throngs. Moreover, this confusion is due not solely to the nineteenth- and twentieth-century researchers but goes all the way back to the Middle Ages.

---

*Away with day,
for the night is mine!

Translation of what the Wild Hunt (Güestia) says in Asturias.

The Journey of the Double

We encounter the first instance of the belief in the Ladies of the Night in a canon attributed to the Council of Ancyra,[5] which met in 314. Yet this canon's first known appearance was in 872, in the capitularies of Charles the Bald. It was picked up anew in 899, in a treatise by Regino, the abbot of Prüm: "This also is not to be omitted, that certain wicked women, turned back to Satan, seduced by demonic illusions and phantasms, believe of themselves and profess to ride upon certain beasts in the nighttime hours with Diana, the goddess of the pagan, or Herodias, and an innumerable multitude of women, and to traverse great spaces of the earth in the silence of the dead of night, and to be subject to her laws as of a Lady, and on fixed nights be called to her service." This text, known as the *Canon Episcopi,* inserted around 1066 by Burchard of Worms in his *Decretum,* offers evidence that the church attacked an allegedly pagan belief that was still vigorous enough to be viewed as dangerous: "Have you believed what many women, turning back to Satan, believe and affirm to be true, as you imagine in the silence of the night when you have gone to bed and your husband lies in your bosom, that while you are in bodily form you can go out by closed doors and are able to cross the spaces of the world with others deceived by the like error and without visible weapons slay persons who have been baptized and redeemed by the blood of Christ."[6]

Burchard records here a belief that is the source of the witches' Sabbath: certain women possess the ability to propel flesh and blood Doubles of themselves to roam for great distances, committing evil deeds, killing people, eating them—placing pieces of wood or straw in the place of their hearts, then reanimating them. He goes on more explicitly: "Have you believed, as certain women are accustomed to believe, to wit that by virtue of other limbs provided you by the devil* you have crossed in the silence of the quiet night through closed doors to fly into

---

*[Christian interpretation of creating a Double. —*Trans.*]

the clouds where you have waged battle on others,* both inflicting and receiving wounds."

These women who roamed the night fought the same battle as the sixteenth-century Benandanti, who performed a third-function ritual.† Here the representatives of good and evil, the fertility and sterility of the land, confront each other. The wicked individuals of one of these bands stole the seeds; the others, working for good, tried to hold the wicked in check. The victory of the "good folk" over the wicked ones made it possible for the coming year to be fruitful.[7]

Alongside the chapters of the *Decretum* that link these women to Satan we find another note on the same subject. It introduces a well-known figure from folk belief who persisted into relatively recent times: Holda, or the Benevolent One. "Have you believed that there is any woman who can do that which some, deceived by the devil, affirm that they must do of necessity or by his command, to wit with a host of devils transformed into the likenesses of women, she who common folly calls Holda, must ride on certain beasts during special nights and be counted as members of the company of demons."[8] Burchard does not understand the phenomenon of a split personality and attributes it to a "necessity" or a "command." In fact, it is a gift, an atavism. According to the beliefs of earlier times, every human being possessed several souls[9]—and, in this instance, the word *soul* means "vital principal." Among these souls there is the external soul, which the ancient Scandinavians called the *hamr* and which Latin texts refer to as *animus* or *spiritus*. This soul is able to quit the body when it is sleeping, is in a coma or a trance, or is afflicted by a serious illness. It can then go about in the form of an animal or human. The clerics were unable to grasp this, observing only

---

*Women.

†[The third-function is a reference to the tripartite division of ancient societies into castes, one of warriors, one of priests, and one of producers, which in the oldest societies were primarily peasants, those who worked the land. Later caste systems, adapting to social evolution, added classes such as the merchant class, but the three-class system persisted even into modern times. France's ancient regime is the best-known example, and it only ended with the French Revolution of the late eighteenth century. —*Trans.*]

that the body was still present before their eyes, and they attributed the stories of people whose Double had rejoined their bodies to a trick of the devil.

The notion of a troop appears in these three extracts from the *Decretum:* the women involved gather together in the night, when they travel across the earth and through the air led by Holda, Diana, or Herodias.

Diana and Herodias

This Diana is certainly not the same as the Roman Diana whose cult, according to Margaret Murray, survived into the Middle Ages.* According to Martin of Braga, she might be the sylvan and rural goddess worshipped by fifth- and sixth-century peasants.[10] In fact, commingled here are Diana of antiquity and Di Ana, a Celtic goddess who is also called Anu. The existence of a god Dianum speaks to this hypothesis. This deity, who was perhaps the Asturian Dianu,[11] no doubt came from Di Anu, who was taken to be a masculine figure.

Herodias is a well-known figure from Christian legend: it was believed that she played an instrumental role in the decapitation of John the Baptist. She is the preeminent anti-Christian. The *Ysengrimus,* twelfth century and attributed to Nivardus, knows her as Pharaildis and explains how she was condemned to travel through the air.

[A]nd the virgin Pharaildis condemned to unjust punishment by a saint . . . Herod was famous because of this child and could have been happy thanks to her, but an unhappy love was also the misfortune of this young woman. This virgin burned to share the bed of John the Baptist, and had vowed to give herself to no other man but he. Her father, having discovered his daughter's passion, became angry, and

---

*I can find no basis for postulating the survival of her worship into the Middle Ages. Furthermore, *Diana vel Herodiade,* which appears in Burchard, indicates that the bishop of Worms attempted to convey a local belief with the help of Roman names. To Burchard, the use of two names customarily served to close in on an autochthonous concept.

he cruelly ordered the innocent saint decapitated. In despair, the young woman asked to see the severed head, and one of the king's servants bore it to her on a platter. She tenderly clasped it between her arms and bathed it in her tears, which she wished to accompany with her kisses. The head fled from her embrace and repelled her by blowing at her, and *she was carried off by the opening made in the roof by the whirlwind* [*illa per impluuium turbine flatantis abit*] exhaled by the saint. Since that time, she has been pursued through the empty reaches of the sky by the anger of St. John the Baptist in the form of his breath, because he dwelled too fixedly upon the past. Dead, he tormented her, and alive, he did not return her love. Yet fate did not let her die entirely: honors sweetened her mourning, and respect softened her punishment. One third of humanity serves this afflicted sovereign who rests upon the oaks and hazel trees during the second half of the night until the final crow of the black cock. Today, her name is Pharaildis. She was formerly known as Herodias.[12]

This legend is also found in Spain, where Herodias was given the same posthumous punishment: *de la dansa aéra á que están condenadas las Herodiadas por la muerte del Bautista* (the aerial dance to which Herodias was condemned for having caused the death of John the Baptist).[13] E. Charbonnier[14] notes that the nocturnal journey of Herodias is reminiscent of witches who ride through the sky. The fact that she is followed by "one third of humanity" (*par hominum meste tertia seruit here,* v. 91) is a detail of Rather of Verona (d. 974) and one we find connected to Dame Abonde in the second part of *The Romance of the Rose,* which Jean de Meung finished around 1280: "Many people's senses deceive them, and they believe they are witches [*estries*] wandering the night with Dame Abonde; and 'they say that one of every three children of this land exhibit this condition and go forth three nights a week, wherever fate takes them,' entering into houses, for neither locks nor bars can stop their passage, and they can enter through a chink or cat hole; their souls can quit their bodies [*se partent des corps les amis*] and they accompany the Good Ladies into other places and into other houses while their bodies remain in bed."[15]

Should we presume that men and children make up the other two-thirds? The presence of the black cock can be explained: the night was then divided into seven parts: *crepusculum, vesperum, conticinium, intempestiva, gallicinium, matutinum,* and *diluculum.* Only the middle of the night (conticinium) was propitious for the magic journey. This was also the most favorable time for apparitions, because it was the time men no longer spoke and the roosters were not yet crowing. Pharaildis/Herodias gathered her companies during the third part of the night, rested during the fourth, and returned the women to their homes at cock's crow. It is common knowledge that the crowing of the cock sends the spirits of the night fleeing. The first warning is given by a white rooster, the second by a red one. By the time the black cock crows, all spirits have vanished.

The *Ysengrimus* therefore tells us, in its distinct fashion, how Herodias becomes one of the leaders of these nightly phalanxes. We should note that a folk tradition (*wulgariter dicunt*) maintains that the head of John the Baptist slew Herodias with its breath.[16]

John of Salisbury (ca. 1115–1180) knew of this rumor spread about Herodias and repeats it in *Polycraticus* (II, 17): "They claim that a *noctiluca* or Herodias or a witch-ruler of the night convokes nocturnal assemblies at which they feast and riot and carry out other rites, where some are punished and others rewarded according to their merits. Moreover, infants are set out for lamias and appear to be cut up into pieces, eaten, and gluttonously stuffed into the witches' stomachs. Then, through the mercy of the witch-ruler, they are returned* to their cradles. Who could be so blind as not to see in all this a pure manifestation of wickedness created by sporting demons? Indeed, it is obvious from this that it is only poor old women and the simpleminded kinds of men who enter into these beliefs."

---

*In one piece.

Here, John of Salisbury lumps together current beliefs on lamia:[17] ogresses who, along with the other Ladies of the Night (Herodiad, Abundia, Satia), devour children. Thanks to William of Auvergne (1180–1249) and Gervase of Tilbury (ca. 1152–1221), we do in fact know that lamia were thought to be styrges that entered houses in the dead of night to feed on little children.[18]

The nocturnal prowling by a certain kind of woman enjoyed wide diffusion by means of the clerical literature for which this kind of woman became almost common place. The intermediary that assured them great publicity was the *Decretum Gratiani,* whose final form essentially took shape around 1142, which fed the decalogues and cat-echetical works throughout the entire Middle Ages before assuming a prominent place in the manuals of the Inquisitors.

The Feast of the Ladies of the Night

Just what did these troops of women do to occupy their time? John of Salisbury has already provided us with some elements of the answer: they feasted.

In his *De universo,* the bishop of Paris, William of Auvergne, indulges in a sharp critique of the pagan rites and beliefs that were widespread in his century, and, of course, he, too, speaks of nocturnal hosts.

> The same is true of the spirit that, under the guise of a woman who, in the company of others, visits homes and services at night. She is named Satia, from *satiety,* and also Dame Abonde, because of the abundance she bestows upon the dwelling places she visits. It is this very kind of spirit that the old women call *the ladies* and in regard to whom they maintain this error to which they alone give credence, even in delusional dreams. They say that these ladies con-sume the food and drink they find in homes without consuming them entirely, nor even reduce their quantity, especially if the dishes

holding food are left uncovered and the containers holding drink are left uncorked when left out for the night. But if they find these containers covered or closed or corked, they will not touch either food or drink, and this is the reason why the ladies abandon these houses to woe and ill fortunes without bestowing either satiety or abundance upon them.[19]

William revisits this theme to scold the foolishness of women with the help of a theme familiar to the clerical mind: "It is our old women who, through lack of wisdom, have, in astonishing fashion, spread this detestable belief that they have maintained and fixed almost ineradicably in the minds of other women. It is especially women whom they have persuaded in the existence of the ladies of the night and their beneficial qualities, as well as of the attribution of great good to the houses said ladies frequent."[20]

The feast of the Ladies of the Night is also vouched for on the eastern side of the Rhine, but the leader of the host here is named Percht or Perchta. Bertold of Regensburg (Ratisbonne) (ca. 1210–1272) violently condemns the beliefs of the Bavarians and commands his flock in a Latin sermon: "You should not believe at all in the people who wander at night [*nahtwaren*] and their fellows, no more than the Benevolent Ones [*hulden*] and the Malevolent Ones [*unhulden*], in fairies [*pilwitzen*], in nightmares [*maren, truten*] of both sexes, in the ladies of the night [*nahtvrouwen*], in nocturnal spirits, or those who travel by riding this or that: they are all demons. Nor should you prepare the table anymore for the blessed ladies [*felices dominae*]."[21]

This last sentence is explained in another sermon: "The foolish peasant women indeed believe that the ladies of the night and nightwalking spirits visit their homes and they set a table for them."[22]

It was around 1350, that this practice was made more precise. An anonymous pamphlet titled *Mirror of Souls,* not to be confused with the work of the same name written by the preacher and Inquisitor Martin of Amberg, finally names the woman who visits these homes: "Sinning also are they who, on the night of Epiphany, leave food and drink upon their table so that all shall smile upon them over the coming year and good luck will grace them in all things . . . Therefore also sinning are they who offer food to Percht and red snails [or shoes] to the Howler [scrat] or to the nightmare."[23]

In German-speaking countries Percht is the equivalent of Abundia and Satia. Their identical nature was clearly established by Thomas von Haselbach (ca. 1420–1464), professor of theology at the University of Vienna, who provided other names for these nocturnal visitors: Habundia, Phinzen, Sack Semper, and Sacria.[24] Phinzen is the personification of Thursday, Sack Semper is a bogeyman, a member of the Christmas processions as well as the personification of Sempertac, which falls eight days following Three Kings Day (Epiphany). The Dominican Johannes Herolt, who died in 1468, incorporated Percht into Diana, and a penitential, inspired in part by Burchard of Worms's *Decretales,* states that Percht and the Parcae (the Fates) were the same.[25] Among the numerous accounts coming out of the later Middle Ages, that of the *Thesaurus pauperum* (1468) merits our attention.

> The second type of superstition is the idolatrous custom of those who leave out vessels filled with food and drink at night intended for the ladies expected to visit, Dame Abundia and Satia, or as the people call her, Fraw Percht or Perchtum, because this lady always comes with her retinue. They leave these out so when they find these dishes holding food and drink in open sight they will later refill them and grant abundance and riches upon the household. Many believe that these ladies led by Fraw Percht will visit their homes during the holy nights between the birth of Jesus and the night of Epiphany. There are many who leave out upon their tables during these night bread, cheese, milk, eggs, wine, water, and foodstuffs of all sorts, as well as spoons, plates, cups, knives, and other similar objects with the visit of Fraw Percht and her troop in mind. Their hope is this lady will find it pleasant there and consequently look

with favor on the prosperity of the household and the conduct of its temporal affairs.[26]

Leaving containers open is clearly a pagan custom, according to the Bible: "And every open vessel, which hath no covering bound on it, is unclean."[27] We can also note that these ladies visited only orderly households.

The historian and writer Johannes Praetorius (1630–1680), who studied at Leipzig University, obtaining the grade of magister, notes: "Diana travels on Christmas night with her furious band of warriors."[28] Later he states that Dame Holle or Holda begins wandering on Christmas, which underscores the identical nature of these two individuals, although the nature of the members in the procession can be quite different.

A Rite of the Third Function

What can we deduce from all these different accounts? First, a troop of women travel through the night and stop at houses for restoration. Second, they are led by a *domina* who bears several names often connected to her duties (Abundia, Satia) or to the date on which she appears: Percht undoubtedly personifies the transfigured night (*giberahta nacht*), Epiphany. The most detailed texts all agree on the date this ritual occurs: between Christmas and Epiphany—that is, within the twelve-day Christmas cycle, when it is said that spirits have free rein to leave the otherworld and wander about the earth, performing various tasks. We will see that the Wild Hunt appears most frequently during this time of the year.

The movement of this host of women was connected to a rite of the third function that falls into the category of omens. If the visitors were satisfied with the food offerings, they would bring prosperity and fertility to the household. Thus taking shape in the background was a calendar-based rite belonging to the mythology of beginnings: whatever happens on this date foreshadowed what would happen over the New Year. This rite accrues greater meaning for us once we know the Romans celebrated it. Setting a table during this time of year was a religious rite connected to ancestor worship, for the dead were considered the dispensers of the fertility of the soil and the fruitfulness of men and beasts. In Rome this table was known as the table of souls or the table of the deceased.[29]

This custom was observed throughout the entire Middle Ages, as the clerical literature testifies. It is mentioned by Césaire of Arles (died 542), St. Boniface (675–754), the pseudo-Augustine (eighth century), Atto de Vercelli (died 960), Yves de Chartres (d. 1040), and Gratien (d. before 1179), and others.[30] The canonists and clerics note that offerings or gifts are placed on the set table (*mensas cum dapibus vel epulis in domibus preparare*). Sometimes the rite is referred to by two words: *mensas ornare*. A Munich manuscript from the Alderspach Monastery alludes to those who "garnish their table for Percht."[31]

It is probable that our medieval authors were inspired directly or indirectly by the Roman custom, but there is no doubt that such a rich flowering of testimonies would not exist if the custom had been completely foreign. If we examine local traditions, we see that traces of similar rites existed throughout the medieval West.

Parallel Mythologies
Fairies and the Dead

In medieval Scandinavia winter, more specifically, Jól (Christmas), the great feast of the dead and the ancestors of the majority of Indo-European peoples, is also the feast of spirits and therefore carries the name sacrifice to the elves (*álfablót*). Elves collectively denoted living beings of the otherworld and, most specifically, good ancestors.[32] The sacrifices performed on a certain date were intended to procure a year of peace and fertility, thus a table was prepared for the invisible guests. Other customs were connected to this rite: Christmas gifts (*jolagjöf*) and the games of Jól (*jolaleikar*), with masquerades, have partially survived into the present. The Celts dedicated the cycle of twelve days at Christmas and after to the Matronae, the mother goddesses, and the Venerable Bede called Christmas the night of the mothers [*modra nect*],[33] with "mothers" designating said goddesses, who were also regarded as the dispensers of fertility and fecundity. We encounter elsewhere the same attitude: mythology of the beginnings and worship of invisible powers for a good year.

The Matronae were quickly incorporated into the goddesses of Fate, into the Parcae, and, by means of etymology, into the dead. One of them was named Morta, according to Varro and Aulus Gellius (*Attic Nights*, III, 10, 16), and they were also quickly identified with midwives as well. It was believed that *parcae* shared the same root as *parere*: "to bring into the world." Successors to the Parcae and the mother goddesses, medieval fairies, inherited their attributes and were in turn mother goddesses, deities of fate, and messengers of death. This feature is found in Melusine, for example, who is also a white lady, a *banshee*.[34] Kin to the good women of the Abundia, Satia, and Percht, but with a much more pronounced ominous nature, the Dises (Dísir) of the ancient Scandinavians were believed to fly through the air in a group. They were often confused with the Norns, the Germanic Parcae, the Valkyries, and the Swan Women. In *The Lay of Volund* (*Volundarkvida*, strophe 1)—Wayland the Smith—their number is not specified:

> *The maidens fly from the south*
> *Through the mirkwood,*
> *Young, all wise,*
> *For deciding destinies.*

The Lay of the Lance, transmitted by *The Saga of Burnt Njal* (chapter 157), relates an event that takes place on the eve of the battle of Clontarf (1014). The Irish king Brian perishes: "A man named Dorrud walked outside and saw twelve people riding together to a women's hut, and then they all disappeared inside. He went up to the hut and looked inside, through a window there, and he saw that there were women there, and that they had set up a loom. Men's heads were used for weights, men's intestines for the weft and warp, a sword for the sword beater, and an arrow for the pin beater."[35]

These women spin death, and when they are done they tear the cloth into pieces, one for each of them. Holding their piece of cloth, they mount their horses and ride away, six to the south and six to the north.

The *Second Lay of Helgi Hundingsbani* (*Helgakvida Hundingsbana II*, in the *Poetic Edda*), says that Högni's daughter, "was a Valkyrie and rode through sea and air."[36] An interesting link is implicitly established between the riding of the Valkyries and the storm: "Helgi assembled a great fleet and went to Frekastein and braved, on peril of their very lives, a violent storm. Then lightning flashed from above and the bolts struck their ships. They saw nine Valkyries riding in the sky and recognized Sigrun among them. The storm then subsided, and they made their way to shore safe and sound." (See prose after strophe 18.)

We can therefore see that entities of all kinds with a direct connection to fate haunted the skies. In contrast with the Latin and German texts, the Scandinavian testimonies do not specify if these troops rode at night except in the *Story of Thidrand and Thorhall* (fourteenth century) passed down to us by the *Flateyarbók*.

> Thidrand organized the feast of Winter Nights* on which a bull had to be sacrificed for the ritual meal. He forbade anyone to leave because this would have been dangerous. But suddenly someone knocked at the door; the noise was repeated twice. Thidrand drew his sword and stepped outside. He saw two troops of nine women, one clad in white, riding white horses [*níu konur allar ljósum klædum ok á hvítum hestum*] arriving from the south, the other clad in black and riding black steeds, coming from the north. Attacked, Thidrand valiantly defended himself, but he was mortally wounded and it was believed that the Dísr had sought revenge on him for

---

*Around October 14.

Figure 1.1. Witches preparing to depart for the Sabbath. We can see already they are en route, riding a billy goat. Hans Baldung Grien, 1510.

being neglected and that they had come to take him as a sacrificial victim.[37]

The absence of Celtic testimonies may surprise us. In fact ancient Ireland, as best we know, does not seem to have experienced this kind of phenomena except for the Sidh Army (*Sluagh Sidhe*), which showed itself to humans when it marched across the lands on Samhain (November 1). The inhabitants of the Sidh (mound) were, according to the texts, ancient gods, fairies, or the dead, conveniently called residents of the otherworld.[38] In Spain, finally, we discover that one of the nightly hosts was called *buena genta,* "the good folk" (Asturias), which should certainly offer comparison to the *bona res* of the thirteenth century.

Demonization

All the traditions I have mentioned, which were condensed and then focused on fairies, were demonized.[39] In the *Malleus Maleficarum*

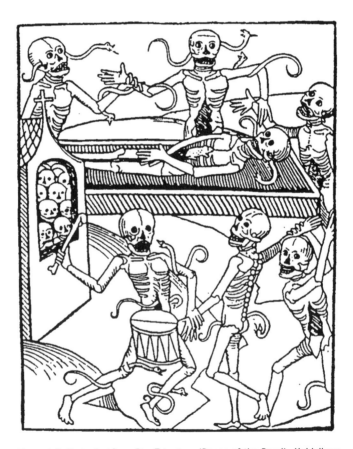

Figure 1.2. Engraving from *Der Totentanz* (Dance of the Dead), Heidelberg, H. Knoblichtzer, verse 1488

(The Hammer of the Witches), printed around 1486 or 1487 in Speyer, the Inquisitors Jacques Springer and Henrich Kramer regard "riding with Diana or Herodias, as roaming with the devil who had adopted this form and name . . . and that an imaginary ride like this occurred when the devil disturbed the spirit of the person enslaved to him by lack of faith in such a way that she believed what took place in dream was physically occurring" (I,1). A little farther (I, 10), the two echo the text of the *Canon Episcopi* and arrange this ride anew in the list of satanic deceits.[40]

Renward Cysat, born in Lucerne in 1545 (d. 1614), offers a valuable testimony in his *Chronicle.*

> It is said that the Good Folk (Sälïge Lütt) and the Furious Army
> (Guottisheer) are made up of souls of people who died violent or
> premature deaths, who must wander the earth until the day that
> fate has fixed for their passing; these folk are friendly and kind, and
> enter the homes of those who speak well of them at night, cook,
> eat, and then leave again, but the amount of food does not dimin-
> ish. There are some who have the folly to think that living men and
> women accompany them on their rounds and share their meals in
> order to gain greater good fortune.[41]

Cysat reports the belief in the Good Ladies and their visit and meal—but combines it with that of night demons (*nachtgespenst*) and the dead. In his *Interpretation of the Gospels* (1571), Johannes Mathesius throws into the same bag all creatures that wander the night: "So who then are all these knocking and noisy spirits, unnatural deceits, Dame Herodias or Mother Hulda, the old Percht with her furious army, the Howlers, the sprites, the trolls, the dwarves, if they aren't demons?"[42]

All the contours have been blurred, the various rudiments have been superimposed or piled one atop another, and different elements from each have been brought together and commingled. Our task is to discover the reason for this disorder.

2

The Phalanxes of Demons

IN ORDER TO ADULTERATE beliefs that had become questionable, the church possessed a kind of matrix within the tradition itself. The demonization process did not emerge ex nihilo but instead was facilitated by beliefs that existed long before the conversion of these regions to Christianity. There was another dangerous, night-roaming troop—one that consisted of demons who were totally free to indulge in their activities from sunset to cockcrow.

A Universal Belief

The belief that night attracted demons and the return of day drove them off was universally widespread. The Hebrews believed that the demons of the desert were particularly active from twilight to cockcrow, which signified the return of light and possessed an apotropaic virtue: it broke spells and sent spirits fleeing. For Christians this belief is illustrated by the story of Peter, who stops denying the truth at the third crow of the cock. In the *Confession of Saint Cyprien*, written around 360–370, the rooster interrupts the Sabbath (*Confes. Cypriani* 13), and Prudentius (348–415) explains it this way in his *Cathemerinon* (I, 37–45):

> *'Tis said that wandering spirits [vagantes daemonas] roam*
> *Abroad beneath the dark's vast dome;*

24

But, when the cock crows, take their flight
Sudden dispersed in sore affright.

For the foul votaries of the night
Abhor the coming of the light,
And shamed before salvation's grace
The hosts of darkness hide their face.[1]

The ancient Greeks recorded the movement of demons. Hippocrates (ca. 460–370 BCE) speaks of terrifying images that emerge during the night through the agency of Hecate, the infernal goddess who rules the crossroads. The Greeks turned to charms and purification rites for protection from her. An anonymous author of the fifth or fourth century BCE alludes to the nocturnal host of Hecate that shows itself at night, a point confirmed by a scolia in the *Argonautica* by Apollonius of Rhodes (third century) in which this apparition is given the name Hekateia.[2] In his *Preparations for the Gospel,* Eusebius of Caesarea (ca. 270–340) informs us that the leaders of the spirits that rule the night are the demons Serapis and Hecatez—Beelzebub.

The Legions of Demons

This is how Sulpicius Severus (ca. 363–406/410) describes the invasion of a monastery by invisible demons in his *Life of Saint Martin* (23, 6): "Toward midnight the entire monastery gave the impression of swaying to the muted noise of people walking about; in the young man's cell numerous lights could be seen glittering as well as a dull sound of many people going to and fro, and the murmur of many voices."[3]

Felix of Crowland describes the demons that attack St. Guthlac (674–714) and carry him off *in corpore* to the very gates of hell.[4] One night Guthlac "suddenly sees the whole tiny cell filled with horrible troops of foul spirits [*immundorum spirituum catervis totam cellulam suam impleri conspexit*]. . . . Bursting forth from the earth and the sky,

Figure 2.1. A horde of demons carries off St. Guthlac (twelfth century).

they covered the space beneath the heavens with their dusky cloud . . ."[5]

The lesson of the text is clear: demons rarely traveled alone, and in the twelfth century William of Newburgh recounts the story of Ketell, a man who sees demons: "He observed that they would rove about to afflict men, even in petty ways, and that they rejoiced at having produced the most trifling injury."[6]

William of Auvergne, in his treatise *De Universo,* written between 1231 and 1236, also links the appearance of demons to crossroads.[7] *The Miracles of Saint Eloy* (Eligius), from between 1250 and 1300, presents an army of devils (*diables, li fi Sathan*) who, accompanied by a strong gale, assail an abbey, some of whose monks then cast their robes into the nettles on the counsel of their leader.[8] According to the *Brauweiler*

Annals, two troops of demons are seen waging a battle by cavalry and throwing enormous trunks of oak trees.

In the *Scala coeli,* Jean Gobi cites an interesting case: when bearing a vessel to a miser on his deathbed (*laborantis in extremis*) an old man spots knights on black horses holding torches. These horsemen enter the house through the door, grab hold of the dying man's soul, and bear it off to hell (n°95). A little later Jean Gobi relates an anecdote about demons living as a community: "An abbot and monk became lost on the way and met some monks in the forest who invited them to follow them to their abbey. During the morning, the abbot gave a sermon on angels. When he talked of the first hierarchy, half of the monks left the premises; when he mentioned the second, the other half followed suit. When questioned, one of the monks explained: 'We are members who have fallen from these orders,' and the entire abbey vanished [*tota illa abbatia evanuit*]."[9]

The Dominican Étienne of Bourbon (ca. 1190/1195–1261) mentions demons taking human form in an *exemplum.*

A knight who had lived an evil life refused to go to Rome to make penitence, and his bishop commanded him to keep vigil all night in a church "without speaking to anyone, and without listening to anyone at all except for God and his saints." The knight was let into the church and the doors closed behind him.

The knight kept vigil until midnight, praying peacefully in front of the crucifix. Through the devices of the devil, a gleam of light began illuminating the church, as if day was dawning. He then saw, through an open door, men and women entering as if to pray. He then heard a noise as if numerous carts had pulled up, and he saw merchants enter the church who claimed his wife had sent them. They demanded his assistance, but he refused. They retreated indignantly, and pretending that they had gone to his home, they brought in a devil who had taken the form of his wife and another who had taken that of his son. Despite their entreaties, the knight remained mute. The demons then took on the shape of the bishop and his clerics, saying: "*Benedicte,* my son! May God bless you! How did the night go?" and other words of the same kind. The knight remained impervious. He made the sign of the cross over his breast, and "the confounded demons transformed into hideous figures who hit and tortured him."[10]

Around this same era, *The Book of the Fathers* (Das Väterbuch) shows us how St. Paul delivers a soul who seeks to lead "the furious troop of the devil" (*des tiuvels wuetendez her*). In France is the story of Luque, the cursed witch of Rouen, as told by a certain Boudet.

On the fifth night before St. Peter's, which is called winter beneath Peter [*iver souz* Pierre], Luque took to her bed feeling death was near. She let Hellequin/Hennequin know of this and asked him to come for her, because she wished to be his bride. He decided to wed her before the end of winter, and he sent his auxiliaries to show her what forces he held at his command. They then left to devastate the entire Caux region including Luque's house in Rouen.[11]

The bishop of Orange, Alphonse de Spina (died 1469), speaks of this troop of demons that appears on the roads like a vast army and is accompanied by a great noise (*cum magnis tumultibus*).[12] Michel Wyssenherre picks up this belief in the fifteenth century and uses it in his *Outremer Pilgrimage of the Noble Lord of Brunswick*.[13]

Last, we find a fictional vision of these beliefs in the fourteenth-century tale *Perceforest*. The hero of the story, Passelion, finds himself at the gates of hell, a wild and horrible place of mountains and valleys, where he hears a stupefying noise produced by the souls of creatures who have died since the time of Adam and Eve were created and from whom they were born. The porter refuses him entry, a storm suddenly blows up, and Passelion hears a new noise: ". . . then arose a gust of wind and a tempest to that part because it carried devils coming from Great Britain and neighboring lands with a great number of souls they had collected, who came running while making a very impetuous noise."[14]

This passage includes the essential elements, mainly the storm that accompanies the passage of the army of devils who carry the souls to hell.

We see that the air is the domain of demons that appear primarily during storms. It was claimed in Trier in 1256 that demons were spotted in the sky during a tempest, and in similar circumstances near Limoges, people believed they could hear two demons conversing.[15] These demons were sometimes regarded as the spirits of those who had died prematurely, enemies of fertility.[16]

We are now a long way from the third-function rite mentioned earlier. Its meaning has been reversed. Furthermore, the attempt to decode this phenomenon is so difficult: a wide variety of spirits inhabit the air. The entire body of ecclesiastical literature therefore regards these nocturnal retinues as armies of demons, and it makes no distinction between the living, the dead, or the spirits.

Demons or Revenants?

The Russian *Chronicle of Times Bygone* reports a strange event that took place in the Ukranian town of Polotsk in 1092. Though the different accounts are in agreement about the event, they diverge on the details, which allows us to see how the church distorts a piece of information. The parts of this text in italics are the points that deserve particular attention.

> In the year 6600,* something quite strange took place in Polotsk. It was produced *in the imagination.* At night a loud noise would be suddenly heard in the streets: devils *galloped* as if they were human beings. If someone tried to leave his house in order to see this better, the devils inflicted him immediately and invisibly with a fatal

*Since the creation of the world.

wound. People no longer dared leave their homes. Next, these devils began to appear during the day on horses, and there were no means to see them. People could see the shoes of their horses, though. They also ate the folk of Polotsk and its surrounding area, so people began to say: "The inhabitants of Polotsk, *by all evidence, are being murdered.*"

This phenomenon first occurred in Drutsk. During this time there was a sign in the heavens, like a very large wheel in the middle of the sky. That summer, the weather was so dry that the earth was consumed thereby and many forests burst into flames by themselves, as did the peat bogs. There were many signs here and there, and a large invasion of Polovtsians. . . . That same summer, Rurik, the son of Rotislav died. At this very same time, many people died from a host of illnesses. So many died that some coffin sellers were prompted to say: "From St. Philip's Day to the beginning of Lent, we have sold 7,000 coffins." Now this all occurred because our sins had multiplied like our iniquities. God inflicted this upon us so that we would perform penitence and turn away from sin, envy, and all other malignant undertakings of the Evil One.[17]

Different texts stress from the first that the troop of devils is the fruit of the imagination. They use words that correspond to *phantasma/phantasia* and *enigma,* and the doubt therefore persists. They diverge from each other on the demons' stampede, and the Hypatien copy notes: "It moaned like human beings." Last, the Radziwill text uses the word *nave* (*nekroi*) to designate what slays the Polotsk residents and to suggest that "[t]he inhabitants of Polotsk were devoured by the dead." The compilers therefore waver between demons and the dead, but we can take a stand for the dead based on a philological element and the context. The word *nave* is relatively rare, and it is apparently regarded as a nonliterary term. It was therefore removed by the copyist of the Lamartine text, and there we find in its place an adverbial expression that means "not in dream, but really, openly," The event recorded by the

Chronicle therefore was believed to have happened in reality and not in dream or the imagination, and it was thought that revenants (corporeal undead) caused such massive fatalities. We can note another hesitation between the creatures that moaned: devils or human beings? The context indicates that the phenomenon was perceived as a manifestation of divine wrath, and the account is recast as a sign of the punishment of sin, obvious evidence of the Christianization of elements whose sources are folk beliefs, as shown by certain details such as the invisibility of the devils and the wounds they inflict and on the partial visibility of their mounts: only the horses' shoes can be seen.

While the stampede is original, *The Chronicle of Times Bygone* contains one of the oldest accounts of the Wild Hunt and the Furious Army, with one detail we find nowhere else but which could be entirely metaphorical: the dead devour the living.

Demonic Animals

We can also note a marginal sideline of this area: the night is also host to the wandering of demoniacal animals. In southern Sweden, for example, Gloso, the glowing sow,[18] appears during the twelve days of Christmas. She has eyes of fire, sparks spring from her bristles, and she travels like a burning flame. To insure a good harvest, people offered her gruel and fish so that she would not harm anyone. Once the harvest had been brought in, three blades of wheat* were left in the field with the harvester: "These are for Gloso: one for Christmas night, one for the night of the New Year, and one for king's night."[19] Gloso is sometimes interpreted as the specter of a murdered child who was never buried or as the supernatural guardian of a church (*kirkegrim*).

We can find in several provinces of Norway the belief in the movement of fantastical animals. Trettanreidi is described as a flying goat in Hordaland; in Vest-Agder, a billy goat and nanny goat (*julabukk* and

---

*The same is done for other beings in folk mythology, namely the Wee Ladies of the Marshes (Moosweibchen), whom the infernal huntsman pursues.

Figure 2.2. *Chronicles of Times Bygone*

julegeita) have neither blood nor bone, but they do possess eight strong horns; and in Rogaland, a goat (*jula-gjei do*) bites the horses in their stables.[20] The *türscht* in Alemannic Switzerland is sometimes a pack of ghost dogs and sometimes a sow accompanied by its young whose appearance heralds bad weather. When a storm blows up, people say: "It looks like the türscht is going through."[21] Packs of fantastical hounds that bear various names—High Hunt, Glapotê/Glapoté, Minette Dogs, Dogs of Bad Weather—wander through the French Alps.[22]

These threatening shadows, which have sometimes survived in folk traditions even into our days, certainly deserve more extensive study. We must note their presence among the infernal populace that traverses the skies, though they are marginal to our chief concern: the Wild Hunt, which, as we will see, is sometimes accompanied by animals.

3

The Troops of the Dead

Es stehn die Stern am Himmel,
Es scheint der Mond so hell,
*Die Toten reiten schnell . . .**

Like demons, the dead who have not found rest or who are suffering the punishments of purgatory often moved about in a troop. The Greeks believed that the revenants returned to Hades with the dawn, and Propertius (ca. 47–15 BCE), in *Elegies* (4, 7, 89), puts these words in their mouths: "By night we range in wandering flight; night frees the prisoned shades, and Cerberus himself strays at will, the bar that chains him cast aside. At dawn hell's ordinance bids us return to the pools of Lethe."[1]

An Orphic hymn that perhaps dates back to the third or fourth century CE alludes to Hecate, daughter of the Titan Perses, who wanders the night with a retinue of the dead and dogs.[2] As described in the *Register* of Inquisitor Jacques Fournier, bishop of Pamiers (who led the persecution of the Cathars of the Upper Ariège region around 1320), the beings who roam the night are neither fairies nor demons; they are dead people

---

*The stars sparkle in the firmament
the moon shines clear
the dead ride fast . . .

From the folk song "Lenore," which inspired the poet G. A. Bürger (1773) and which tells how a dead man returned for his fiancée.

33

who "do not frequent sordid areas and do not enter poorly kept houses" (*mortui . . . nolunt venire ad loca sordida nec intrare domos immundas*),[3] a detail we shall see again in the testimony of Renward Cysat.

An Itinerant Purgatory

In his *Book of Visions,* Otloh (ca. 1010–1070) recounts how two brothers see a large troop in the sky (*viderunt tubam magnam in aere*). Crossing themselves for protection, they ask these people who they are. One of them discloses his identity as their father who is being punished for enjoying the use of someone else's property. He will find redemption only if and when his sons return this land to its rightful owners.

Wipert, archdeacon of Toul, writes in his *Life of Pope Saint Leo* (Vitas. Leonis pape) around the year 1060:

> Some years before the death of St. Leo, a vast company of individuals garbed in white was seen advancing toward the city of Narmi. They marched in ranks from morning to almost three in the afternoon before settling down at the fall of night. The citizens of Narmi grew alarmed, believing they were under attack by enemies. One man, more courageous than the others, noticed in the crowd an individual he knew and went out of the city and asked him the identity of this troop. The other responded: "We are souls who have not yet atoned for our sins and because we are not pure enough to enter [h]eaven, we are visiting the holy sites as penitence. . . ." Our brave man was so terrified by this vision that he remained ill for an entire year.[4]

In 1135, Hugues de Mans relates the story of a knocking spirit (poltergeist). It concerns a deceased individual who has a request that he desires to give to his family.

> "Alas," said the voice, "since coming from remote lands and through many perils, I have suffered from storms, snow, and cold! So many

fires have burned me, and so much bad weather I have tolerated in coming here! Nicholas, my brother; my sister-in-law; my nephews; and other friends—have no fear, for the power to cause anyone harm is not granted me. You should, however, protect yourselves by making the sign of the cross over your brow and over your heart. It is a fact that a wicked throng that is eager to work evil has come in with me and will retreat with me when I leave. So that I may leave the pernicious road they travel and fully enjoy eternal rest, please celebrate a Mass for me tomorrow. . . ."[5]

The text is clear—it alludes to a journey in the company of a troop of those who are apparently demons to which the dead sinner belongs. The fact that it is possible to escape from this host suggests that it is in some way an itinerant purgatory.

Ekkehard of Aura notes this in his *Chronicle* for the year 1123:

During a certain number of days in the province of Worms, many armed knights were seen coming and going and gathering in groups, as if for a pleasant encounter, sometimes here and sometimes there, and returning around the ninth hour to a mountain from which they had been seen leaving.

One of this land's inhabitants eventually approached one of these extraordinary reunions, but not without fear and only after seeking protection by making the sign of the cross. Soon he implored, in the name of the Lord, one of the people he found there to reveal the reason for their assembling like this. The individual he addressed told him: "We are not ghosts, as you are thinking, nor are we the knights we appear to be to your eyes. We are the souls of slain knights. The arms, horses, and clothing that were once our instruments of sin are now tools of torture for us, and in truth, all you see about you is dead, although this is not something you can see with your eyes of flesh."

It was in a reunion like this that there appeared Count Emicho, who had been killed several years earlier, and who let it be known he could be delivered from his punishment by prayers and alms.[6]

The Spirits' Mass

There is another common theme that strongly emphasizes how the dead assemble in a group: the Mass celebrated by spirits, a long-standing theme, which appears in the historical work of Gregory of Tours (538–594), and which we can find throughout medieval Europe.[7] Here are several of the most significant examples.

Bishop Thietmar of Merseburg records a "true" story in his *Chronicon* (I, 11–12): The priest of Walsleben Castle is on his way to sing Matins at the church, but on entering the cemetery (*atrium*), he spies a crowd of people (*videns in eo magnam multitudinem*) that makes offerings to a priest, and the members of the crowd stand at the door of the building. He stops, makes the sign of the cross, and enters the chapel. A woman he knows who has died recently asks him what he is doing there, and he tells her. She then lets him know that he has not much longer to live.[8]

A similar experience occurs to a priest of Deventer. He reports the event to the bishop, Balderich, who then commands him to spend the entire night at the church. The dead then throw him out of the building along with his bed (*cum lecto . . . sequente nocte a defunctis eiectus est*). Another night he brings holy relics with him and sprinkles holy water about the church, but the dead emerge at their customary time (*solita hora venientes*), grab him, and burn him. Balderich explains that the day belongs to the living and that the night belongs to the dead: *ut dies vivis, sic nox est concessa defunctis.*

In his book *Miracles and Apparitions,* written between 1063 and 1072, Peter Damian cites the case of a woman who mistakenly attended a Mass of the spirits in the basilica of Santa Maria of Campitella on the night of Assumption, and a recently departed gossip tells her she has no more than a year left to live.[9]

Encountering the dead is fraught with danger. In the *Life of Jón*

Figure 3.1. A living woman who attended a Mass of revenants attempts to escape death.
Illustration from *Tales*, collected by P. C. Asbjørnsen and J. Moe. Based on
R. Grambo, *Gjester fra graveren* (Oslo: n.p., 1991), 26.

Ögmundarson (bishop of Holar, in Iceland, who died in 1121) monks
interred in a church attack an old woman who comes in to pray.[10] In
1516, a woman attends a spirits' Mass by chance and recognizes one of
her neighbors, who warns her that she should leave the church before

the consecration and flee without looking back. To stay means the dead will tear her to pieces. The old woman follows this advice, but the dead, in their pursuit of her, rip away her coat. The next day, she sees that a piece of her coat is on each of the graves.[11]

The Message of the Deceased

Nevertheless, the most frequent theme remains that of the return of a dead person to ask for suffrages or to right a wrong he or she committed in life. The *de cujus* is sometimes alone and sometimes accompanied, as in this story from the book *On Miracles* (1135–1142) by Pierre de Cluny: the knight Guigo de Moras-en-Valloire (Dauphiné) dies and is buried. Around noon the chaplain, Étienne, walked near the castle, and he hears behind him a sound akin to the noise of a large army (*quasi immensus exercitus strepitum post terga mea audio*). Stricken with terror, he enters the nearby forest, where he sees a large host of men at arms march past. Among them he recognizes Guigo, who explains to him the sin for which he is atoning.[12]

In another story (I, 28) Pierre tells how a dead man named Sanche comes to deliver him a message, and Sanche is joined by another dead man who urges Pierre to leave the premises and get back on the road, because "the troop of their companions awaited them outside, occupying all the roads and byways" (*omnes vias . . . sequens nos exercitus sotiorum implevit*).[13]

The *Book of the Miracles of Sainte-Foi* (1108–1155) recounts how the knight Walter of Diebolsheim customarily performs penance at night outside of a monastery.

> One night, he saw two hordes: pilgrims dressed in white who emerged in one of the monastery's courtyards, and a throng of red-clad knights mounted on horses of the same color. Walter addressed one of these pilgrims, who turned out to be his late lord, Count Conrad. The count charged him to perform several missions, for

example, obtaining the suffrages of Bishop Otto of Strasborg. Conrad also asked that he restore to St. Foy what he had bequeathed to the monastery. Walter asked Conrad about the Whites and the Reds. The first were the souls of those who had lived chastely and escaped the tortures of hell but did not yet enjoy rest. The second had scorned divine and human law and died in battle without having done penance and were thus condemned to the fires of hell.[14]

The following story is told by Conrad, monk of Clairvaux, then abbot of Eberbach (died September 18, 1221): Following Mass, a monk emerged from the church and leaned against it, looking east. He suddenly became seized by terror: the hair of his head stood up on end, his eyes opened wide, and he found himself unable to move. He could see a large throng of people of both genders and of all ages and rank, walking and riding. Among them were some he had known while they were still alive. One of them, Baudoin, a monk of Clairvaux, told him they were souls of the dead who were condemned to roam the earth, because of their sins.[15]

The anonymous continuer of the *Chronicle of the Dominican of Colmar* (1308–1314) tells of the return of a dead man thirty days following his death. The deceased asks to speak to his friend Sereius, who refuses to meet with him. Several days later, while walking alongside a river in search of a bridge, he sees a troop of riders that he recognizes as knights who have died in battle. They cross the river in silence, but one approaches him—it is his dead friend, and Sereius is compelled to listen to what the dead must say. His friend demands that he ask Count von Schwarzenburg to leave on Crusade. Sereius performs the mission with which he is charged, but the count scoffs at him and is slain shortly thereafter.[16]

We must linger for a moment over the thirty-days motif, for it repeatedly appears in the stories of apparitions. Heirs could not take possession of the goods of the deceased before the passage of this span of time, because it was believed that the dead person remained near his or her body for thirty days. This was the reason for the festivities at the gravesite on the third, seventh, and thirtieth day following death, as well as on the anniversary date of death every year. A twelfth-century manuscript claims that because the deceased had yet to reach the beyond during this time, he or she could be interrogated through the intermediary of a priest.[17] The liturgist and bishop of Mende William Durand (1230/31–1296) believed that "some people observe a service of thirty days or celebrate the thirty-first for the dead because the number of days required for the course of the moon through space is thirty days, so at this time the works of the dead are thus fully before the Lord."[18]

Several texts tell how an ill monk sees a procession of phantom monks crossing through the infirmary where he is convalescing. We can find this story in the writings of Jean Gobi, prior of Montpellier from 1302 to 1304, and in those of Vincent de Beauvais.[19]

The Dead Gathered Together

The novelistic literature of the romances and sagas provides important corroboration to the writings of the clerics and shows that the theme of troops of the dead is not the prerogative only of edifying scriptures.

The *Saga of Snorri the Godi*,* a kind of rural chronicle written in 1230, which relates the events that took place from 884 to 1031, tells the story of Thorolf Twist-Foot, a wicked man who returns after his death and causes the death of the inhabitants of Hvamm. He first causes the deaths of the mistress of the house and a shepherd, then that of other men: "He killed men, and it was seen that the dead traveled with him."[20] The same saga speaks of another series of deaths: Thorir dies, slain by an undead shepherd, then returns and begins haunting the premises in the company of that same shepherd. Thorodd and six other people drown when their ship goes down, and they all return to take part in their funeral feast.[21] In folk beliefs, the dead had a tendency to gather, form a band, and choose as their chief or leader the one who was first to perish.

---

*[Also known as the *Eyrbyggja Saga. —Trans.*]

In his *Histories,* written between 1028 and 1049, the Cluny cleric Ralph (or Rodulfus) Glaber puts these words in the mouth of an undead member of a large throng, which the revenant addresses to Brother Wulferius: "We are all professing Christians; but as we defended our homeland against the Saracens, we were separated by the sword from our mortal flesh. A divine dispensation has been made to take us into the company of the blessed, and, as it happens, we were due to pass through this region, because many from this region are shortly to join our company."[22]

This belief in a gathering of the dead[23] into a throng before the final voyage closely agrees with and feeds a Christian myth that claims that between the moment of death and the time of Christian burial, the soul must undertake a journey to its place of judgment, where its fate will be fixed while it awaits Final Judgment. Often this stopping place occurs at or involves crossing over the Bridge of St. James—Santiago de Compostela*—and is connected to the Milky Way as the road of souls.[24] Those who pilgrimage there find that their souls are exempt from having to travel this pathway after their deaths.

The literature of diversion has also left us curious stories such as the *Lay du Trot* (thirteenth century) and the *Lord of Würtemberg* (Der Württenburger), written sometime between 1198 and 1393. The following is from the first text.

A Breton knight named Lorois de Morois set off by himself one day to listen to the song of the nightingale. On the edge of the forest, he encountered a group of noble ladies accompanied by gallant men. Each of the couples were embracing and kissing. Hardly recovered from his surprise, Lorois then caught sight of a second troop that pursued the same activities. Suddenly, the forest echoed with the sounds of moaning and groaning, and from it emerged about a hundred women clad in rags, all thin and wretched, who were soon followed by the same number of knights in a similarly pitiable state.

*[*Santiago* is the Spanish word for Saint James. —*Trans.*]

Lorois asked one lone woman what this all meant, and she told him that the happy couples were those who had been wise enough in their lifetimes to love truly while the others had been too haughty and proud, *ne ainc ne daignierent amer.*[25]

The didactic intent of this text is quite clear, and it is fairly reminiscent of what Andreas Capellanus says in his *De amore,* written around 1180–1190. What we see here again are the dead who have not found rest and are on earth to atone for their sins. The internal contradiction of the text will not escape readers: What are the first two retinues doing here, for their members have nothing for which to be condemned? They are obviously evoked for the needs of the narrative, as *tertium comparationis.*

This German text is quite close to the French lay.[26] The knight Ulrich goes hunting and becomes lost and then sees, coming toward him, a couple on horseback, followed by a group of five hundred men and as many women. No one responds to his greeting. Only one of the women agrees to answer his questions. "We are dead," she tells him. "My body perished thirty years ago; it has rotted and what you see is naught by a reflection." She explains that she betrayed her husband and sinned without paying penance. Ulrich accompanies her to the castle, where the dead are sharing a meal. He grabs a fish that sets fire to his fingers (re-emergence of the theme of the food of the otherworld being forbidden to the living).

Thanks to the testimony provided by both the clerical and the secular literature, we can see that the dead often traveled in hordes, had occupations such as attending Masses reserved for them alone, and danced in cemeteries,[27] as is the case in the story by Rudolphe of Celestat in which Lord Berthold von Stauffen and the provost Thierry von Spechbach witness such a spectacle. The dead in the tale have not found rest for a variety of reasons—lack of penance, unfulfilled vows, misdeeds that must be set right, will provisions that have not been respected by their heirs, a message to deliver[28]—and they come from purgatory, hell, or some unspecified third region located on the earth, which reflects

Fig. 3.2. The dead dancing, Hartmann Schedel, *Liber chronicarum* (Nuremburg: n.p., 1493)

folk beliefs in which the otherworld was thought to be the tomb, the mound, or a hollow mountain.[29]

Survivals

Folk traditions have preserved this belief in the gathering of the dead who, on certain dates—the Ember Days,* the night of November 1, St. Hilaire's Day (January 14),[30] and especially in winter (Advent, Christmas)—traveled in processions over the earth. In Switzerland, for example,[31] these retinues were called Processione dei poveri morti (Misox, Italian-Catholic Switzerland); Gratzug (Valais), because it was

---

*[In the liturgical calendar the Ember Days are four sepatate sets of days within the same week, specifically Wednesday, Friday, and Saturday, at the beginning of each season that are set aside for fasting and prayer. —*Ed.*]

necessary to transport the dead over the ridge (the German *Grat*) of the mountain; *Til dils morts* (Engardine); *Totuchrizgang; Nachtschar; Nachtvolk* (Procession of the Dead, Night Troop, Night Folk); and *Totâgeigi*[32] (Music or Fiddler of the Dead, Alemannic Switzerland), because the passing of these dead was accompanied by music, a theme we will see again in the Wild Hunt. In Rovio the dead rose during the night of November 1 and paraded through the village, stopping in the houses and sitting near the stoves to eat what they found there. Even today some people leave the lights on and their fires burning on this night and leave food upon their tables. In Upper Savoy, it was said that on Toussaint* there were as many souls on earth as there were *chalavrons* (hemp stems) and that on this evening, processions of souls traveled the roads. In Galicia roamed the Procesión de las animas en pen.

In Scandinavia, Gongfoela and Gongferda designated a diabolical host that consisted of the souls of the dead that spent the night above the earth, without ever touching it, and when it was present people heard an almost songlike murmur. They had to then lie down, fully stretched along the ground, in order not to be carried off. Other testimonies recommend leaving the area, because the dead must be allowed to pass (*lad de døde fare vorbi*).[33]

---

*[All Saints' Day. —*Trans.*]

4

The Phantom Armies

AMONG THE EXTRAORDINARY PHENOMENA that have never ceased stirring the imagination and have had considerable influence over the formation of the legends and myths of the Middle Ages is that of the phantom armies, which presents two facets.[1] On one hand, there are the dead who continue to wage their battles after their deaths,[2] and on the other hand are armies that loom up in the skies on the eve of a conflict or on certain dates that commemorate a bloody confrontation.[3]

The Dead Continue to Battle

Damascius (fifth–sixth century) tells how Attila wages a terrible battle beneath the walls of Rome, after which the souls of the dead still fight there with singular ferocity for three days and nights. Around 150, Pausanias mentions the ghost soldiers of Marathon: "At Marathon every night you can hear horses neighing and men fighting. No one who has expressly set himself to behold this vision has ever received any good from it."[4] Paulus Diaconus (ca. 720–787), the historian of the Lombards, notes that during the year 590, marked by a great pestilence, the noise of battle trumpets, and a noise like the sound of an army can be heard both night and day.[5]

In May 1236, Matthew Paris, chronicler for St. Albans Abbey, states that it is possible to see a battle that takes place in the skies over the land of Wales.[6] Felix Malleolus (1309–1456), Christoph Besold (1577–1638), and Jacob Thomasius tell us this: "After defeating Ottokar, Rudolph of Habsburg spent the night on the battlefield. Toward midnight, spirits could easily be seen, and strange sounds and rattling noises were made by the dead who had fallen in battle. These were diabolical glamors, but the folk of this time were convinced that they were souls of the slain continuing to fight."[7]

The Eternal Battle

Alongside these tales is the testimony of Snorri Sturluson (1178–1241), which forms part of another tradition but belongs to the same thematic family. In response to the question: Why is the battle called

Figure 4.1. Army in the sky. Conrad Lycosthenes, *Prodigiorum as oastentorum chronicon* (Basel: n.p., 1557).

Hjadningar's Storm or Tempest (Hjadningar vedur eda él), Snorri says this in his *Treatise on the Poetic Arts:* "Hedinn abducted the daughter of King Hogni and carried her away on his boat, and the latter pursued him until they met on an island. Their battle raged throughout the day, and at dusk both kings returned to their vessels. But during the night, Hild, the daughter of Hogni, went out to the battlefield to revive the dead by magic. The battle will thus last until Ragnarok."*[8]

This theme is recast into romantic literature. Gerbert de Montreuil, for example, offers us the following adventure in the *Fourth Continuation of the Story of the Grail:* "Perceval met anew with Gornemant, whose castle was attacked every day by forty knights who would resume combat the next day after being slain. Perceval vanquishes these knight-revenants, but before dying, the last tells him, 'We have no dread of death.' Seeking to learn how the slain knights can come back to life, Perceval remains at the site of their demise despite warnings from his companions. He witnesses the arrival of an old hideous woman [*plus est noire de nul fer* (verse 5586)]. She carries two small barrels containing two magic balms, and with these, she can resuscitate and heal the cadavers."[9]

We can connect to this same complex of legends the tourneys of the slain for which Caesarius of Heisterbach offers us two examples: "One twilight, in the Hesbaye, in the province of Liège, near the castle of the count of Looz, a priest saw a large tourney of dead men and heard shouted the name of a dead knight, Walter of Milene. The priest drew a circle around himself [*circulum circa se fecit*], and the vision disappeared." [See *Dialogus miraculorum* XII, 17.] "The night following the death of the duke of Louvain, who was slain by the liegois, a valet of the count of Looz, who passes close to Montenake, the place where the battle took place, sees there a large tournament of 'demons' [*tornamentrum demonorum*]." (See *Dialogus miraculorum* XII, 16.)

---

*[The twilight of the gods. —*Trans.*]

We can note a detail that distinguishes these armies from the Wild Hunt: the spectator has no contact with the returning dead. There are no dialogue, no revelations, and no requests for suffrages or reparations. The phenomenon is completely amputated from the world of human beings. It is a manifestation from the otherworld that offers evidence that death does not bring an end to life's activities.

Wonders and Omens

Among the number of marvels that heralded the death of Caesar, Ovid cites "the rattling of weapons in the black clouds, the sound of terrifying trumpets and horns in the sky."[10] Virgil reports that "in Germany the clash of weapons could be heard resounding through the heavens. . . . Ghosts of an odd pallor could be seen at the fall of night."[11] Pliny the Elder notes earlier that during the campaign against the Cimbrians "the din of weapons and the sound of a trumpet were heard in the sky." He also tells of the appearance of armies in the sky in the third consulship of Marius, "the people of America and Tuder saw heavenly armies marching from the west and east to join battle. The army from the west was put to flight."[12] Lucan (39–65) cites among the marvels that preceded the civil war the perception of the sounds of trumpets in the skies and a clamor such as that produced in battle.[13]

Around 1048, the monk Ralph (Rodulfus) Glaber finished his five books of history at Cluny, and he dedicated them to Abbot Odilon. Among the wonders he records, he mentions this:

A pious priest named Frotterius was living at Tonnerre. . . . One Sunday evening, he walked across to his window before dinner to pass the time, and, looking out, he saw an enormous multitude of riders drawn up as though in a battle line, moving steadily from north to west. After he watched them closely for some time, he became alarmed and called out to a member of his household to come and see them, but as soon as he had called out, the figures dissolved and disappeared. He was so shaken by the sight that he was hardly able to keep from tears. Later that same year, he fell ill and died, ending his life in the same godly manner in which he had lived.[14]

Ralph Glaber specifies that this omen was fulfilled the following year. Henry, the son of King Robert, attacked the town with a large army, and a huge massacre took place. Gerald of Wales (ca. 1146–1223) records:

It happened that while the army was in Ossory they camped one night on a certain old fortification, and these two men were lying in the same tent, as was their custom. Suddenly, there was a great noise, as though a thousand men rushed in upon them from all sides, with a great rattling of arms and clashing of battle axes. Such spectral appearances frequently occur in Ireland to those who are engaged in hostile excursions.[15]

In 1123, armies of dead warriors showed themselves in Molsheim, Colmar, and Freiburg-im-Breisgau, causing the deaths of many people. In 1432, during the war between the count of Katznellenbogen and the Nassau country squire John of the Hat, people in Westphalia saw knights in harness riding through the sky. The apparition lasted for two days around St. John's Day that summer. Similarly, in Saverne in Alsace, six thousand men were seen traveling through the sky, and people could see even the sparks made by the shoes of the horses. On April 29, 1506, in Nordfeld, near the Jungenberg, people saw an army of headless knights, all dressed in red. Coming to meet it was another army, all in white, that attacked it and put it to flight, whereupon the white army pursued the red into the Hart Forest. These fighters were so huge that they strode over the trees. The apparition could be seen at noon for four weeks without interruption, to the great terror of the entire region.[16] In 1520, in Wissemburg on the Rhine, a strange noise was heard in the sky around noon. It was a terrible din of crashing arms and shouts like those made by soldiers mounting an assault. The inhabitants thought they were

Figure 4.2. Battle in the sky, a marvel of the year 1554. *Feuille volante*
(Nuremberg: Georg Merckel, 1554).

under attack by an enemy, and they hastily retrieved their weapons.

In 1531, two armies were seen fighting each other in the sky, and boats filled with unknown warriors were seen on the lake bearing the banners of the five cantons. Then they all disappeared.[17]

In 1742, one hour after nightfall or one hour before sunrise, Jeremy Daum heard a large din of horses and chariots every time a war was soon to break out.[18] Similar examples are not unknown in France.[19]

A Critical Piece of Evidence

We should note the extremely critical testimony provided by the bishop of Paris, William of Auvergne (1180–1249). In his criticism he wonders if these armies are "of spiritual substance," and if they "are good or malign." He responds: "they are not flesh or real, they have no bodies, they are invulnerable, they are the mystifications of demons, and it is wrong to say they appear only at crossroads."[20] William then concludes with an interesting debate that continues on into the sixteenth century:

> On the point that these knights appear in the shape of men, I say: of dead men, and those most often slain by iron, we can undoubtedly, based on the advice of Plato, consider that the souls of men thus slain continue to be active the number of days or the entire time it was given them to live in their bodies, if they had not been expelled by force.
>
> You should know, however, that the souls of those who have been killed in this way—in other words, by violent death—roam, according to Plato, around the mounds and do not indulge themselves in excursions like those we have discussed. According to this same author, when the requisite number of days has passed, they return to stars of the same value [?] and, inasmuch as these souls sometimes appear singly or either, especially, those whose lives have been cut short by arms, in the form of these armies—the common folk call them Coupés-par-le-fer*—it is believed they perform penance with arms, because they were the instruments of their sins. This is why they sometimes make demands of those who were dear to them—so these might aid them by their prayers or other favors, and they also inform them this way of the means they can be freed of the punishments they are suffering, on condition the help they are given is effective.[21]

William bases his acceptance of the dead returning on a very ancient belief, which maintains that a man receives a certain duration of life at birth—seventy years, according to some—and is not able to reach the beyond until the assigned term has fully elapsed. Those who die prematurely are therefore condemned to roam the earth until that date. Yet

---

*[Those whose lives have been cut short by iron or, in other words, weapons. —*Trans.*]

William does not think these souls have bodies. He believes they are images, semblances of bodies that also come from purgatory, which is revealed by his final allusion to suffrages.

Some Conclusions

Examination of the texts provides evidence of the existence of a variety of nocturnal hosts, as testified by a thirteenth- or fourteenth-century German charm, which lists the demonic creatures who haunt the night: pixies (*pilewizze*), witches, Good Ladies, nightmares, elves, and the Furious Army whose members are criminals that have been broken on the wheel and hanged.*

Thus roaming across the earth are phalanxes of demons, legions of damned dead, and the throng of Doubles of sleepers who gather under the guidance of a leader—Diana, Herodias, Percht—in order to perform tasks closely connected to the third function as defined by Georges Dumézil, which rules fertility and fecundity. Dealings with the dead also fall into this category. Though the troop formed by the Good Women allegedly brings prosperity with it as long as the rites are respected, the passing of phantom armies is a bad omen: it heralds either some catastrophe or war. Sometimes, people see even gods ride through the skies. In the saga that bears his name, Viga-Glúm dreams this:

> *The ring-giver saw them riding*
> *A snapping of swords must happen*
> *It's come, the grey spears' greeting*
> *As the gods ride* [godreid] *fast through the pasture*
> *Odin exults to see*
> *The Valkyries eager for battle*
> *Those goddesses dripping forth gore*
> *Drenching the lives of men.*[22]

---

*See appendix 6.

Figure 4.3. *Der todten Dantz* (The Dance Macabre) (Munich: 1500-1510)

As for the dead who have escaped purgatory, their duty is one of an entirely different nature, both edifying and terrifying. Their task is to let sinners know what fate awaits them beyond the grave and to serve in some respect as guides for the living. It is obvious that what we are dealing with here is the recuperation by the church of beliefs that it was incapable of eradicating and which it twisted to serve didactic and catechetic ends.

A simple comparison of the accounts in the clerical literature and those of the sagas, historiography, and the romances provides us with a stark, contrasting image. In the clerical accounts, the dead are involved in stereotypical activities, and it seems we are reading the same thing over and over. In the other accounts individualistic dead pursue lives close to those they led while still alive. They visit those who were dear to them, they do not hesitate to meddle in clan and family business, to display their unhappiness, to win revenge upon those who displeased them or reward those they esteem or love. The church contrived a formidable reduction in the heart of the rich palette of the activity of the dead in folk belief and retained only those actions that served its purposes. It systematically eliminated everything that contradicted the dogma, denied the fundamental ideas that gave structure to the notions of yore—for example, that a person could reach the beyond only at the end of the term of life originally granted him or her by destiny, thus condemning revenants to wander the earth, awaiting this date in the event of a premature death. On the other hand, the church appropriated the belief according to which those who commit suicide or are those slain by arms cannot find rest and that wizards and witches are destined to transform into revenants and therefore become part of the nocturnal hosts.

PART TWO

The Supernatural Hunters

5

The Diabolical Huntsman

Ex remoto vox quasi venatoris terribiliter
buccinantis nec non et latratus canum
*venaticorum praecedentium audiuntur.**

CAESARIUS OF HEISTERBACH,
"THE PRIEST'S CONCUBINE"

The terms *hunt* and *hunter* used in folk traditions are remnants of an ambiguous and often inappropriate use, and they have therefore caused numerous errors of interpretation. Figuring near the top of the list is the commingling of supernatural hunters and the host of the dead and the Furious Army. For the sake of classification, I propose these definitions:

- *The diabolical huntsman,* the subject of this chapter, is a demon that sets off in pursuit of a person; he appears mounted on horseback and is most often accompanied by a pack of hounds.
- *The wild huntsman,* whom we will examine in chapter 6, is a being of folk mythology (a daimon) who primarily victimizes supernatural creatures. He owns no dogs except in traditions that appear after the Middle Ages. Indeed, he is a tracker.

---

*[From the distance there came the terrible sound of a hunting horn and the barking of a pack of hounds. —*Trans.*]

Figure 5.1. The devil bears away the witch of Berkeley after her death.
Olaus Magnus, *Historia de gentibus septentrionalibus*, Rome: Giovanni Maria Viotto.

- *The cursed huntsman,* whom we will look at in chapter 7, is a man on horseback who, with his pack of dogs, pursues a prey that eternally eludes him.

The similarity of the elements among these three should not cause us to overlook some fundamental differences: In the first two cases, the prey of the supernatural hunter is a human being. In the second case, mainly found in folk traditions, this human being is usually a minor figure of the supernatural world. In the third case, the hunter's prey is an animal. The hunter is at times a demon and sometimes a devil; the prey is most often a revenant, a sinner, or a damned soul.

During the thirteenth century we find mention of a diabolical huntsman (*infernalis venator*) in the exemplum "The Priest's Concubine" written by the Cistercian monk Caesarius of Heisterbach:

I have been told by a pious man about the mistress of a priest who, when she was on the brink of death, demanded forcefully that the finest quality shoes should be made for her. As she expired, she said, "Bury me in them. This is of the utmost importance to me." This was done, and the next night, in the light of the full moon, well before dawn, a knight and his squire were riding along the highway, when they heard a woman screaming. They wondered what this might be, and the figure of a woman ran toward them, crying for help. At once, the knight dismounted and, brandishing his sword in a circle about him, took the woman under his protection. The woman, whom he recognized, was dressed only in a shift and the new shoes. Suddenly, from the distance there came the terrible sound of a hunting horn [*vox quasi venatoris terribiliter buccinantis*] and the barking of a pack of hounds [*latratus canum venaticorum*]. When she heard this, the woman trembled greatly, and when he saw what was the matter, the knight handed his horse's bridle to his servant, wrapped three locks of her hair around his left arm, and held his sword upright in his right hand. When the infernal huntsman drew near [*approximante infernali illo venatore*], the woman cried to the knight, "Let me go, let me go. Look: he is coming." And although the knight tried bravely to hold her back, the poor creature resisted him, hitting at him with her fists and eventually she escaped by tearing her hair loose.

Then the devil [*diabolus*] chased her and caught up with her and threw her across his horse with her head and arms hanging down on one side and her legs on the other. The hellish horseman rode back past the knight as he carried his prey off into the darkness. In the morning, the knight returned to the manor, told the household all he had seen and showed the handful of woman's hair, which remained in his grasp. They dug open her grave and found that the woman had lost her hair [*aperto sepulchro feminam capillos suos perdidisse repererunt*]. This happened in the archbishopric of Mainz.[1]

An abbreviated version of this narrative can be found in Jean Gobi's *Scala Coeli,* but the word *diabolus* has disappeared, and the scene takes place near a woman's grave (*juxta sepulchrum ejus*) under the light of the moon (*splendente luna*). It is specified that the priest's mistress asked to be buried with her shoes on (*sepelitur cum eis*).

The essential part of Caesarius of Heisterbach's story is retained here—notably the mention of the moon,[2] which frequently intervenes with regard to the Infernal Hunt—because it holds a separate place in the tradition of the theme, which Tubach's index[3] indicates by giving the narrative a different shelf mark than the group of texts that follow.

Around the same time, another Cistercian, Hélinand of Froidmont (died after 1229), tells another story that is quite similar, but has its own distinguishing features: "One night, as a charcoal burner of the count of Nevers was tending his fire, he saw a naked woman pursued by a knight riding a black horse. Brandishing his sword, the knight stabbed her and hurled her into the fire. He then pulled her body out of the flames, set it on his horse, and carried it away. The charcoal burner witnessed this drama repeated for several nights, then reported it to the count, who accompanied his servant to the scene to watch. On this occasion, though, the count asked the knight why he inflicted this punishment upon the woman. He told the count that he had committed adultery with this woman while he was still living upon the earth."[4]

The Hélinand exemplum was recorded around 1250 by Vincent de Beauvais in his *Speculum historiale* (XXIX, 120) and was recorded anew at the beginning of the fourteenth century in the *Alphabetum narrationum*[5] (n°629), a collection of exempla, in the fifteenth century in John Bromyard's[6] *Summa predicantium* (XVII, 2) and, a century later, in Johannes Pauli's *Schimpf und Ernst.*[7] The tradition was essentially clerical and exemplary until the end of the sixteenth century. Through sermons it fell into the public domain and was given a new lease on life. A number of alpine legends feature a priest's mistress abducted by the devil to serve him as a mount. Often, this diabolical rider appears at a blacksmith's in the night to ask that his mount be shod. When the blacksmith fulfills this commission, a plaintive voice asks him not to drive the nails too deeply, and he recognizes the voice as that of a relative, an aunt or sister, depending on different versions.[8] We should not be surprised to meet a soul in the shape of a horse. In *Thurkill's Vision* (written at the beginning of the thirteenth century), a devil tells the visitor: "Don't be astonished that I've changed this soul into a horse to ride here. We are allowed to transform the souls of the damned into any creature we choose.*

Let us now return to Helinand. In addition to supplying the substance of the famous novella in the *Decameron* (verse 8), which Boccaccio wrote between 1349 and 1351, his story can be found in *The Mirror of True Penitence* (Specchio della vera penitenza; written in 1354) by the preacher Jacopo Passavanti (1300–1357).[9] This rebuilt mirror is a collection of sermons given in Florence before 1354, and Hélinand story appears in the chapter titled "How Fear Dissuades Men from Performing Penance" (III, 2).

> There lived a poor man in the earldom of Nevers; he was a good and god-fearing man, and made his living as a charcoal burner. Once, after lighting his charcoal pit and sitting in his hut to supervise the burning, he heard great cries at midnight. Going outside to see what it was, he saw, running toward him, a naked and frenzied woman pursued by a black knight on a black steed who held a knife in his hand. Burning hot flames flared from the mouth, eyes, and nose of both the knight and his horse. When she reached the burning charcoal pit, the woman stopped, not daring to cast herself within, but as she raced about its edge, her pursuer caught up with her. While she screamed, he grasped her by her unbound hair and struck her fully in the middle of her chest with his knife. She fell to the ground, gushing blood. He then picked her up again by her blood-covered locks and cast her into the hot pit of burning charcoal, left her for

---

Dampnatorum animas licet nobis in quasilibet formas et species transformare.

several minutes, then pulled out her burned and flaming body, which he then placed over his horse's neck. He then galloped away in the direction from which he came. The charcoal burner witnessed this spectacle a second and third night. . . . He then told the count of Nevers the vision he had seen three days in a row.

The count returned to the pit with the charcoal burner, and while they watched from the hut, the woman arrived at the customary time, uttering terrible cries, with the knight pursuing her. The two saw all that the charcoal burner had seen before. Although frightened by this horrible spectacle, the count gathered all his courage, and as the cruel knight was about to ride off with the burned woman he had tossed across his steed, the count called out and beseeched the knight to stop and explain the vision he had just witnessed. The knight turned his horse back to face him, and weeping greatly, he answered, "Count, because you seek to learn of our torments that God has wished to show you, know that I am Geoffroi, one of your knights raised in your court. This woman to whom I have shown such cruelty is Lady Beatrice, wife of your dear knight Beranger. Both of us found pleasure in a dishonest love, which led us to commit sin, and in order to perform this evil deed more freely, the lady slew her husband. . . . Just before dying, she first and then I repented, and, having confessed our transgression, God granted us his mercy and changed the eternal punishment of hell into the temporary punishment of purgatory. Know then that we are not damned. What we do is for our punishment, and it will be lifted one day." The story continued with an explanation of the punishments.

According to Hélinand and Passavanti, the horse is a demon entrusted with the duty of torturing the human beings (*diabolus qui nos ineffabili vexatione torquet*). The Tuscan preacher develops the story more fully, adding the names of the protagonists and many gory details, transforming Hélinand exemplum into a veritable novella. The underlying theme of the Hunt is indicated in this story by one detail:

Figure 5.2. The devil carried off the priest's concubine. L. Petzold, *Kleines Lexicon*
(Munich: Beck, 1990).

toward midnight, the charcoal burner and the count hear this knight
vigorously blow his horn (*buccinantem fortiter*). Though Caesarius of
Heisterbach speaks of a devil on a horse, the other tales turn the steed
into a demon, because they exploit a story in which both sinners must
be punished. Caesarius makes no mention whatsoever of any punishment for a lusty priest, but a legend collected in Normandy around
1800 recounts this: "A priest, who enjoyed impure relations with a
nun and who died before performing penance was condemned, along
with the poor sister, to race through the sky. . . . The priest and nun,
as redress for their illicit love, were changed after their deaths into
devils so hideous and frightening that their colleagues could not suffer their presence. The entire Infernal Host followed closely on their
heels, driving them forth from their dark abode at night and pursuing them through the sky, while giving bent to frightful cries, until
the return of day, during which time the entire diabolical procession
returned to its home in hell."[10]

Figure 5.3. The devil carries off the priest's mistress. After Alfonso di Nola, *Der Teufel: Wesen, Wirkung, Geschichte* (Munich: DiederichhsVerlag, 1990).

German legends kept alive the memory of this theme into the nineteenth century. For example, one legend tells how a noblewoman who committed a great many injustices was pursued by a pack of infernal hounds. In the sixteenth century the *Zimmern Chronicle*, written between 1564 and 1576 by Count Froben Christoph von Zimmern and his secretary Johannes Müller, stars a diabolical huntsman who is undoubtedly inspired by Caesarius of Heisterbach:

Many years ago, the servant or housekeeper of a priest of Hansen, near Andelsbach, went to Bittelscheiss one evening. While making her way there, she encountered the Furious Army, as has often happened, but this may well be only an illusion. The way this apparition appeared was as if a hunter seized the housekeeper by force and then drove her before him like prey. The intrepid woman defended herself and yelled for help, but there was nothing that could aid or hold her back, and she was forced reluctantly to submit to the huntsman's will.

A lone soldier—some claim he was a vagabond student, as once were so plentiful, and others maintain it was a peasant named Jacob Algewer—ran into the housekeeper and the ghost. She cried to him for aid and asked him in God's name to free her, and she indicated that he should trace a circle around her and her phantom abductor with his naked blade. Only then would she be saved.

It is said that this soldier was so courageous that he confronted the ghost and did what the housekeeper asked of him, but in his haste, he traced the circle only around her. Although she was now in the circle, she was unable to detach herself from the ghostly hunter. The soldier, student, or whoever he was then struck this phantom with his sword, which knocked the horn from its mouth. The horn fell into the circle, where it stayed. The huntsman and his entire retinue rose into the air with a great din of jangling and shouts, then he and his band vanished. The housekeeper found herself freed. As an eternal souvenir of these events, the horn was housed in the church of Bittelscheiss, where it remained on display for many years, but it disappeared a few years ago—no one knows where.[11]

The soft focus of this story shows through. The narrator seems to hesitate between diabolical huntsman and Furious Army, and it is hard to see how the housekeeper could have been saved, because the soldier did not draw the circle correctly. The author undoubtedly blends several versions, creating uncertainty about the fate of her savior.

6

The Wild Huntsman

Fasolt and Wunderer

Around 1250, in the regions east of the Rhine, the first stories appear that describe a diabolical and often gigantic figure who hunts fairies or dwarves. In the *Eckenlied* (Song of Ecke), Dietrich von Bern—in other words, Theodoric the Great—meets in the Tyrol forests a wild maiden named Babehilt. She rules a kingdom in the sea (*im mer han ich ain schoenes lant*) and is pursued through the forest by its lord and his pack of hounds. "He is named Fasolt, and he rules over the wild lands." This figure is a giant who blows a horn, is clad in armor, and wears his hair braided like a woman. When he catches sight of Dietrich, who protects Babehilt, he enters into a rage and says, "You have taken my maiden from me. . . . I have pursued her today from yon far mountain. . . . What gives you the right to steal my prey?"[1] Because Dietrich is wounded, however, Fasolt does not engage him in combat. Fasolt and Babehilt are both supernatural creatures, but the anonymous author offers no reasons for this Hunt. We should note, however, that a certain Fasolt appears as a weather demon in a charm from the end of the fifteenth century.

All is made somewhat clearer when we refer to the *Virginal* and to its variations *Dietrich and his Companions* and *The First Adventure of Dietrich,* a romance and adventure story from the end of the thirteenth century, centered on the adventures of Dietrich von Bern and

65

Virginal, queen of a populace of dwarves who live in the caves of the Tyrol. Each year, Virginal must deliver a young girl as a tribute to a giant named Orkîse, whose name brings to mind the picture of an ogre. Once selected, the victim enters the forest, where she will be pursued by Orkîse and devoured. Here the story matches the legends connected to place spirits who tolerate only those who regularly offer them sacrifices in their territories.[2] The legend can also combine with that of the master of animals, a genius loci, as in this example:

> Near Lüneberg lived a man whose son, on Christmas night, slew prey pursed by the pack of the wild huntsman [wilder jäger]. Hence-forth, the man had to offer a cow during each part of the Hunt.* The animal would be taken away and never seen again. One day, he had had enough of this sacrifice and kept the cow. The pack first entered the stable and sniffed at the animal, which went stark, rav-ing mad. Because the door remained closed, a tempestuous wind gusted and shook the house so strongly that it seemed the structure would collapse at any moment. Trembling, the peasant opened the door, and because the cow immediately took flight with its tail up, he cast after it a curse, "In the name of the three devils, away with you" [na denn lop in Dreedüwels Namen]. Ever since this time, the diabolical huntsman has not crossed through the house again, even when the doors and windows are open.

This indicates that the wild huntsman is a spirit of place, the owner of a specific territory and the wild animals found therein. These ani-mals are his herd, and hunting them is his pastime. This also involves the theme of the master of the animals.[3] The explanation for the final sentence of the story: when you hear the wild huntsman, you must close your doors and windows and avoid looking outside.

The final medieval testimony comes from the Wunderer, which is undoubtedly from the same era but is known only through its later versions

---

*Therefore, each year during the twelve days of Christmas.

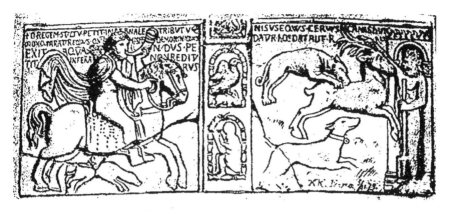

Figure 6.1. Theodoric the Great as wild huntsman.
Bas-relief from the Basilica of San Zeno, Verona.

of the fifteenth and sixteenth centuries.[4] Here, too, the hero is Dietrich von Bern, and the action takes place in the Tyrol Mountains, but the female figure is now Dame Fortune (Frau Saelde)—in fact, a fairy or supernatural being known in the Tyrol region as Salige—and her pursuer is a giant called the Wunderer. The name of the woman allows us to venture an interpretation: This is undoubtedly a literary vision that has been transposed into the courtly world of the struggle between good and evil and, on an older and more rural level, that of the battle between the powers—the spirits of the local land who govern the prosperity or misfortune of human beings.

The principal elements of the three stories of the Wunderer can be summed up in this way: The enemy of the maiden is an ogre who has exterminated her family or that of the queen. His dogs attack the victim, and the sound of his horn sparks terror in the heart of the maiden over whom he claims to have rights. The Wunderer claims that Frau Saelde has been promised to him and that he shall wed her.

Behind this story that appears to be the avatar of a myth there is a hierogamy whose purpose is to guarantee the prosperity of a region. We should note that this theme of the pursuit of a supernatural being is very widespread. For example, in Värmland, in western Sweden, the wood spirit (*skogsrå*) adopts the guise of a woman with drooping breasts who is tracked by a hunter accompanied by two black hounds.

The Testimony of Renward Cysat

Renward Cysat, town clerk of Lucerne, tackles the theme of the diabolical huntsman on several occasions, and two passages from his work are quite significant.

> Another ghost lingers in the mountain near Lake Pilatus. He gives shepherds no end of trouble and bothers the animals, especially in areas where people live dissolute lives with no fear of God. This is the infernal or diabolical huntsman [*der höllische oder Tüfflische Jeger*], who is called Türst. At the fall of night, he goes out with his pack of hounds and descends on poor livestock, which then scatter and stop giving milk. He blows his hunting horn, and the poor beasts are compelled to come to him. Then there are his diabolical dogs, who run on three paws, barking with a hollow and unnatural sound as if it were muffled. When they hear them, the animals scatter. . . .
>
> Often heard in our mountains and in the thick forests is the night huntsman [*nacht jeger*], an evil spirit [*ein böss gespenst*]. He hunts at night with his dogs, blowing his horn, and with other companions, as men are accustomed to do while hunting. His dogs have been seen running on their three paws and baying in muffled, hoarse, and terrifying voices. They are a great peril for livestock, which become terrified when they hear them, then scatter and sicken.[5]

A new motif appears in this legend complex: three-footed dogs. This monstrous detail is intended to solidly anchor the dogs' infernal nature: from the end of the eleventh century, many made allusion to this mutilation among the dogs and horses of the nocturnal hosts. When listing demonic glamors, the jurist Philippus Camerarius (1537–1624) cites three-legged rabbits with eyes of fire that lure hunters toward dangerous areas; he also includes ghosts (*phantasmata*) who could be seen in the sky and upon the ground, hunters with their dogs who had the appearance of those long dead (*formas hominum ante defunctorum*).[6]

The local name of the diabolical huntsman is not without interest:

Türst (the Alemannic Türscht), which we saw earlier (page 32), meaning "pack of phantom hounds" or, originally, "giant,"[7] proves that this figure clearly served as a model for diabolical huntsman of the exempla.

In Denmark, Odin sets out in pursuit of a supernatural being. In a long article, Hans Ellekilde addresses the theme of the wild huntsman, called Odin here, and other related figures (Grøn Jette, Groen, Valdemar, Kong Volmer, Natjoegeren, etc.) in the traditions of the Isle of Møn and other Danish islands.[8] The case file he assembles and analyzes emphasizes the importance of the horn and dog motifs,[9] and the testimonies he cites show how the theme of the wild huntsman blends and intersects with that of the king sleeping in the mountain (*Klintekongen*), the priest's mistress,[10] and the cup stolen by the spirits or bestowed by them. We find, for example, the pursuit of a supernatural being, an ondine (*havfrue*)[11] or an elf (*ellefrue*).[12]

The kinship of the theme of the wild huntsman and the diabolical hunter—each time the victim is a woman pursued by a demonic being[13]—seems to indicate that Caesarius of Heisterbach and Helinand borrowed the framework of their examples from folk epics in the vein of the *Eckenlied*. Though it was clearly possible for Caesarius to have been inspired by German folk traditions, it is less certain that this is true of Hélinand for the ancient testimonies are lacking, unless we accept that the original strata of the complex is represented by the sacrifice offered to the local place spirit. We can retain this hypothesis, because French legends have preserved the memory of similar events.

Traditions and Innovation

One of these legends recounts this: "Once upon a time, the young girls of Ennordes, in the Berry region, drew lots to learn which of them would have to go to the monster that awaited them in the heart of the forest. One day, an intrepid knight met one of these distraught victims, accompanied her, and slew the monster."[14]

The borrowing is quite clear if we refer to later legends (from the sixteenth to nineteenth century). Around 1635, Hans Kreppel, a peasant from the Saalfeld region, goes out to cut trees. A small marsh woman appears and asks him to make three crosses on the trunk of the last tree he cuts down, but he fails to honor her request. The next day, the woman appears again and tells him, "Alas, man, why did you not mark the trunk with three crosses? You would have benefited thereby, and it would have given us aid, because the wild huntsman pursues us from noon into the night without cease, and slays us miserably. We shall have no respite unless we are able to sit upon trunks that have been marked this way. He cannot remove us from them, and we are safe." The man still refuses to draw the crosses, whereupon the woman leaps upon him and grips him so tightly that he falls ill. Since that day, he never neglected to draw the crosses.[15]

When the inhabitants of the Mountains of Giants (Riesengebirge) in Bohemia hear the yell of the huntsman, the blast of his horn, and the din of wild beasts at night, they say: "There's the night huntsman," and they specify that he has set off in pursuit of tiny women clad in moss,[16] who are sometimes viewed as condemned souls that undergo punishment.

The meaning of these stories is unclear: who are these tiny women, and why are they hunted? In their present state, these legends look like the vestiges of an ancient belief whose meaning is now lost, but which seems to have a close connection to the notion of regional place spirits.*[17]

The Union of the Cock and the Dog

Philippe Walter has recently proposed a new interpretation of the facts based on his analysis of the forms of the Hennequin, one of the names for the leader of the Infernal Hunt. He suggests that the name can be read as cock dog (German *Han, Henne* + Norman *quin*).[18]

---

*A certain kinship exists between the wild huntsman and another mythic hunter, Orion, who is also a giant and who, according to Hygin, tries to rape Pleione when she travels through Boetia. Jupiter casts them both into the sky, which is why Orion still seems to pursue her. The *Premier Mythographe du Vatican* (ca. 875–1075) distorts this information and talks of seven young girls pursued by Orion (III, 32), which permits its author to explain the origins of the Pleiades.

To lend weight to his hypothesis, he studied the possible role played by the rooster and the dog in ancient beliefs, and he unearthed an important fact provided by Thietmar of Mereseburg: "in January, every eight years, the inhabitants of the Lejre region—in other words, Roskilde, in Sjaelland (Denmark)—sacrifice dogs and cocks to the gods. This is no isolated testimony. We can find a Christianized version of it in the legend of St. Tropez: when his decapitated body came ashore, those who discovered it found a rooster near it."[19] These tales indicate that two animals were connected to a sacrificial and funereal rite that took place during the Christmas season— Thietmar mentions the day after the "theophany of the Lord." Philippe Walter concludes from this that Hellequin/Hennequin is a roving spirit, a giant psychopomp that oversees the seasonal journey of souls, which offers a new and plausible explanation for the figure of the hunt leader.

The symbolism of the two animals seems relatively clear if we refer to archaeological findings. A group of three clay statues was found in a field of Gallo-Roman urns that depicted a Matrona with a child, a rooster, and a dog.[20] On a symbolic level, the dog represents death and the cock stands for resurrection. We can recall the Swedish saying "the dead are put to flight by a red rooster."* The Latvians slew a black cat, black dog, and black rooster when they believed they were threatened by Meris, the Plague Virgin. The blood of these three was used to coat a rope twisted backward, which was then used to gird the house.[21] As a symbol of resurrection, a chicken (or goose) egg was placed in Celtic tombs and, more specifically, in ossuary vessels that contained the remnants of cremated bodies. We can also note that the body of a woman who was forty to sixty years of age was found in a Celtic tomb in the Valais canton, in a wooden coffin that also held, among other objects, a cup with five chicken eggs.[22] In Geren, in the Upper Valais, a depiction of a woman showed that on the front of the lower half of her body was an anthropomorphic figure and a rooster.[23]

This is how Phillipe Walter decodes the myth of the death of the cock and dog: the name (The Union of the Cock and the Dog) reflects the

---

*För tuppar röda springa de döda.

coupling of the two holy animals charged with the duty of expressing the sacred cosmological act and the hierogamy that establishes universal order at the moment of renewal when the solstice takes place. The pursuit of a supernatural being by the wild huntsman "would be nothing less than the hunting of the Virgin Mother (Great Goddess) for the purpose of a divine hierogamy realized by the union of the cock and the dog." This utterly new reading of the legend returns the wild huntsman to a mythological and religious context, which clearly reflects that of its origins.

Walter's hypothesis does not contradict the notion of the place spirit. Instead, it shows that there cannot simply be one lone, canonical, reading of these myths transformed into legends. My considerations reflect instead the ambiguities of folk traditions that do not stop evolving over the course of time.

Punishments

The legend therefore continuously welcomes new motifs: such as that of the hardy spirit who, on hearing the wild hunter passing, wishes the hunter good luck or shouts out a request for a piece of the booty. Later, this rash individual may receive a part of a human being or find a man nailed to his door. We find attestation for this motif in Alsace, the Ardennes, Berry, Bourbannais, and Morvan, as well as in Normandy, Poitou, Saintonge, and the Vendée,[24] and, undoubtedly, it forms part of the legacy of all Europe.

Here is an example collected in north Germany, near Saalfeld: a peasant travels into the mountains to cut wood, and while he is there, the wild huntsman passes by. The huntsman is invisible, but all can hear the baying of his hounds. For fun, the peasant shouts that he wants to help him hunt. The following morning, when the peasant returns to his stable, he sees hanging there a quarter of the corpse of a marsh woman—in other words, his part of the hunt.[25] In the Cholet region, if someone shouts, "Galerie Hunt, leave me a piece of what you are hunting," when the hunter passes, the next morning, the shouter may find near his house the arm or leg of a little child.[26]

Next is the motif of curiosity punished: "A young lad of Petze who gathered wood late one evening was much too curious. He had heard that a person could boldly look at the wild huntsman if he did so through a key. He thus hid a key on his body, and when the hunt passed overhead—Giff, gaff! Hoho, hoho!—he closed one eye and looked up at the sky with the other through the opening of the key. What he saw then he has never told a soul, because he has been mute ever since, and ten horses could not drag him back into the woods. He also lost an eye and became a ward of the commune."[27]

Percht herself has been introduced into the theme of the wild hunter. In some stories she travels with a cart full of people and hurls death at those who demand their share of the booty.[28] In others she plants her ax in the knee of anyone who hides to spy on her when she passes, accompanied by her seven dogs. The following year, she returns to retrieve her tool.[29]

Folklorization

Though we temporarily bring this wild huntsman theme to a close, we must note that the folkloric strata, which is visible through the surface of the *Eckenlied,* was Christianized at least once on the English side of the Channel. In the beginning of the thirteenth century Gervase of Tilbury recounts this story:

A knight who lived near Penrith in the Cumberland hunted one day in the woods. . . . He was caught by surprise by a sudden storm that blew with violent thunder and lightning. Through the thunderbolts that set the forest alight here and there, he saw by the gleam of the lightning flashes a large dog that spit fire from its jaws. Terrified by such an extraordinary apparition, the knight then luckily spied approaching him a knight who held a hunting horn. Fraught with fear, he ran toward the newcomer and explained to him the reason for his fright. "Have no fear," the other reassured him, "I am St. Simeon, whom you called upon in your prayers in the midst of the lightning. I give you this horn, which shall protect you and yours forever. . . ." Then St. Simeon

Figure 6.2. Death as a hunter. Johann von Tepla, *Der Ackerman aus Böhmen* (Bamberg: n.p., 1461), detail.

asked if the knight had seen anything that had inspired his awe or astonishment. The knight answered that he had seen a dog that spit thunderbolts from its mouth. St. Simeon, continuing along his way, disappeared, leaving the horn to the knight in memory of this high deed. . . . Meanwhile, the dog of this tale entered the house of a priest who lived near the village in question, and then, leaving through another door, burned down that house along with its very illegitimate family.[30]

St. Simeon, who purportedly comes to protect the knight from the storm, appears here as the huntsman, as shown by his horn. Yet he does not pursue the thunderbolt-spitting hound, contrary to what Gervase suggests. Instead, he is following it, because he is hunting with it and has come to punish with fire the illicit household of a priest. Thus freely inspired by the theme of the wild huntsman and connecting it to that of the lustful priest, Gervase blurs the elements and transforms the substance of legend into an exemplum.

The legend of the diabolical hunter, which fits into the large cycle of the punishment of sin, is therefore highly Christianized, but rare testimonies inform us that the figure is not of Christian origin, but the cursed hunter is a creation of the church.

7

The Cursed Hunter

THE LEGEND OF THE CURSED HUNTER remains, beyond all transformation, an exemplum intended to illustrate the postmortem fate of a sinner. It presents no major difficulties, because, contrary to texts we have uncovered, its structure is closed, and the possibilities for interpolation remain weak, although all the paradigms (or almost all of them) may vary.

Sin Punished

One of the first testimonies we focus on is from a Meistersang by Michel Beheim (ca. 1416/21–1474/78). It illustrates the danger of ill-considered words reminiscent of the biblical admonition "You shall not take the name of the Lord in vain."

> One fine day, Count Eberhart of Wirtenberg went by himself to hunt in the forest. He soon heard a loud uproar and saw an alarming creature appear in pursuit of a stag. In terror, he fell to the ground and sought refuge in a copse, where he asked the apparition if he intended to do him harm. The unknown figure answered, "No, I am a man like you. I was once a lord who was passionately fond of hunting, and one day, I asked God if he would permit me to hunt until Judgment Day. To my great misfortune, my wish was granted, and it has already been five hundred years that I have hunted this

single stag." Eberhart then asked him, "Show me your face that I might possibly recognize you." The other uncovered his face. It was the size of a fist and as wrinkled and dry as a dead leaf. He then rode off in pursuit of the stag.[1]

This story occupies its own place in the corpus of the cursed hunter. The hunter is punished for hunting on Sunday, for damaging crops, for slaying a stag in a church. His passion for hunting is punished and condemns him to the eternal hunt, without any break or rest, until the day of Last Judgment. This type of legend was extremely popular, and Paul Sébillot has collected a large number of them:[2] "The noises of the Chasse Hennequin* are the baying of the pack of the hunter who was cursed for hunting during holy services and profaning the Sabbath. Now he is condemned by God to hunt through the night without cease. . . . Also heard are the sounds of riders and trumpet calls."[3]

When the notion of sin is absent, what appears is that of spirit—proof that the theme of the cursed hunter derives from that of the wild huntsman. This point is clear in the *Histoire de France et des choses mémorables* by Pierre Matthieu, printed in Paris in 1605, which relates this event, which occurred in 1598: "The king† was hunting in the vast Forest of Fontainebleau when he heard, as if half a league away, the yapping of dogs and the cry and horns of hunters. In a moment, this noise that seemed to be quite far off appeared about twenty feet from his ear. He requested his lordship, the count of Soissons, to push forward through the brush to learn who this might be. He little liked that there was someone so bold that he would meddle with his hunt and disturb his pastime. Advancing, the count of Soissons heard the noise, but he did not see from where it was coming. A large man in black appeared in the thickness of the brush, and he shouted: "Hear me," before suddenly disappearing. . . . The shepherds of the area said that it was a spirit who hunted in this forest—one they called the great huntsman. Others maintained that it was the saint,

---

*[The name of the Wild Hunt in the Baugé region, in Maine-et-Loire. —*Trans.*]
†[Henri IV. —*Trans.*]

Hubert Hunt, who could be heard in other places."[4]

Abraham Gölnitz[5] speaks of a *phantosme* and a *roaming spirit* that shouts "Mend your ways!" He states more explicitly: "the manual laborers, charcoal burners, woodchoppers, shepherds, and peasants of the area reported seeing a large black man leading a pack of dogs." In the Rousillon and in Catalonia, the black huntsman (*caçador negre*), still called *mal caçador* and *gran caçador,* comes from the same legend, but these names also apply to the autumn squalls in the Pyrenees, which bring to mind Fasolt of the *Eckenlied.* In the Catalan Ripollès, the mal caçador was condemned to hunt a prey he would never catch, because he left Mass at the time of Communion to hunt with his dogs.[6] Arnaut, Count of Pallars, who ruled over the upper valleys of the kingdom of Majorca in the thirteenth century, allegedly seduced the mother superior of the Convent of St. Joan of the Abadesses. Unmasked as the author of this sin, he was condemned to die without a grave and to spend eternity roaming the skies after nightfall. In addition, we can note the case of the parish priest Esteben de Garibay: he was punished for accepting assistance from the devil and must eternally wander the skies over Lower Navarre. The notion of sin is dominant in this entire legend complex.

Johann von Trittenheim, also known as Johannes Trithemius (1462–1516), Benedictine and abbot of St. James in Würzburg, leaves us this account:

On December 21, 1354, Walram, count of Spanheim, died and was buried. The following night, Gottfried, his castle chaplain, "heard a voice in the forest like that of a hunter exciting his dogs to pursue a beast of prey." A man clad in fire [*igne vestitus*] and riding a black horse was surrounded by a vast number of black and terrible dogs. This man spoke to him: "My lord Gottfried, have no fear! I am the soul of Count Walram, and I suffer this punishment for the pleasure I have taken in the hunt and for devastating the fields and vineyards of my serfs. Tell my sons they should have thirty Masses said in thirty days for my deliverance, and they must feed as many poor people during the same number of days." Walram also made other requests.

This version, which is centered around the punishment of a sin, belongs to a vast complex that has produced many legends: that of the man in the moon[7] (a man who was gathering wood on a Sunday was cast onto the moon, where we can now see him with his bundle of firewood); that of the wandering Jew[8] (for having demanded of Herod the condemnation of Jesus, the cobbler Cartaphilus, Buttadeus, or Ahasver must wander the earth for eternity, and it is said that the soles of his feet are covered by a layer of horn two fingers thick); and finally, that of the Flying Dutchman (Fliegende Holländer),[9] which the French know as the Vaisseau fantôme,* a theme immortalized by Richard Wagner.

The Repetition of the Sin

Yet the theme of the cursed hunter is not limited to stories about damned huntsmen. Hunting, which in fact represents a perpetual wandering and the repetition of one act, has also been, since the Middle Ages, the punishment for other sins. In the *Vision of Thurkill,* written at the beginning of the thirteenth century and sometimes attributed to Ralph of Coggeshall, we see a theater on the stage of which sinners regularly repeat their sins, a performance, which the devils would not miss for all the world.[10]

This legend has certainly been contaminated by that of the Wild Hunt, as shown in an exemplum by Étienne of Bourbon (Stephen of Bourbon), whose composite structure makes it worth citing in extenso.

> I have heard say that a peasant, who carried a bundle of firewood beneath the moonlight in the area of Mont du Chat† saw an immense pack of hounds that seemed to be baying on the trail of their prey. A throng of footmen and riders followed them. When he asked one of them who they were, the man responded, "Knights of King Arthur,"

---

*[Ghost ship. —*Trans.*]
†In Savoy.

and that they were on the way to his nearby court, where a fine time was promised to all. The aforementioned peasant followed after them into a palace full of large, magnificent chambers, and there he saw knights and their ladies playing, dancing, eating, and quaffing fine drink and delicate dishes, before being offered a bed. He was led to a chamber in which stood a richly decorated bed. In this bed lay a most beautiful lady. He took his pleasure and fell asleep beside her, but on awakening in the morning, he found himself lying on his bundle of firewood. The whole experience had been a hoax.

Étienne of Bourbon illustrates some diabolical cheats: the demons sometimes adopt "the appearance of knights going on a hunt" (*in similitudine militum venantium*), he says in an epigraph, and this is the first trace of a connection between Mesnie Hellequin (a name for the Wild Hunt in France) and a simple hunt, and his syballine story combines the themes of the Infernal Hunt and the cursed hunter.

King Arthur

There is also a tradition making King Arthur the leader of the Furious Army (a German name for the Wild Hunt) or a cursed huntsman.[11] We must note, however, that Étienne of Bourbon says nowhere that these are the dead. It is up to the reader or listener to deduce this by relying on other traditions.

For his part, Gervase of Tilbury notes (*Otia Imperiala* II, 12): "The forest guard,* whom the common folk call foresters—in other words, the guardians of the hunters' nets, the game reserves, or the royal woods—recount how they often see on certain days, around the noon hour† and during the first half of the night, when the full moon is shining, a com-

---

*Of Great Britain and Brittany.
†We should not be surprised to see this diurnal hour: it is just as dangerous as midnight and witnesses the appearance of the noon demon, Meridiana. Both the middle of the day and the middle of the night are temporal portals that establish a connection between this world and the other.

pany of knights hunting, accompanied by the din of hounds and horns. They answer those who question them that they are the retinue and house of Arthur."[12]

When speaking of the *familia* Arturia, Étienne of Bourbon forges a link to a tradition that maintains that this monarch did not lead an exemplary life, as *The Prose Lancelot* informs us.[13] He is described here as caught *flagrant delit,* committing adultery, the reason why he was excommunicated. The Modena manuscript of *The Legend of the Holy Grail* has handed down another tradition in which we can see King Arthur after his disappearance to the Isle of Avalon:[14] *"li Bretons . . . cuidaient tos que il revenist. Mais tant sachiés vos que li au quant l'ont puis ve es forès chacier, et ont oï ses chiens avec lui."**

Folk traditions have preserved the memory of Arthur's damnation: in the Maine region, the Chasse Artu[†] designates the passing of demons carrying the body of a reprobate.

From Sinner to Hunter

Undoubtedly influenced by popular legends about the diabolical hunts-man and the cursed hunter, and through reliance on a particular accep-tance of the verb *jagen,* "to move quickly"—in Norwegian the phrase *å jage av sted* means "a movement" often with no determined purpose—a new group of narratives began transforming into hunters men who had died in a state of sin. The explanation for this was surely the posi-tion taken by the medieval church on hunting, which it condemned and anathematized on many occasions. Here is a significant example of the infernal coloration that gradually began affecting the theme of the hunt:

Abel, second son of Count Waldemar of Denmark, slew his brother

---

*"The Britons . . . all believe he shall return. But many are those known to have seen him hunting in the forest, and they have heard his dogs with him."
†[Arthur's Hunt. —*Trans.*]

in 1250 then fell in 1252, when fighting the Frisons. He was buried in St. Peter's Church in Schleswig, but numerous hauntings occurred. His body was removed from the religious building and submerged in a swamp in the Pöl Forest, near Gottorp, after the coffin had been pierced through with a stake. During this time, the area became haunted and those who passed near it heard the sound of a hunting horn and saw a man. Everywhere, it was said that the man was Abel and that his mouth and his body were black and that he rode a small horse of the same color and that he was accompanied by three dogs glowing like fire.[15]

We can find this testimony by Brother Boissen, counselor to Duke Johann Adolph of Holstein-Gottorp (1575–1611), in the *Schleswig Chronicle*. It shows, moreover, that a proven precaution—piercing the coffin and body through with a stake—had no effect, doubtless because fratricide was too great a crime to prevent the deceased from leaving his final resting place: a swamp. Swamps were considered preeminent malefic spots, and the ancient Germans once tossed certain criminals in them.

Conclusions

The legends of the diabolical huntsman, the wild huntsman, and the cursed hunter form a complete set for which we can sketch an outline of specific time categories. Originally, we find a supernatural being, an ogre or giant, in pursuit of another fantasy creature, a lady of the woods, a fairy who has been promised to him. Because she refuses his suit, he wishes to kill and devour her.

Philippe Walter has shown that the supernatural being was a composite mythical creature—a goddess of the dead or psychopomp?—connected to the rooster (or the chicken) and to the dog. This sets off the debate again about the name of the leader of the Wild Hunt and suggests that the Herla component is not original. Instead, it is likely a fabrication of Walter Map or his source, the invention of a mythical king of the ancient

Bretons, introduced into the story to give it some historical heft.

The leader of the Wild Hunt was undoubtedly the avatar of an ancient, ambivalent deity who presided over death and resurrection—exactly like the Celtic Dagda, who killed men with one end of his staff and resuscitated them with the other, and whose attributes included a rooster and a dog, which symbolically reflected his dual function. This deity likely provided the name Hennequin. The story of King Herla is, then, only an etiological legend intended to shed light on the origin of the Wild Hunt. Drawing from the same sources but merging them with other mythical traditions, the story by Walter Map does not share the same intention as that of Orderic Vitalis and those of clerical literature. It is political, whereas the others are edifying and fall into the context of redemptive propaganda and a pedagogy based on fear.

Predicated on the mythological canvas and adopting the image of the devil/hunter, the ancient deity was demonized and transformed into a demon pursuing a soul in punishment, that of a sinner. We should recall that the image of Satan as hunter was established in the fourth century, in opposition to the figure of the sinner, which smacks of Christian representations. Early on St. Augustine called the devil "the worst hunter in the entire universe."[16] Yet the devil does hunt in the conventional fashion, which would correspond to the civilization of the earliest testimonies describing him as a hunter. His weapons are instead ties and hooks (laquei) and, more rarely, nets (retia) or even stingers, picks, and arrows. This image of the hunter was partially transposed upon death, which was personified and depicted as a huntress carrying a horn that she blew devilishly while pursuing her prey. She can be seen wearing this guise in Hélinand of Froidmont's *Verses on Death*.[17]

From the legendary narrative, we now move to the exemplum. The events were reinterpreted by Christianity and inscribed within a new reality. From this point, it was easy to make into sinners those individuals who were condemned to wander eternally, for these wanderers, as we have seen, were referred to with the verb *jagen* and the noun *jagd*, which facilitates their incorporation into hunters *stricto sensu*. At a given moment, the word *hunter* metonymically designated the sinner.

We can easily identify each group of this corpus centered on the notion of hunting, for each is characterized by one or more specific and recurring elements. In the case of the diabolical huntsman, this element was the active intervention of a living individual who attempted to save the hunted person, failed, and then saw the devil carrying off his prey, which he tossed across his saddle. In that of the wild huntsman, the nature of the protagonists, first and foremost, distinguishes this group of stories from the others. Another distinguishing element is the motif of a share in the hunt. In the case of the cursed hunter, the explanation provided by the dead person transforms the narrative into a pedagogical exemplum. We can note one constant: the appearance most often takes place in a forest.

Some stories remain unclassifiable, because we do not know the nature of the hunter—as is, for example, the case with Herne, the name of a ghostly huntsman well known in the Berkshires, who appears in Shakespeare's *Merry Wives of Windsor* (IV, 4, 28–38). There are a number of traditions that maintain that he was a forest warden who committed suicide.

> There is an old tale that Herne the Hunter,
> Sometime a keeper in Windsor Forest,
> Doth all the wintertime, at still midnight,
> Walk around about an oak, with great ragged horns;
> And there he blasts the tree, and takes the cattle,
> And makes milch-kine* yield blood, and shakes a chain
> In a most hideous and dreadful manner:
> You have heard of such a spirit, and well you know
> The superstitious idle-headed eld
> Received and did deliver to our age
> This tale of Herne the hunter for a truth.[18]

---

*Milk cows.

This tale, however, does not mesh with our typology, and we should undoubtedly view it as the reminiscence of a much older myth.*

Stories are not fossils. They permanently combine and evolve. They are reworked in accordance with the literary genres that adopt them[†] and become harder and harder to classify. Starting from the fifteenth or sixteenth century, we can note fusions and contamination, and only the indexing and analysis of medieval testimonies make it possible to track down the corpus of legends collected in the nineteenth century.

I close this chapter by offering the future of this legend based on two examples collected in Savoy in 1964 and 1965:[19] the Resseran is a man who preferred hunting rabbit with his two dogs on Christmas Day rather than attending Mass, as everyone advised him to do. When he reached the Rochas, his gun went off accidentally, killing him. Since that time, on Christmas Day and even at other times of the year, people can hear the Résseran's two dogs wildly pursuing a rabbit (St. Nicholas-la-Chapelle).

The Rachaseran—another name for the same individual—was a hunter accompanied by a pack of hounds who crossed the mountains with the speed of a lightning bolt. Misbehaving children were told, "The Reçhasséran is going to get you!" One night, a man yelled out, "Reçhasséran, give me a piece of what you are hunting!" The Reçhasséran immediately tossed a piece of meat down the chimney of his house. The meat began swelling to an inordinate size until it filled up the entire house, forcing the occupants to leave (Saint-Georges-d'Hurtières).[20]

---

*Worth singling out are two elements: Herne represents the malefic pole of Dumézil's third function (fertility, fecundity), and his appearance is harmful to plants and animals. He bears horns on his forehead, which brings to mind the myth of Actaeon, whom Diana transformed into a stag after he surprises her naked (Ovid, *Metamorphoses* III, 138*ff.*). The goddess with the quiver "endows his brow . . . with the antlers of a mature stag, lengthens his neck, sharpens the tips of his ears to narrow points, replaces his hands to hooves and his arms with legs, and garbs his entire body with a dappled hide," after which Actaeon is killed, slain by his own hounds.

†The finest example is that of the eighth story in the fifth volume of Boccaccio's *Decameron*.

PART THREE

The Wild Hunt

8
The Legend of King Herla

BEFORE VENTURING FURTHER in our study of the Wild Hunt, we must remind ourselves of what distinguishes it from the troop of the dead and phantom armies. The members of the Wild Hunt possess a leader, they wear the guise they wore during their final hours of life, and only one of them responds to a questioner. Here, we enter the core of the subject, and the preceding details make it possible to establish distinctions and how elements have been mixed.

There are two fundamental texts to which we should refer: one by Orderic Vitalis and the other by Walter Map. The two narratives are akin yet quite different: both are essential for considering the origin of the belief. Because these texts are most often summarized or only partially cited, I have decided to reproduce them in total so that we may not isolate a single element from its context.

The Testimony of Walter Map

The legend of King Herla has made its way down to us through Walter Map, born in Wales between 1135 and 1140 (died 1209 or 1210). In his *De nugis curialium* (The Courtiers' Trifles), written between 1180 and 1186, we read this: ". . . A king of the most ancient Britons, Herla it is said, was interviewed by another king who was a pygmy in respect of his low stature, not above that of a monkey. This little creature was mounted

Figure 8.1. Depiction of elves and the night dance of specters.
Olaus Magnus, *Historia de gentibus septentrionalibus* (Rome: n.p., 1555).

on a large goat, says the tale, and might be described in the same terms as
Pan. His visage was fiery red, his head huge. He had a long red beard that
reached to his chest, which was gaily attired in a spotted fawn's skin. His
belly was hairy and his legs declined into goats' hoofs."[1]

We should not attach too much importance to this depiction of a
dwarf king: it is entirely borrowed from scholarly Roman literature and
has no correspondence whatsoever with autochthonous elements. We
should note, however, that the Latin *pygmaeus* was commonly used to
translate the word dwarf (*zwerc, dveorg, dvergr*) and that Herla is invited
by a dwarf king who paid him a visit one day. According to legend, pygmies rode rams and goats when they headed into battle with cranes. We
should regard this goat, then, not as a mythological component, but as
a symbol of the pygmy's nature, because, in the entire body of medieval
literature, this animal represents lust.[2]

Herla found himself tête-à-tête with this being, who said, "I am the king
over many kings and princes, an unnumbered and innumerable people,

and am sent, a willing messenger, by them to you. I am unknown to
you, it is true, but I glory in the renown which has exalted you above
other monarchs, inasmuch as you are a hero and also closely connected
to me in place and descent, and so deserve that your wedding should
be brilliantly adorned with my presence as a guest, as soon as the king
of the Franks has bestowed his daughter upon you. This matter is
already being arranged, though you know it not, and the ambassadors
will be here this very day. Let this be a lasting agreement between us:
I shall first attend your wedding and you mine on the same day a year
hence." With these words, swifter than a tiger, he turned and vanished
from view. The king returned home, struck with wonder, received the
ambassadors, and accepted their proposals.[3]

Several details merit our attention. The dwarf is a powerful sovereign whose people have in some way chosen Herla as a worthy ally, and
he declares they are kin. These syballine assertions become clearer once
we know that dwarves are, among other things, a representation of the
dead who continue to live as they once did, thus retaining their social
and familial organization.[4] Their otherworld is not in the beyond. What
we can take away from the story thus far is that the principal reason for
the dwarf's vision is to conclude a pact, but Herla does not know exactly
to what he commits. This is something we, and he, learn later.

Another legendary theme emerges in the background: the double
invitation.[5] Several witnesses recount a dead man's visit to his surviving
friend's wedding, and the pretext for the return invitation is sometimes
the marriage that the deceased contracts in the beyond with a supernatural entity.[6]

When he took his place in state on the wedding day, before the first
course, the pygmy made his appearance with so vast a crowd of similar
beings that the tables were filled and a larger number sat down outside
the hall than within it, in pavilions brought by the pygmy, which were
set up in a moment of time. Out of these pavilions darted servants

bearing vessels, each made of a single precious stone by some not imitable art, and the servants filled the palaces and tents with plates of gold and jewels. No food or drink was served in silver or wood. Wherever they were wanted, they were at hand: nothing that they brought was from the royal stock or elsewhere. They lavished their own provision throughout, and what they had brought with them more than satisfied the utmost wishes of all. Nothing of Herla's preparations was touched: his own servants sat with their hands before them, neither called for nor offering aid. Round went the pygmies, gaining golden opinions from everyone. Their splendid clothing and jewels made them shine like burning lights among the company. They were never importunate and never out of the way, yet they vexed no one by act or word. Their king, while his servants were in the midst of their business, addressed King Herla in these terms: "Noble King, I take God to witness that I am present at your wedding in accordance with our agreement. Yet if there be anything more of your contract than you see here that you can prescribe to me, I will gladly supply it to the last point. If there be nothing, see that you do not put off the repayment of the honor conferred on you when I require it." And so, without awaiting a reply, he swiftly betook himself to his pavilion, and about cockcrow, he departed with his people.[7]

This entire passage shows the wealth and power of the dwarves, stereotypes of medieval literature that nonetheless correspond to a well-established belief: the otherworld is full of riches; it is a veritable land of plenty—which is why so many heroes attempt to get there. Those who succeed on entering and returning are rich or have been given a mighty gift. The dwarf king returns to the notion of a pact, which emphasizes its importance and shows that the gifts of food evoked so emphatically are binding and equivalent to a veritable potlatch: the dwarf has honored his commitment, and it is up to Herla to do the same.

In one final detail we clearly see the existence of a connection between dwarves and the dead: the visitors disappear at cockcrow.

Multiple German testimonies state that the light of the sun petrifies dwarves. They are chthonic and nocturnal beings. Yet the term *dwarf* may be out of place here, because the text tells us these visitors are as resplendent as lights, which would correspond more to luminous and helpful beings, such as elves.[8]

> After a year had passed, he suddenly appeared before Herla, and called on him to fulfill his agreement. To this, Herla consented, and after providing himself with supplies sufficient for an adequate repayment, he followed whither he was led. The party entered a cave on a high cliff, and after an interval of darkness, passed in a light that seemed to proceed not from the sun or moon, but from a multitude of lamps, to the mansion of the pygmy. This was as comely in every part as the palace of the sun described by Naso.* Here, the wedding was celebrated. The pygmy's offices were duly recompensed, and when leave was given, Herla departed laden with gifts and presents of horses, dogs, hawks, and every appliance of the best for hunting or fowling. The pygmy escorted them as far as the place where darkness began, and then he presented the king with a small bloodhound, strictly enjoining him that on no account must any of his train dismount until the dog leaped from the arms of his bearer. And so he took leave and returned home.[9]

We should pay particularly close attention to the elements of this passage, because they contain the core of the narrative. We see that Herla has plunged into a hollow mountain (in a high cliff), which contains several different areas: a dark no-man's-land, which serves as an airlock, then the place where the dwarf's palace stands. The details concerning the ambient light are confirmed by other texts:[10] the light of the otherworld is different from that of ours. The romances explain it from time to time as due to the presence of carbuncles that illuminate this underground space. We can note that the gifts foreshadow the

---

*[From Ovid. —*Trans.*]

transformation of King Herla and his companions into hunters. Most important, the dog occupies a very special place: he belongs to the dark region. "Within a short space, Herla arrived once more at the light of the sun and at his kingdom, where he accosted an old shepherd and asked for news of his queen, naming her. The shepherd gazed at him with astonishment and said, 'Sir, I can hardly understand your speech, for you are a Briton and I a Saxon—but the name of that queen I have never heard, save that they say that long ago, over the very ancient Britons, there was a queen of that name who was the wife of King Herla, and he, the old story says, disappeared in company with a pygmy at this very cliff, and was never seen on earth again, and it is now two hundred years since the Saxons took possession of this kingdom and drove out the old inhabitants.'"[11]

We can note in this that the time spent at the dwarf's is equivalent to several centuries,[12] which means that Herla truly visits the otherworld, and this detail confirms that the hollow mountain is a kingdom of the dead,[13] a widespread representation in the Germanic world.[14]

So what are the consequences of this sojourn? "The king thought he had made a stay of but three days. He could scarce sit his horse for amazement. Some of his company, forgetting the pygmy's orders, dismounted before the dog had alighted, and in a moment, they fell into dust. Whereupon the king, comprehending the reason for their dissolution, warned the rest, under the pain of a like death, not to touch the earth before the alighting of the dog. The dog has not yet alighted."[15]

On contact with the ground of this world, time takes back its rights and does its work. The crumbling into dust of several knights indicates they are dead and can live only in the otherworld. Here, again, we are in the presence of extremely ancient beliefs, which maintained that death was not an ending, but the transition from one state to another: a person dies in this century, but he or she continues to lead the same life somewhere beyond the grave.[16]

Walter Map's tale includes this conclusion: "And the story says that this King Herla still holds on to his mad course with his band in eternal wanderings, without stop or stay. Many assert that they have often seen the band. Recently, it is said, however, that in the first year of the coronation of King Henry, the band ceased to visit our land in force as before. In that year, it was seen by many Welshmen to plunge into the Wye, the river of Hereford."[17]

Contrary to what we might expect, Herla and his men are considered not hunters, but an army. This detail makes sense, though, and their endless ride has nonetheless come to an end. This final point, well explained by J. C. Schmitt, testifies to the recuperation of the legend for political purposes.[18]

Walter Map revisits the story of King Herla and provides us with another version of the legend. While the first is etiological in nature—it explains the origin of this fantastic army—the Map story provides us with the perspective of its witnesses.

In Lesser Britain (Brittany) there have been seen droves of spoil by night and soldiers driving them—and they always pass in silence, and the Bretons have often "cut out" horses and beasts from among them, and made use of them, some with fatal results, others without harm to themselves.

The nocturnal companies and squadrons, too, which were called Herlethingus, were sufficiently well-known appearances in England down to the time of King Henry II, our present lord. They were troops engaged in endless wandering, in an aimless round, keeping an awestruck silence, and in them, many people were seen alive who were known to have died. This household of Herlethingus was last seen in the march of Wales and Hereford in the first year of the reign of Henry II, about noonday. They traveled as we do, with carts and sumpter horses, packsaddles and panniers, hawks and hounds, and a concourse of men and women. Those who saw them first raised the whole country against them with horns and shouts, and as is the wont of that most alert race, a large force came equipped with every weapon and, because they were unable to wring a word from them by addressing them, made ready to extort an answer with their arms. They, however, rose up into the air and vanished on a sudden.[19]

Here, the Mesnie of Herlethingus, named for the first time, does not plunge into the Wye, and the Mesnie is much more populated than in the first story. It is now a veritable army with its *impedimenta*. Contrary to many testimonies, it moves silently and not only at night. The increase in the number of its members is suggested by one detail: "many people were seen alive who were known to have died," which means that this is a troop of the dead and confirms that Herla and his companions are also dead.

We must note one last detail: Walter Map mentions two different hosts: the one seen in Wales and the one appearing in Brittany, about which he has not much to say except that the Bretons sometimes steal their animals, at times with harmful consequences. We should keep this detail in mind, for it also appears in the account by Orderic Vitalis.

Toward an Interpretation

The dwarf's participation in Herla's wedding can be read on two levels. On a historic level and in the feudal context, it is an honor, an acknowledgment of the king's grandeur, the manifestation of an alliance, which matches with a theme from the romances: the appearance of supernatural beings at the hero's wedding in order to emphasize his virtues[20] and his legitimacy as sovereign or lord.

On a mystical level appears the idea that sovereignty can be legitimate only when recognized by supernatural powers, by the otherworld. We should not forget that the king combines the three functions defined by Dumézil, and that the prosperity of the kingdom is dependent upon beings from the otherworld. The sovereign concludes a pact with them, or these individuals accept him because they know his true worth. This is the theme of choice, of election. The mythic background is extremely rich here, for these figures from the otherworld can be deceased

ancestors, and, as in Germanic beliefs, these ancestors are often confused with dwarves or elves.[21]

The visit of the dwarf conceals, however, an intention that is scarcely
obvious: it amounts to a binding gift, the nature of which emerges
only with the invitation to visit the cave. Herla has no distrust of this
dwarf whose presence heightens his prestige and flatters his vanity. He
should, however, because of an important detail that survives in Walter Map's story: this particular dwarf is redheaded, and this color had
an extremely negative connotation during the Middle Ages. As early as
the eleventh century, it is counseled in the Ruodlieb never to form the
bond of friendship with a redhead: *Non tibit sit rufus umquam specialis
amico.*[22] This phrase appears in the legend of Pope Gerbert—*Rufus est,
tunc perfidus*—and this is still proverbial wisdom in the Tyrol ("A red
beard rarely hides a good nature"—*unter rotem Bart stecjt ke gute Art*)
and in the Upper Palatinate ("Red hair and firewood never grow in a
good soil"—*Rauds Huar und Jarhulz wachsn af koin gouden Buadn*).

Furthermore, the fact that dwarves are crafty and perfidious is almost a
constant of medieval romances.[23] Herla has double reason to be cautious.

Entering the cavern—in other words, the hollow mountain—is
synonymous with death if we take at its word the Germanic literature.
The best example of this literature is furnished by the legend of King
Sveigdir, who follows a dwarf into a boulder and disappears never to be
seen again.[24] Further, "to enter the mountain" is used for "to pass away."
Numerous tales tell how a dead man invites a living man to follow him
into a hollow mountain, a veritable purgatory[25] in which the living man
finds sinners gathered in expiation for their transgressions.[26] Walter Map
treats death euphemistically—it is not even a question, but the otherworld nevertheless remains that of the dead. Two details demonstrate
this: time does not flow at the same speed there as it does in this world,[27]
and this world takes back its rights after return from the otherworld, and
causes death for those who taste earthly food or touch the ground.[28] This
motif is already vouched for in *The Voyage of Bran,* an ancient Irish tale:
"Gone in search of a land he spied in a dream, Bran and his compan-

ions, suffering from homesickness, returned several years later, though they thought they had been gone for only a year. Although the Queen of the Isle of Women had warned them that no one should step foot from the boat, Nechtan leaped from the coracle and fell forthwith into a heap of ashes 'as though he had been in the earth for many hundred years.'"[29]

In a small book with a great wealth of motifs of great antiquity, Felix Karlinger has collected numerous testimonies of journeys into the beyond that offer evidence of a distortion of time and witness the hero falling into dust.[30] In all these stories, the person who extends the invitation is a dead man, a fairy,[31] or a supernatural bird.

When Herla and his companions take their leave of the dwarf, the dwarf heaps them with presents. This act corresponds to feudal custom, but it possesses another function: the horses prevent the visitors from making contact with the ground. They therefore have the duty of psychopomps and insure the survival of their riders in our world.

The dog offered by the dwarf certainly plays the role of a guide or indicator, but it is also a guardian: as long as he does not leap to the ground, Herla and his people remain prisoners of the otherworld—in conformance with the well-known infernal nature of dogs, as vouched for by Cereberus of classical antiquity and by the dog that guards the entrance of Hel, the world of the dead for the ancient Germans.[32]

The structure of Walter Map's story shows a construction that leads to a climactic finish: the dog occupies a central place and plays a leading role. This is the pivotal point of the tale. In his decision to leap to the ground or not, he holds in his paws the fate of Herla—and thus his life. The dog gives material substance to an element already present in the legend of Orpheus: the beyond does not give back what it has taken. We can return under certain conditions, on certain dates, but we remain its prisoner. The dog therefore gives concrete expression to captivity in the otherworld. At the same time, he is the guarantor of these very particular living individuals, for they are in fact dead, in the etymological sense of the term, without truly having truly died. The dog does not jump to the ground, knowing that to do so would prove fatal to his new master who, in this case, is reduced to dust—as proved by the example of some of Herla's companions.* Justification for this hypothesis can undoubtedly be provided by an archaeological element mentioned earlier: on a field of first-century Gallo-Roman urns, a set of three statues was found that depicted a Matrona with a child, a dog, and a rooster. On a symbolic level, the dog represents death and the cock symbolizes resurrection.[33]

Among the dwarf's gifts, the dog holds a special place: it alone is so differentiated. We can ask why the dwarf gave it to his guest, but the answer can be only hypothetical: the dwarf wishes to protect Herla, his relative, and his men from dissolution—those who touch the earth crumble into dust and no longer enjoy any posthumous life—or he means that they belong to him. Whatever the truth may be, the dwarf is an ambiguous character, just as are his fellows in medieval literature: sometimes he is benevolent, sometimes he is wicked, and rarely is he neutral.

The story of the dwarf's visit to Herla can be read this way: he announces the imminent death of the king at the same time as he is admitted into another paradisiacal world, a kind of heaven of noble warriors. The dwarf therefore performs the duty of psychopomp, similar to that of the Valkyries, who collect those Odin has chosen to inhabit Valhalla (Vahöll). The primary myth is based on a complex of well-known beliefs: several worlds beyond ours exist, and not all men go to the same worlds.[34] There are the elect, and there are the common dead. The total dissolution of the body is definitive death, without any hope of return in the form of a revenant or, through the agency of reincarnation, an imprisonment in Hel. Preservation of the body makes it possible for the dead to show himself and act in this world, to come and go between the worlds without, however, being able to stay on this earth for more than a certain amount of time.

Herla's disappearance in the mountain overlays another mythic theme: the sleeping sovereign who leaves his underground home when his

---

Quidam autem ex sociis suis ante canis descensum . . . descenderunt et in puluerem statim reloluti sunt.

Figure 8.2. *Everyman* (London: John Scot, 1530).

country needs him. Folklorists have named this *absconditio* (*Bergentrück-ung, bergtagning*),[35] and we can compare it to the dormition theme in Christian legends such as that of the seven sleepers of Ephesus. It has also been applied to Frederick Barbarossa, Charlemagne, Waldemar, and other kings who have left a positive remembrance in the popular memory, which explains the recuperation of the legend for political ends. Herla's Mesnie no longer appears in a country where exists a strong central authority and the rule of order, as noted by Jean Claude Schmitt.[36] Let us look at the apparition that is recorded in both the Anglo-Saxon "The Land Chroni-cle" and that of Hugh Candidus in 1127: "Immediately thereafter, many men saw and heard many huntsmen hunting. These hunters were black and big and ugly, and all their dogs were black and ugly with wide eyes, and they rode on black horses and black goats [*svarte hors and swart bucces*]. This was seen in the deer park itself in the town of Peterborough and in all the woods between Peterborough and Stamford. And the monks heard the horns blowing, which they blew at night. . . . This was seen and heard from the time he* came here, all that Lent up to Easter."[37]

The explanation? In 1127, King Henry I gave Peterborough Abbey to his cousin, Henry of Poitou, a sneaky and greedy prelate. The appearance of this Hunt coincides with his taking office.

---

*[The new abbot Henry of Poitou. —*Trans.*]

9

The Mesnie Hellequin

Orderic Vitalis's Story

We owe the first account of the Infernal Hunt[1] to the monk Orderic Vitalis from St.-Evroult Abbey in the Lisieux diocese. He was born in Attingham, England, around 1075 and died in 1140. Orderic compiled an *Ecclesiastical History,* the seven chapters of which form a history of Normandy.[2] Among many memorable events, he recounts the following encounter.

I cannot ignore or remain silent about an event involving a priest of Lisieix diocese on New Year's Day. The priest was named Walchelin, and he had responsibility for the Church of St. Aubin the Confessors, a former monk who became bishop of Angers. On the night of January 1, 1091,* this priest was called out to attend a sick man, as was his duty, in an outlying area of his parish. He was coming back alone, through an isolated part of the country, when he heard the kind of sound that is made by the passage of a great army. He assumed it was the personal guard of Robert de Bellême, which made a hurried approach to the siege of Courcy. The moon shone brightly under the constellation of the Ram, and the road was clear. Wachelin was a young man, courageous and strongly built and adroit, but when he heard the kind of sound made by a rabble of

---

*[Or 1092—it varies in different translations. —*Trans.*]

soldiers, he became fearful. He remained there, uncertain whether to flee and so avoid being attacked and robbed by ruffians or to stand his ground and defend himself. He noticed four medlar trees standing in a group some distance from the path, and he decided to hide in this little grove until the mounted horsemen had passed, but a figure of enormous size, wielding a large club, stood in his way, and holding the weapon over his head, the man cried, "Stay where you are. Do not move."[3]

The tale goes on: "The priest immediately stood still and supported himself on his staff. The grave figure who carried the club took up a position beside him, without doing him any ill, and together they waited for the army to pass."[4]

This introduction provides all the essential details: place, an extremely precise date, and the name of the witness. It introduces a motif that contradicts Walter Map's tale: a large commotion, a motif destined to enjoy a long life. Combined with the notion of an army, this tumult explains the German name for the Wild Hunt or the Furious Army. We should not regard as merely empty detail the mention of the four medlar trees. Until the very recent past, the wood from the medlar tree was used for protection from enchantments. In the Vendée and in Anjou, it was said a medlar staff would put witches to flight. Likewise, in the Ain region, a branch of this tree on the ceiling of stables protected the livestock from evil spells. What next occurs has given rise to countless speculations and has misled many researchers. In this detail we move far from the source legend and fall into the Christian exemplum: "A large crowd [*turba*] appeared on foot, and on their shoulders and draped around their necks they bore the animals, clothes, furniture, and household possessions that make up the plunder of every raiding army. Yet they all complained bitterly and chivvied each other onward. Walchelin saw among them many of his fellow villagers who had died recently, and he heard them lamenting the fact that they were in torment because of their sins."[5]

We can note the kinship of this passage and that in *De nugis curialium* (IV, 13) by Walter Map. In both texts a large throng of people carries objects, and witnesses see individuals they know to be dead but now form part of the crowd. The Christian incorporation of this legend is heralded by the final sentence:

> Next came a group of pallbearers, whom the giant suddenly joined, supporting the weight of some fifty biers. Two men carried each bier. On these biers were seated dwarfs with huge barrel-shaped heads. One gigantic tree trunk* was carried by two Ethiopians† on which a hapless man was tightly lashed and undergoing severe torture and screaming aloud in his pain. A terrible demon that sat astride this trunk dug into his back and thighs with red-hot spurs so that the blood flowed freely. Walchelin immediately recognized the man: he was the nurderer of a fellow priest called Stephen, and Walchelin understood that the man was being tortured for the crime of spilling the blood of an innocent man only two years before, so that he had not had time to complete the penance for such a terrible misdeed.[6]

The giant joins the pallbearers, which suggests he plays the role of a psychopomp. This has caused some researchers to see in him an ancient Gallic deity, Ogmios or Sucellos, god of the club and the dead.

The second point of contact between Orderic Vitalis and Walter Map is the presence of dwarves with large heads. Though the clerical literature sometimes depicts the dead as individuals who are the size of dwarves,[7] the motif of the large head appears only in the work of these two authors. We can compare this motif to that of the demons with heads the size of cooking pots, like those appearing in the *Vision of Saint Fursy*. Let us, however, get on with our story.

> Next came a group of women who seemed to the priest to be innumerable. They rode side saddle, in the fashionable manner, but with their saddles studded with red-hot nails. As the gusts of night air

---

*Funeral stretcher.

†Meaning devils.

caught them, they were lifted a few feet out of the saddle, and then were dropped back on the pointed nails. In this way, their thighs and buttocks were tortured by the burning nails, and so they loudly called out, "O woe, O woe!" in lament for their sins which had caused them such punishment. The sensuous lechery in which they had indulged when they were on earth caused them now to undergo the flames and stench and torture. They complained of their punishment with such loud cries. Walchelin noticed a number of high-born ladies among this group, and he also noticed that there were horses and mules belonging to many who were still alive. These animals drew women's carriages, which were as yet empty.[8]

The torture of the nail-studded saddles is a common feature in the exempla.[9] What is new in this instance: the wind that lifts the sinners in the air, the mention of which can be found nowhere else. Was Orderic inspired by another legend, which he alters, or is the motif intended to demonstrate the incorporeal nature of the souls of the dead? The answer is not certain. According to some traditions, souls are light as feathers, which may have influenced some accounts of the Wild Hunt, which traveled not over the ground but through the air. Yet according to the *Vision of Barontus* (chapter 4), the soul is so light that a gust of wind can carry it away: when it leaves the body, Barontus's soul is the size of a freshly hatched chick, but it keeps the appearance of a miniature human and receives an ethereal body. What appears here, as we know now, is the Double of the dead individual.[10] It is certainly corporeal in folk belief, and this is what the church finds unacceptable. The church prefers to talk about souls with the semblances of bodies.

We should not be surprised by the fact that the living may appear in the midst of the Wild Hunt or the Infernal Hunt. "This is the sign of an imminent death, and this motif has a long history."[11] We should note that this reinforces the didactic nature of this story in which emerges finally the notion of sin.

Figure 9.1. *The Infernal Hunt.* School textbook illustration, 1926.

The priest remained there, trembling, and he began to ponder the meaning of these awful visions. The next group to come along was an assembly of clerics and monks, and he could see their leaders, bishops and abbots, carrying their pastoral staffs. The clerics and their bishops wore black capes. The monks and abbots were dressed in black cowls. They moaned and complained, and some of them even hailed Walchelin and beseeched him to pray for them in the name of their former friendship. The priest said that he noticed many highly regarded figures, who, according to the respect in which they were held by their fellow humans, were generally believed to have joined the saints in heaven. He even saw Hugh, bishop of Lisieux, and the famous abbots Mainer of St.-Evroul and Gerbert of St.-Wandrille, along with many others whose names I cannot remember.[12] The estimation of humans is often wrong, whereas nothing can be hidden from the sight of God. Men's judgment depends on external appearances. God searches the very heart of things. In the kingdom of eternal bliss, an eternal light illuminates everything, and a perfect holiness, with a delicious savor, is triumphant among all the children of heaven. There, no disorder can be found nor stain find entry. There, never can any villainy be encountered nor any action occur contrary to honesty. All that is irksome of the carnal bond is consumed by a purgatorial fire and purified by diverse expiations, in accordance with the provisions of the eternal Censor. Further, just as a vessel, its rust removed by fire and meticulously cleaned, is stored in the treasury, so shall the soul, which has been rid of the contagion of all the vices, be admitted into heaven and enjoy complete bliss, where it finds joy and is freed of all fears and worries.[13]

Orderic now reveals his true design: to cause fear in order to inspire repentance, and the tone of his tale is that of a sermon whose exordium could be the previous paragraph. While describing the religious individuals among the procession, he gives free rein to an acerbic criticism of the clergy's habits and reveals the hypocrisy that can fool men but never God.

Shaking with fear and amazement at these dreadful spectacles, the priest steadied himself by leaning on his staff, and he awaited further even more terrible sights. Next to come was a great troop of knights with no colors except that of darkness and flickering flame. All the knights rode enormous horses, all of them were armed as if charging into battle, and all of them bore pennants of the deepest black. Among this troop were Richard and Baldwin, the sons of Count Gilbert, who had recently died, and many others whom I cannot name. Landry of Orbec, who had been dead less than a year, addressed the priest in a loud shout, gruffly ordering him to take a message to his wife, but the other soldiers around him in the troop shouted louder and said to the priest, "Do not listen to Landry. He is a liar." This Landry was once sheriff and advocate of Orbec, and he had risen from humble birth by virtue of his intelligence and personal qualities. In the court cases in which he was involved, however, he decided the outcome according to his own advantage, and took bribes, being more committed to corruption and personal gain than to justice. Thus he merited the shame of open torment, and deserved to be called a liar by his companions in torment. That was a judgment in which there was no flattery or supplication for his clever casuistry. Indeed, because he had closed his ears against the laments of the poor during his time of authority, now in his suffering he was not even accorded a hearing.[14]

Here, the first part of the narrative comes to an end. It is marked by the passivity of Walchelin, a simple spectator who watches file past the representatives of abuses of power and sins. Of course, not all of feudal society is presented: the types are chosen based on their representativeness. In the second part, Walchelin becomes an actor in the drama, and he takes on an important role that takes place in two movements. Let us look at the first.

After this great army, thousands upon thousands strong had passed by, Walchelin began I tell himself, "Without a doubt, this is the retinue of Herlequin [familia Herlechini]. I have heard from those who claimed that they had seen them, but I used to mock those who told such stories and did not believe them, because I had seen no firm evidence. Now I myself can see the specters of the dead with my own eyes, but no one will believe me unless I can take back some proof to show the living. I will seize one of the spare horses that follow the troop and ride it home, in order to ensure that my neighbors believe me when I show it to them." At this, he grasped the bridle of a jet-black horse, but it broke free and galloped after the dark army as though it had wings, and it rejoined the troop of Ethiopians. The priest was vexed at being unable to fulfill his plan. He was in fact a young man of bold and subtle mind with a sturdy, agile body. Not daunted, the priest stood in the middle of the track and held out his arm to stop another of the approaching horses. It paused and waited for him to mount, letting out a great breath of steam, which took the shape of a large tree. Walchelin set his left foot into the stirrup, and he held the rein and grasped the saddle. Immediately, however, he had the sensation of burning fire under his foot, and the hand that held the rein sent a shiver of icy cold straight to his heart.[15]

The notion of proof is a fundamental element in the stories of visions, true journeys of the soul into the beyond, and those whose plots are centered on an encounter between the living and the dead. A thousand stories tell us that the individual who comes in contact with the dead comes away from it with a souvenir in the form of a burn mark, either because he touches a revenant or because the undead individual perspires due to the fire that consumes it, and it lets fall a drop of that sweat on the hand of the other party.[16] One exemplum explicitly states the meaning of this detail: "Touched on the arm by the dead man, skin and flesh were seared through to the bone so that this sign may serve as a constant reminder of your promise," says a deceased who has come in search of help from a living man."[17] In narratives collected during the nineteenth century, when the grateful dead man takes leave of the person who helped him, he holds out his hand, but the living individual avoids taking it and extends a log in the place of his own hand. This log is completely scorched by the encounter and serves as proof of the events.[18] The immense troop—"thousands upon thousands strong"— smacks of epic exaggeration, and it is followed by riderless horses. As a general rule, these horses are intended for those next to die or, potentially, for the living encountered by the Mesnie Hellequin and abducted. The combination of heat and glacial cold that Walchelin feels when he touches the horse refers to the two primary places of purgatory, fiery ditches and frozen lakes, which are presented in almost all the accounts of the visionaries who, guided by an angel, visited this site of penitence. In the Valais region of Switzerland, it was still believed in the nineteenth century that souls in torment atoned for their sins in the glaciers, and in the Grisons region, purgatory is called Scaläratobel. In addition, we can note the reference to a common oral tradition about the Mesnie Hellequin—Herlechin here—which brings to mind Walter Map's Herlethingus. In the manuscripts the letter *t* can easily be confused with the letter *c,* so the transition from one letter to the other could be the explanation for the name variations.

Walchelin receives messages to pass on to the living. The members of this roving purgatory want redemption and request the help or suffrages of their kin.

> At the same time, four dreadful knights approached and thundered at him, "Why are you troubling our horses? Come along with us. You have not been hurt by any of our companions, but you try to take what belongs to us." Dreadfully frightened, Walchelin released the horse, but as three of the knights were about to seize him, the fourth said, "Leave him alone and let me talk to him, so that I may send messages to my wife and sons." Then he addressed the frightened priest, "I pray you, listen to me, and take this message to my wife." Walchelin replied, "I do not know who you are, and nor do I know your wife." The knight said, "I am William of Glos, son of Barnon, who was well known as steward of William of Breteuil and before him, his father William, earl of Hereford. I was responsible for unlawful judgments and seizures while I was alive, and I have carried out more sinful actions than I can tell you. Yet I am troubled most of all by the sin of usury. When I was alive, I made a loan to a poor man, and I was given his mill as security for the loan. He was unable to repay me, and so I kept the mill and displaced the heir by bequeathing it to my heirs. You may see that in my mouth is the burning shaft of a mill wheel which weighs upon me more heavily than the tower of Rouen. You must give a message to my wife, Beatrice, and to my son Roger: they should bring me comfort by returning this security to the rightful heir. They have benefited from it far more than the amount of the original loan." The priest replied, "The death of William of Glos occurred a long time ago, and no one who truly believes could carry

a message such as this. I have no idea who you are or who are your heirs. If I was to give such a message to Roger of Glos and his brothers and mother, they would mock me as a fool. William, however, implored him, insistently and forcefully. He made a large number of very obvious signs. Although the priest clearly understood what the knight was asking, he pretended to ignore him. Finally, however, overcome by the other's pleas, he accepted and promised to do what he had been asked. William recapitulated all his requests, and in a long speech, he repeated each point in review. The priest, however, thought that he would never pass on to anyone the instructions of a dead man. "It is not suitable," he said, "to let others know such things. Under no circumstances will I carry out your orders or deliver your message." Enraged, the knight reached out and seized the priest by the throat, pulling him and making as if to attack him. The priest felt that he was being held by a hand that burned like fire, and in great fear, he called out, "Blessed Mary, Mother of Christ, come to my aid!" As soon as he implored the help of the glorious and compassionate Mother of the Son of God, help came to him, in conformance with the arrangements established by the All-Powerful. There appeared another knight who bore in his right hand a sword. Wielding the drawn sword as though he were prepared to strike, he said, "You miserable wretches, why are you threatening to kill my brother? Be off and leave him alone." They left immediately and rejoined the army of Ethiopians.[19]

We are no longer in the domain of the profane legend (*sage*), but in that of the Christian legend (*legende*), and the intertextuality is particularly rich. In addition to the request for aid, which is a distinguishing feature of souls in purgatory, one phrase is a stereotype: "The burning shaft of a mill wheel, which weighs upon me more heavily than the tower of Rouen." This is what the dead say in the *legendae* when they bear a cope or a burden that symbolizes their sin.[20] Walchelin's reaction to this request is interesting: he fears being taken for a madman, which suggests that not everyone believes in revenants, or else it is a literary device intended to make the story more real. What would you have done in the priest's place?

When the other figures departed, the knight stood alone with Walchelin in the track and asked, "Don't you know who I am? I am Robert, son of Ralph the Fair-Haired. I am your brother." As the priest stood there, astonished at this unexpected news and troubled by all the sights and sensations of the evening, the knight began to recall their time together as boys and to bring forward many proofs that he was indeed who he said he was. The priest remembered everything that he spoke of, but did not dare to admit it, so that eventually the knight said, "I am astonished at your hardheartedness and stupidity. I raised you after our father and mother died, and took more care of you than anyone alive. I sent you to France for your education. I provided you with apparel and livelihood, and I helped you in many other ways. Now you pretend not to remember any of this and refuse even to acknowledge me." With such sincere truths spoken to him, the priest tearfully acknowledged that the revenant was indeed his brother, who continued, "It would have been right if you had died and been carried away with us, for you foolishly tried to take things that belonged to us. No one else has ever attempted this, but your celebration of Mass earlier today has saved you. In addition, I have been allowed to appear to you and show you how wretched I am. After we spoke for the last time in Normandy, I departed for England without consulting you. There, my life ended, as my Creator ordained, and I have undergone severe punishment for the weighty sins which bore so heavily upon me. The weapons that we carry are burning hot, and they give off a terrible stench and bear down upon us with an unbearable weight and smolder on forever. Until this time, I have undergone terrible torment, but after you had been ordained in England and had celebrated your first Mass for those who had died in faith, your father, Ralph, was released from his torment,

and the burden of my shield, which had been a cause of great torment to me, fell away. You can see that I still bear this sword, but I
faithfully await release from its burden this coming year."[21]

We must note one surprising detail: in the clerical texts, the living
very rarely meet a dead person who reveals his or her identity in one
way or another—whereas in the folk beliefs recorded in the chronicles,
the recognition is immediate. A homily by St. Augustine on the Psalms
contains a very revealing phrase: "Such as you are at the moment you
leave the world, so you shall be in the next life."

This story finds its place in the literature of revelations, for the clerics undoubtedly wished for the dead to speak. In typical Christian fashion, the Mass is mentioned. When a person has either heard it or said it,
or if an individual has taken Communion or prayed to or invoked God
or his Mother or his saints, then he or she has invoked one of the surest
means of protecting ourselves from the undead. Yet this detail does not
quite correspond to the reality of the beliefs. When testimonies have
been barely or not at all tainted by Christianity, we see that protection
against revenants is procured by charms,[22] iron, or by drawing a circle
around a pursued individual. Yet these methods sometimes prove inef-
fective, and it then becomes necessary to fight the dead person physically. The theme of weapons that become instruments of torment is also
a standard element of the clerical critique of the *milites,* and one we
have already seen earlier in the work of Ekkehard of Aura.

We can note another detail: the troop moves away and one of its members remains behind. We have encountered this motif earlier in the *Würt-
temberger* and the *Lai du Trot.* It frequently appears in the Wild Hunt:[23]
"The Lord of Rechenberg encountered the Furious Army. 'One person
lagged behind the main body of the troop holding a saddled and bridled
horse with no rider. Rechenberg asked him who they were and where they
came from. He was told, 'The Furious Army that comes out of hell.'"

This is combined with the motif of the pitcher filled with tears:[24]
a person, usually a child, wearily trudges behind the procession while

carrying a jug filled with water and asks the living witness to tells his parents that they should cease weeping, because their tears fall into his pitcher, whose weight is unbearable.[25] This motif is a variant of the motif of the shirt soaked in the tears of the living who mourn the dead person wearing it,[26] which we also find in *The Golden Legend* (chapter 27) by Jacobus Voragine, Thomas of Cantimpre's *Apiarius* (II, 53), and the *Mirror of Great Examples* (V, 119).

> When the knight had said all of this and more, and the priest had examined him closely, he noticed that there seemed to be a great clot of blood shaped like a human head attached to the spurs on the heels of the knight's feet. The priest was horrified and asked, "Why do you have that great mass of blood around your heels?" His brother replied that it was not blood, but fire, and that it was heavier than Mont-St.-Michel. "I am rightfully forced to carry this enormous weight on my heels, because I once wore shining, pointed spurs in my eagerness to spill blood. Burdened unbearably by this weight, I cannot even begin to tell you how painful is my punishment. Those who are still alive should always remember such things and should take care not to risk such awful punishment for their sins. Yet I cannot speak any longer with you, my brother, for I have to hurry onward with this troop of the damned. Pray for me, I implore you. Remember me in your prayers and your alms-giving. Exactly a year after Palm Sunday, I hope I will be saved and freed from torment by the compassion of my Creator. Look to your own salvation. Amend your own way of life, for it is stained by many misdeeds, and you must surely understand that this cannot last. Do not tell of all that you have heard or witnessed or reveal it to anyone for the next three days."[27]

Here, Orderic reveals his didactic intentions: amend your ways otherwise this is what awaits you! Robert's request for a three-day silence may surprise us, but it is fairly common for the dead to command the living to respect some precaution, as if the encounter removes the living from this world, and a certain time should elapse before he sets foot back on it. In one of the stories by the anonymous monk of Byland (fourteenth or fifteenth century), the deceased states, "Keep your eyes on the ground and do not look at a physical fire for at least this night."[28]

Orderic Vitalis's narrative closes in this way: "With these words, the knight rode off. The priest Walchelin was taken gravely ill and remained unwell for a whole week. As he began to recover, he went to Bishop Gilbert of Lisieux and told him of all that had happened to him, and was given by the bishop everything required to restore him to health. He lived on for fifteen or more years in perfect health, and I myself heard from him everything that I have written down, and I saw the mark on his face that was made when he was touched by the dreadful knight. It is for the edification of my readers that I have written this tale, so that the righteous may be strengthened in good and the wicked turned away from evil."[29]

Here again, the illness that strikes Walchelin is commonplace. Meeting the dead is never without peril, and one of the stories by the anonymous monk of Byland closes thus: "And when the tailor at last returned home, he remained sick for several days." On the other hand, Orderic takes some liberties with the belief by granting Walchelin another fifteen years of life. Ordinarily, death follows on the heels of the encounter.

A Reversed Vision

Orderic's story is a fabrication based on pre-existing elements. Our monk based his story of an Infernal Hunt on the Wild Hunt and a vision—in other words, on a journey into the beyond, something already noted by Edmund Mudrak, but here we have a reversal of the myth.

In a vision, the man "carried away in spirit" (*raptus in spiritu*) travels through the next world under the guidance and protection of an angel. His journey takes him through purgatory and lets him see the "pits of hell" and, in the distance, paradise. In the story of the Mesnie Hellequin, Orderic transports purgatory to earth and thereby eliminates the journey into the beyond. He retains the notion of recognizing the individuals we can see in these places and combines it with a motif taken out of the exempla: some of the deceased make requests of the living individual to be saved once they have made good the wrongs they have caused or when they have sufficiently atoned for their sins. These requests for help and suffrages are frequently encountered in Christianized ghost stories, and Jacobus de Voragine provides an example in chapter CXLIII of his *Golden Legend*. Orderic transposes the angel-guide into the giant who warns the priest and protects him by preventing him from moving forward. The theme of the gigantic devil is not absent from clerical literature. In the *Gesta Karoli* (I, 31), written around 886–887 by Notker the Stammerer, an officer of the palace in Aachen dreams of a giant who is looking for the prefect of the palace so that he can escort him to hell. Valerio of Bierzo, (d. 695) says in his story of the *Vision of Bonellus:* "Then three fallen angels appeared. One of them was a giant."[30] Hariulf (1060–1143), the abbot of Olden-burg, includes in his *Chronicon Centulense* (III, 21) the *Vision of Charles the Fat,* written around 890, in which King Charles states: "I turned toward the dark part that emitted flames, and there I saw some kings of my race in extreme torture. Frightened beyond measure by this and reduced to great distress, I expected to be immediately thrown into these torments by some very black giants who made the valley blaze with every kind of fire."[31] Even dwarves can appear in a vision, such as in that already mentioned by Guibert de Nogent or as seen in this exemplum: a holy man celebrates a Mass for the dead when "he suddenly saw the church fill with dwarves the size of a finger [*homuncionibus ad mensuram digiti*]."[32]

We can note another detail from the visions: Walchelin is attacked by the knight, William of Glos, who attempts to strangle him and leaves on his throat an indelible mark, proof of the truth and reality of the encounter: "[I] saw the mark left on his face when he was touched by the dreadful knight," writes Orderic. It is common in these visions for the angel to leave for a moment. Thus the visitor is alone. The visitor is then attacked by demons, who grab him and try to carry him off, but the angel returns and sends them fleeing. Here is a passage from the *Visio Tondoli,* written in 1149 by an Irish monk of Regensberg named

Marcus:[33] "The angel disappeared again, and Tondale fell into the fire, with nothing to defend him . . . and the devils circulating through the flames descended upon him, surrounding him from every side, jabbing with the tools they used to torture souls. . . . Impatient to wreak evil, they strove to capture this poor soul and cast him into hell, but the angel of Our Lord appeared and set them fleeing in confusion."

We can also read this from a vision of a Holstein peasant named Godescalc, December 20 to December 24, 1189: "Then when I drew near, the flame touched me by chance on the left side. Terrified and very doleful, I implored the help of my guides. They grabbed me immediately and pulled me from the fire. . . ." On his return to his body, Godescalc "was stricken with a sharp pain on the side, which he explained this way: when he had gone near the furnace, the flames had burned his side."[34]

In all these accounts, the notion of proof is fundamental. Without it, no one accepts the verity of these torments from beyond the grave.

Orderic's narrative is therefore quite unreliable. It is a fabrication, a brilliant creation based on various traditions in which clerical literature takes the lion's share. Furthermore, the political intent is just as clear as it is in Walter Map's work. During this time, St.-Evroult Abbey, to which Orderic belonged, was struggling to preserve its independence, which was threatened by the bishop of Lisieux and the nobleman Robert of Bellême. It so happened that the familia Herlechini showed what fate awaited the prelates and lords who committed sins. This message can be read in the background: the Wild Hunt puts in an appearance during troubled times. It has the value of a warning sign (*portentum*).

Toward the Origin of the Belief

Could the legend of Herla be a more trustworthy guide? Perhaps not, for it also draws from sources for which it provides an explanation. It is an etiological legend whose elements—the dead returning in a throng—are scarcely explicit, and it tries to pinpoint the origin of the phenomenon.

Orderic and Walter Map refer to a story whose tone seems to have been clearly furnished by the *De nugis curialium* IV, 13. Because there is no rational way to envision a genetic bond between the two authors' testimonies, the common points refer to their common source, the archetype if one exists. We must therefore employ the same method used by the critical editions of manuscripts if we want to find a way out of this impasse, but we must not forget that the legend or myth would not be the addition of all the variations that we have encountered. What are these common points?

First is the family name of the principal protagonist, Herla, who gives his name to the apparition Herlethingus, familia Herlechini. Next is the fact that we are dealing with a troop of the dead, and finally, we can note the theme of horses and the attempt to steal one of them. If we leave to one side the Christian garb of Orderic's account, the narratives disagree with each other on the following points: the passage of the familia Herlethingi is entirely silent, but that of the Mesnie Hellequin is accompanied by a loud commotion. The familia Herlethingi appears during the day and the Mesnie Hellequin appears at night—but this detail is hardly conclusive, because we find both these indications of time alternating in medieval legends. The elements on which we can base an analysis are extremely slim, so we must refer to other accounts while we locate the intertextual play, borrowings, and influences—that is, while we trace the genetic and typological connections. Let us begin by examining the name of the troop's leader.

I can offer a hypothesis on one of the names of Wild Hunt. In Walter Map's work, the name was taken from that of its leader, Herla, and his men. We should not liken Thingus with the Norse *thing*, "assembly of free men," but rather with the Old English *thegn* (the Middle High German *degen*), "warrior," which has been Latinized and distorted, a conjecture for which we can find confirmation in the variation of the troop's name as Herlewinus, meaning "the friends, of Herla," "the men of Herla," or "the soldiers of Herla." Herlethingus therefore grasps the outer aspect of the complex, and is therefore an exact translation of the phenomenon of the continuous wandering of Herla and his warriors. In the work of the

Norman cleric Orderic Vitalis, the Mesnie Herlequin, while originating from the same mythic lode, apparently draws its name from another and undoubtedly much older evaluation of the facts. Philippe Walter told me that even today in Norman patois, *quin* means dog. Hellequin therefore means "Herla's dog," which takes into account one of the elements I have earlier designated as one of the key motifs of the legend. This explains the ongoing failure of all linguistic attempts to link *thingus* and *quinus,* a kinship that already in the Middle Ages was the object of scholarly inter- pretations. Hélinand de Froidmont and Vincent de Beauvais see in Helle- quins a distortion of Karolus Quintus,* an interpretation that has a canon of clerical literature. Evidence for this can be provided by this example in this passage from the fifteenth-century *Exposition of the Christian Doc- trine*: "Of the Mesnie Helquin I tell you plainly they are devils who wan- der in the guise of men riding horses at a trot. And this is what Sautiez means when it says *ab incurso* [Psalms 90, 5*ff.*]. It is a kind of trotting. But from where does this word Helquin come? You should know, my child, that the fifth Charles who was in France waged a great battle wherein he perished. After his death, there were several on the battlefield who saw what appeared to be a large assembly trotting to Charles, and it is said that it was King Charles who was dead and that he had returned to the field where he had died, both he and his men, and that is said Charlequin, which means the fifth Charles, for which one says Helquin."[35]

The name Herla has excited the sagacity of researchers, but today we widely accept, contrary to what some still assert, that it has no relationship to Hel, the goddess of the dead worshipped by the ancient Scandinavians. This hypothesis was seductive, but it flew in the face of etymological laws. The name simply means "army chief," and it designated a function before becoming a man's name. It was used in this way by our witnesses, and it essentially serves to provide the etiological legend with a historical basis. This event took place in the remote past, before the Saxon invasion of England, which also reinforces the connection between Herla's disappear- ance and the theme of the sovereign sleeping in the mountain.

---

*[Charles V. —*Trans.*]

Figure 9.2. *Der Doten Dantz mit Fuguren: der Doit, der Kauffman* (Death and the Merchant) (Munich: n.p., ca. 1485)

We can imagine another hypothesis by basing our conjectures on the notion of familia and *mesnie*. In Old English, *cyn(n)* is the exact semantic counterpart of these two terms, but also means "people," "race," or "folk," like the High German *künne*, from which derives the word *König*, "king." Familia Herlethingi is thus a pleonastic formation in which familia replaced the misunderstood cyn(n), which can be found in Hellequinus the Harlekinus. The origin of the Wild Hunt is therefore sought among a particular people, a tribe, a troop led by a certain Herla, or among a people whose name provided the basis for the word *herla* in medieval Latin. In this last case, this alleged people must have left a deep imprint in people's memories, especially in the memories of clerics. In 1857, F. von Schönwerth[36] offered the hypothesis that this would be a souvenir of the great invasions. This trail bears checking, for it could give up one of the historical roots of the legend.

We still must examine other ancient witnesses—that is, those not overly contaminated by legends, which, while also connected to the dead, are independent.

10

The Evolution of the Legend

Cando éramos vivos,
andábamos pol-os camiños;
e agora que somos mortos
andábamos por entre os hortos
tocando nas campanillas
e commendo pimentos . . .*

William of Malmesbury

Toward 1125, William of Malmesbury recounts the legend of the statue
of Venus, which was immortalized by French author Prosper Mérimée
in *La Vénus d'Ille:* A young man places his wedding ring on the finger of a statue, which then considers herself his wife and prevents him
from consummating his union with his legitimate wife. He seeks out
the priest Palumbus, who is well versed in necromancy (*nigromanticus*

---

*Song of a troop of revenants in Manzaneda, Trives (Orense, Galicia):

When we were living
we traveled along the paths;
today when we are dead
we walk between the gardens
striking our bells
and eating peppers.

artibus instructus), to be freed of this nuisance. Palumbus gives him a letter and tells him:

> "Go at such an hour of the night into the high road where it divides into several ways, and stand there in silent expectation. There will pass human figures of either sex and of every age, rank, and condition, some on horseback. Some on figures will be on foot, some countenances will be dejected and others will be elated with full swollen insolence. In short, you will perceive in their looks and gestures every symptom both of joy and of grief. Though these should address you, enter into conversation with none of them. This company will be followed by a person who is taller and more corpulent than the rest and who sits in a chariot. To him you will in silence give the letter to read, and immediately, your will shall be accomplished, provided you act with resolution." The young man took the road he was commanded, and that night, standing in the open air, he experienced the truth of the priest's assertion by everything, which he saw there, nothing but what was completed to a tittle. Among the passing figures, he beheld a woman in meretricious garb riding on a mule. Her hair, which was bound above in golden fillet, floated unconfined on her shoulders. In her hand was a golden wand with which she directed the progress of her beast. She was so thinly clad as to be almost naked, and her gestures were wonderfully indecent. But what need of more? At last came the chief [*dominus*] in appearance who from his chariot adorned with emeralds and pearls, fixing his eyes most sternly on the young man, demanded the cause of his presence. He made no reply, but stretching out his hand, he gave him the letter.[1]

The leader grants this request and obtains consent from Venus to let go of the young man.

This text is not without external influences: the woman depicted in the procession is the Whore of Babylon, illustrated exactly as she appears in certain illuminated manuscripts. It tells nowhere that this troop is made up of the dead, yet its formation bears comparison to the procession in Orderic Vitalis's narrative. This procession features not a leader, but a follower: the demon in a chariot, a new motif that can also be found in more recent Germanic folk traditions. Based on his size and bearing, this demon must be a giant. The ban on speaking can be explained only by the belief that the Wild Hunt carried off any who were careless enough to speak to one of its members. The Christian exempla have eliminated this motif, because for their purposes, it is necessary for one of the deceased to describe his fate in the afterlife. In fact, William uses the theme of the Mesnie Hellequin to embellish his story.

Pierre de Blois

In 1175, Pierre de Blois (1135 to ca. 1200), chancellor for King Henry II, then archbishop of Canterbury, makes a brief mention of the "knights of Herlewin" (*milites* Herlewini) in a letter in which he explains that the court clerics (*curiales*), "martyrs of the century, worldly professors, court disciples," join Herlewin's troop, while the just go to heaven. Pierre therefore borrows the notion of an itinerant purgatory in which sinners are punished for his own purposes. His missive vouches for the diffusion of our legend but brings no new details about it.

Yet the name Herlewinus (Herla + *win-us*) has aroused a variety of etymological speculations, one of which is interesting, though unverifiable. The name has been compared to Herla's wain, the cult wagon of the Angles, which became Charles's Wain, the name of the seven brightest stars in the Big Dipper,* which also cause us to recall the legend of Orion.[2] in addition, a subject of discussion is Hurlewain's kin (Hyrlewaynis *kynne*), "race" or "folk of Hurlewain," used to designate troublemakers.[3] We should note that Hennequin/Hellequin/Crennequin

---

*In the Netherlands the constellation is called Woenswagen, "Odin's Chariot."

was also used in Old French to refer to all sorts of thugs and ribald people.[4]

Hélinand of Froidmont

At the end of the twelfth century or during the first years of the thirteenth century, Hélinand of Froidmont, a Cistercian monk (d. 1230), wrote a series of reflections inspired by the Mesnie Hellequin. He opens with an examination of our fate after death and, basing his speculation on the authority of Gregory the Great, St. Bernard, and Virgil, states that the Roman poet was mistaken when he claimed that the dead continued their lifetime activities: "The same pride in chariot and arms that was theirs in life, the same care in keeping sleek steeds, attends them now that they are hidden beneath the earth."[5]

He was wrong to say they appeared to the living as they were before their deaths, "peasants as peasants, knights as knights." They no longer had any concern for what was once theirs in this life. Therefore, according to Hélinand, Virgil was the source for the mistaken belief shared by the common people about the Mesnie Hellequin. The monk goes on to say: "The bishop Henry of Orleans, brother of the bishop of Beauvais, often told of a marvelous thing that he had heard directly from the mouth of someone who witnessed it, a canon of Orleans named John."[6]

John had ordered to Rome a cleric named Noel (Natalis), to accompany the archdeacon Burchard de Pisy, widely known for his avarice. Before leaving, John and Burchard made a pact: the first to die would reappear to the other within thirty days to let him know of his fate in the afterlife (*quod uter e duobus nobis prius moreretur, intra XXX dies, si posset, ad socium suum rediret*). Not far from Rome, Noel and John quarrel over money, and Noel commends his soul to the devils (*se daemonibus commendavit*).

Shortly after this, he drowns while crossing a river. The following night, when John retires to his bed, leaving the light on because of his nightmares, Noel appears to him, dressed in a splendid lead-colored rain cape (*cappa indutus pluviali, pulcherrima, coloris plumbei*). Surprised to see him back from Rome so soon, John learns from Noel that he is dead and endures great torment for having sworn himself to the devil shortly before he drowned. He asks John for his aid. "The cape I am wearing," he says "weighs heavier upon me than if it were the Tower of Parma" (*ponderosior et gravior est mihi quam turris* Parmensis *si mihi superposita esset*), but its beauty symbolizes the hope of pardon earned him by his last confession. John promises to help him and asks if he has joined the Mesnie Hellequin. No, Noel tells him, because it no longer roams the earth. It has completed its penance.

A later gloss introduced into the text, and contradicting the date of its writing, makes Hellequinus a distortion of Karelquinus (*corrupte autem dictus est a vulgo* Hellequinus *pro* Karlequintus). The militia has disappeared, because Charles V has been redeemed, thanks to the intercession made on his behalf by St. Denis, after Charles atones for his sins.

Hélinand also makes use of the motif of the dying man who promises to return with news of the beyond (M, 252, promise of a dying man to bring news of the otherworld), a very productive motif that was incorporated into many exempla. The Wild Hunt appears marginally, but what remains is its temporary nature of purgatorial punishment. The Cistercian of Froidmont thus combines three different traditions: the pact of friendship, the Mesnie Hellequin, and the careless oath, which is the core of the theme of the cursed huntsman and the ghost ship. In other words, Hélinand essentially demonstrates the use to which the legend has been put: quite simply, it has been made synonymous with purgatory and serves as a means for criticism and edification, at least in the monastic milieu.

The story of Noel is followed by another testimony that Hélinand heard from his uncle Hellebaud. It soon becomes apparent that the narrator sees a connection between the two adventures. Yet the troop that appears here remains anonymous.

> Then, toward noon [*circa meridiem*], my servant and I neared the forest. He was before me, riding quickly so as to prepare my shelter, when

he heard a great din beneath the trees like the neighing of many horses, the sound of weapons, and the clamor of many men launching an attack. In terror, he and his horse turned back and returned to me. When I asked him why he had come back, he answered, "I was unable to make my horse move forward, neither by striking him nor with my spurs, and I was so terrified myself, I could not go forward another step. Indeed, I saw and heard some astounding things. The forest is full of the souls of the dead and demons. I heard them speaking and crying out, 'We have already taken the provost of Arques. Now we are going to take the archbishop of Reims!'" To this I responded, "Make the sign of the cross over your brow and go forward in safety." When we advanced and drew near the forest, the shadows were already increasing. Though I could hear a confused din of voices and weapons and horses, I could neither see the shades nor understand what they were saying. After we had made our way back home, we found the archbishop in his final extremities, and he lived only fifteen days more from the time we heard the voices. It was concluded that he had been captured by these spirits [*ab illis spiritibus*], who had been heard saying they were going to take him. It appears that the devils are the mounts on which we can sometimes see riding the souls of the dead. They are demons who have changed into horses, and their riders are the wretched souls weighted down with their sins and charged with the burden of their shield and weapons. In this regard the prophet says: They will go down into hell with their weapons (Ezekiel 32: 28), which means with the instruments they used to sin.[7]

Although never named, we can easily recognize here the Wild Hunt. We can note that the servant of Lord Hellebaud sees the Hunt, although it remains invisible to his master (but he can hear it). We sometimes find this motif, unexplained until now, in ghost stories. Everything plays out as if the host of the dead and devils choose who shall see them, which may be a surviving influence from revelatory literature.

One of the stories recorded by the anonymous monk from Byland cites the case of a revenant who was active both at night and in the day: "He terrified everyone but was visible to only a few. Most times, in fact, he came into the presence of several people but made himself visible only to one or two of them, while letting all there know of his presence."[8]

Another explanation is possible: some people see spirits because they are gifted with second sight. East of the Rhine and in medieval Iceland, such people are called seers (*spökenkieker* or *ófreskr máðr*). Around 1191, Giraldus Cambrensis* speaks about a certain Ketell, an inhabitant of Yorkshire, who "received one such gift from God so that starting with that day and on all those that followed, demons were visible to him and could not conceal from him all they sought to conceal."[9] According to a very old Scottish belief, someone who sees the troop of spirits can transmit that ability to a companion to whom the troop remains invisible. Simple physical contact is sufficient—for example, the visionary can place his foot on that of his companation.[10] The same belief is held in Galicia with respect to the Santa Campaña, which speaks in favor of its Celtic character, for this region of Spain was once inhabited by the Celts.[11]

We can find here a recurring theme: seeing or hearing the Wild Hunt is a sign of an impending death. The end of Hélinand story borrows, for the author's personal benefit, the critique of arms bearers and churchmen present in the earlier narratives by Orderic and Ekkehard of Aura. Hellebaud's narrative is followed by that of the priest's mistress, source for those of Vincent de Beauvais; Boccacio; Passavanti, already cited earlier (page 60); and the Alsatian preacher, Geiler de Kaisersberg.[12] Hélinand therefore plays a significant role in the spread of this legend.

La Relation de Rein

By the twelfth century, well-established was a Christian legend in which the Infernal Hunt had become only ornamental décor and local color.

---

*[Also known as Giraud de Bari. —*Trans.*]

This process triggered by William of Malmesbury can also be seen in Hélinand of Froidmont's work and in a story known as *La Relation de Rein,* because this manuscript, dating from the beginning of the thirteenth century, was discovered in the Cistercian abbey of Rein, near the Austrian city of Graz. Scholars believe that the text was written between 1185 and 1200.

> Two young clerics of the Cluny order who were bound in close friendship [*ambo cor una et anima una*] left their monastery for the city of Tharsis, where they devoted themselves to necromancy. One of them fell ill and felt his death approaching. He despaired of finding divine mercy, despite the arguments of his friend who encouraged him to repent in order to save his immortal soul. His friend told him, "I beg you to come to me on this high mountain, thirty days after your death," and he named a mountain that stood in a wild and desolate region. "If that is permitted me," he responded, and added that his friend should summon him in the name of the Father, the Son, and the Holy Ghost so that he might reveal to him his fate in the afterlife. The sick man soon died, impenitent and in despair.
>
> Thirty days later, his friend made his way to the mountain, which he climbed fearfully after making the sign of the cross and asking the grace of God and his saints. "In fact, the sign of the cross causes terror to demons as it is the symbol of life."[13]

An extraordinary description follows: "Night fell as the wind gusted and clouds raced through the sky against a backdrop of lightning flashes and the dull rumble of thunder. Darkness enveloped the mountain, and the man was stricken with terror." The terms *horror* and *immensus et terror* repeat like a leitmotiv.

> The man then saw, approaching the mountain from the north, 'for from there evil comes' [*quia ab aquiline pandetur malum*], a cloud of horrible black smoke, and he heard a tumult of confused voices

as if an army was nearby [*quasi exercitus*]. A short while later, he made out a throng of horsemen, all knights who bore arms and shields, as well as knapsacks [*manticas*] and tents. They set up camp. Behind them arrived more knights who set up in three Chaldean squadrons [*tres turmas chaldei*] midway up the slope. There arrived a third host whose members were the princes and rectors of darkness. They installed themselves on seats on the mountaintop, like a tribunal. The dead man was then presented, and he was given permission to converse with his friend. His hands and feet were bound by chains of fire, and he wore a black habit entirely covered in script. The living man had great difficulty recognizing his companion and asked, "Are you not my former friend who died in despair?" He then urged him to share his revelations. The other informed him that he was in hell and that the clothing he wore burned him atrociously, because it was made of fire. A spark leaped off it and fell on the living man's hand, piercing it through. The damned man urged his companion to return to the monastery and change his life, which is what happened.[14]

This entire narrative smacks of Cistercian propaganda. The dead man in fact declares that the Cistercian order "is great and nothing on earth can compare to it" (*magnus hic ordo et nullus in terris equandus sibi modo*). The tale also recycles the theme of the message from the other world (motif E, 374), and combines the Wild Hunt—depicted here by the three hosts of knights—and the theme of judgment on the mountain, a very ancient element of Middle Eastern origin. In Babylonian tradition, for instance, the judges of the otherworld sit on Mount Cedar and determine the fate of the dead. There is every reason to think that this staging of a tribunal on a mountain comes from the literature of revelations. The sole common point of this exemplum and our Wild Hunt is the belief that the mountain represents the home of the dead. We should note, however, that the appearance of the dead man and his tormentors is once again accompanied by dramatic weather displays.

A Reduction of Oderic Vitalis's Narrative

The Cistercian Herbert of Clairvaux (1190), abbot of Mores in the Jura, the archbishop of Torres in Sardinia, left in his *Book of Miracles* of the Cistercian monks an exemplum titled "He Who Saw the Mesnie Hellequin" (De eo qui vidit familiam Herlequini), which was obviously inspired by the story of Orderic Vitalis but which retained only certain aspects of that narrative.

Zacharia, a brother of Vauluisant Monastery in the Yonne, had an experience in his youth that inspired him to become a monk. One night, while he was guarding the harvest, there appeared to him a woman who seemed to come from the neighboring village [*quasi de proximo vico adveniens*]. Thinking he knew her, he engaged her in conversation. There appeared then a kind of man [*quasi homo*] whom he took for a thief, and Zacharia prepared to loose an arrow at him to make him flee, but the woman told him not to, "because you do not know who he is." He then asked her if she had ever heard of "that fantastic troop that the common folk call Mesnie Herlequin" [*quae vulgo dicitur* familia Herlequini] or if she had ever seen it. She responded that she was to meet it that very night, but he should not be scared. As she was speaking these words, he began to hear the ruckus and vociferations of a large crowd approaching. With troubled mind and dreading the spirits of the night, he made the sign of the cross and invoked God, then he saw a terribly noisy troop appear. It was moving rapidly through the air, never touching the ground [*omnes in aere suspensi ferebantur et terram pedibus non tangebant*]. This troop consisted of blacksmiths, metal smiths, woodworkers, stone carvers striking together their axes and hammers [*cum securibus et malleis percutientes*], cobblers, tanners, weavers, fullers, and other "disciples of the mechanical arts" [*sectatores mechanicarum artium*], each acting as if in their studio or workshop. One of them, who carried a ram on his shoulders, approached

Zacharia and said to him, "Keep quiet and have no fear, for you shall not die, but be very careful not to respond to what I tell you. I am your companion, one who was once bound to you in friendship," and he explained what he was doing there. He had stolen this ram from a widow whom Zacharia knew, and he asked him to return it to her, which would free him from these ordeals [*ab ista poenalitate liberare*]. The dead man shared other revelations, and the entire band suddenly vanished [*evanuit*] at the same time. Terrified by this vision, Zacharia decided to enter this monastery.[15]

Nothing remains of the society in miniature depicted by Orderic Vitalis but a troop of artisans.[16] Undoubtedly, the monk Herbert wants to denounce those who work with metals—bringing to mind a cliché often used by preachers: smiths and metalworkers forged weapons that killed men, as Berthold of Regensburg proclaimed—and the mechanical arts at that time were viewed either as marvels or deviltries. Technical progress has always caused fear—which is nothing new.

The novelty of this testimony is the movement of the troop that never touches the ground yet makes a great racket. There are two possible interpretations: it is either a metaphor that stresses the extraordinary speed with which the group travel, or the Mesnie is somehow an aerial army of revenants who have become lighter than air. Herbert, however, also evokes the idea of a tempest by means of the great commotion that accompanies this host. One final point: the dead man forbids Zacharia from speaking to him or answering him. This is a new motif in the story of the Mesnie Hellequin. It is based on a widespread belief that responding to an apparition can expose an individual to abduction. Speech is thus considered a kind of pact. It has the same value as eating the food of the otherworld. Doing either causes removal from this world.

We can find the appearance of the Wild Hunt in another fourteenth-century collection: that of John, abbot of Viktring Abbey in Carinthia, Austria, from 1312–1345: "Around that time,* people in the Carniole

*Which would be in 1343.

Marches witnessed the army of Herquernus fighting in the sky with weapons of fire. Under more extensive investigation, it was discovered that old women had been mistreated and grievously wounded. A priest who heard and saw this apparition was so terrified that he had great difficulty recovering from it."[17]

This passage demands a brief explanation. John suggests that these figures belong to the troop of Herquernus, a corruption of Hellequin, which he identifies as witches. We can recall that Burchard of Worms mentions these women in the retinues of Diana and Herodias (see chapter 1). This reminiscence intersects with the themes of battles in the sky between ghostly armies and with that of Mesnie Hellequin. A remnant of shamanism is concealed behind all this: the Doubles of witches confront one another in ritual combat.[18]

It seems that the imagination of clerics and poets sought to create specialized Infernal Hunts. Herbert of Clairvaux gives us a Hunt of craftsmen; Hans Sachs (1494–1576), Nuremberg cobbler and prolific author, gives a starring role to a Hunt consisting of petty thieves. One of his texts, dating from January 29, 1539, is quite evocative and obviously reflective of the traditions that were widespread during his time.

Once, when Hans Sachs traveled through a forest one Pentecost evening on his way to Osnabrück, the fall of night caught him by surprise, and he was out when the moon rose. He heard the blare of horns in the distance. In fear, he made his way to a crossroads, but then arose "a loud and tempestuous wind, like a sudden squall." The din drew nearer, "accompanied by terrifying noises and rumbles," and "there appeared the atrocious and horrible Furious Army, three hundred men or more, the worst kind of brigands clad in rags." A raven perched on the head of every man there, eating their eyes and stripping the skin from their ears, lips, chin, and cheeks:

> *Oben auff in die raben sassen,*
> *Ir augen außbickten und frassen*

Thetten von irem antlißzwacken
Ihr ohren, lebsen, kyn und backen.

Each wore, about his neck, a noose as well as a clinking chain. They jostled each other, their hands bound. All were shriveled and wizened, and some were black and others pale as corpses. . . . Following them was a man who had been hanged that very morning. He still had his eyes, saw me, and approached to ask what had brought me to this place. A dialog ensued, and Hans Sachs learned that these dead men were in search of true justice without indulgence [*die waren strengen Gherechtigkeyt*], hence their wandering. "We have traveled the world, through towns, marches, villages and cultivated fields, mountains and ravines, empty forests, without ever getting anywhere." Then the petty thief criticized a justice that hanged the petty criminals and honored the big ones . . .[19]

We must note both the site of the encounter—a crossroads in a forest—and the date, a night of Pentecost. The motif of the ravens refers to hanging, and we can immediately recall "The Ballad of the Hanged Men" by François Villon.

Rain has drained and washed us
And the sun has dried and blackened us;
Magpies and crows have carved out our eyes,
And torn off our beards and eyebrows.[20]

It is easy to imagine this as a literary borrowing or, quite simply, to note that this evocation of hanged men was part of the spirit of the times.

Mesnie Hellequin and the Crusades

Among the noteworthy contaminations of the Mesnie Hellequin by other legend motifs, occupying a special place are the narrative forms that connect a troop of dead to Jerusalem. There are two different groups of these: expiatory pilgrimages and the returning Crusaders (AaTh 974).

Johann Nider (ca. 1380–1438), Dominican prior in Nuremberg, leaves us this story:

> A nobleman whose conduct had earned him many enemies, was in the habit of traveling by night to avoid being ambushed. One night, he crossed through a forest near the Rhine with his squire, and, before venturing into a field at the edge of the wood, he sent his squire before him to see if anyone had set a trap for them there. The moon was brightly shining, making it possible to see the surrounding area quite clearly. The squire went ahead and noted a large army of horsemen approaching. He warned his master, who decided to wait in order to see if they were friend or foe. The troop passed, and he left the forest, and he met a knight on a steed leading another horse by the bridle. He asked this rider if he was in truth his friend who had recently died, and the other acquiesced. "Who are those that preceded you?" he then asked. The dead man answered, "They are knights and noblemen, such as he over there, and he there," and he named many of them, "who like me are going to Jerusalem this night to pay penitence." The living man then asked for the purpose of the horse he was leading. "It is for you if you wish to come with me to the Holy Land," and he went on to say that he could mount this steed with complete confidence, for it would return him alive from this journey as long as he followed the dead man's instructions. The knight accepted over his squire's objection, and he vanished from the squire's sight. The next day, the squire returned to the spot where his master had left him, and found him there, safe and sound. The dead man had given his friend a salamander* handkerchief and a knife in a scabbard [*mappulam parvam de salamandra et cultellum*

---

*[Salamander wool is woven with asbestos fiber and is fireproof. —*Ed.*]

in vagina] so that he would not think this had all been an illusion [*ne phantasma omnino fictum illa fuisse credatis*].[21]

The Mesnie Hellequin theme emerges in the background but has already undergone an important alteration: the troop of the dead is not engaged in infinite wandering. It has a goal: the pilgrimage to the Holy Land that brings with it redemption. It is therefore not an itinerant purgatory, strictly speaking. Furthermore, appearing for the first time in this kind of narrative is the theme of magical transport that spread throughout the fourteenth century in France and Germany—the theme, for example, concerning Henry the Lion, whom, legend claims, returned in an instant from the Holy Land with a lion in tow.[22]

In his story *The Pilgrimage of the Lord of Brunswick,* Michael Wyssenherre, an author about whom nothing is known, tells how the prince of Brunswick experiences a variety of adventures while on his way to the Holy Land. He loses his men and his horses, but he wins the company of a lion. This is the theme of Androcles and the lion. He then meets the frightful and monstrous (*gruss und ungehüwer*) Furious Army and begs of it, "You must tell me all you can about what has become of my gentle wife and son in my own land." The spirit answers the lord with great wrath, "You have beseeched me so forcefully that it pains me and I can hide nothing from you. Lord Brunswick, know that your wife is about to take another husband (67, 3–68, 7)."[23]

The demon then takes the lord and his lion back to Brunswick, which they reach in time to prevent the marriage. This is how the theme of the Wild Hunt was transformed into a literary motif that writers integrated into fairy tales and other narratives about the wondrous. In fact, the Furious Army appears here only as a *deus ex machina,* but legends of this type usually involve only a single demon.

The story of Richard Sans Peur (Richard the Fearless, fourteenth century) has come down to us in the form of a romance in unrhymed verse and recorded in the *Chronique de Normandie* by a certain Benoît and printed in 1487. In addition, either directly or indirectly, it is based on the legend of Henry the Lion, which was also widespread throughout Eastern Europe.

Another very marvelous adventure happened to the duke Richard Sans Peur. He was in his castle of Moulineaux sur Somme, and when he went forth after supper to walk in the woods, he and his men heard a marvelous noise and a horrible sound of a great multitude. This tumult drew ever nearer, and when the duke and his men heard it close at hand, they hid behind a tree, and the duke sent one of his people to spy out what it was. One of the squires perceived that those who had made this uproar had halted under a tree. He watched their doings and their government, and he saw that it was a king who had with him a great company of men of all sorts, and they were called, in common speech, the *mesgnie Hennequin*. In truth, however, it was the *miené* of Charles V, Whilom, king of France. . . .* This adventure happened constantly, thrice a week . . . and Duke Richard thought that if he might, he would know what people they were who held such assemblies on the land without his leave. He summoned his trustiest knights to the number of a hundred, or six score, of the prowest and boldest that he could find in all Normandy, and told them how on his lands, hard by his castle of Moulineaux, in the evening twilight, there came from time to time a king accompanied by people of many sorts who made a marvelous great noise, and rested them under a tree. . . .

So it befell that Richard Sans Peur and his knights came to Moulineaux and made their ambush in the forest close to the tree under which the king and his meiné had halted. As evening drew on, and it was the hour between dog and wolf, they heard so great and horrible a noise that they wondered. And they beheld how two men took a cloth of many colors, as it seemed to them, which they spread upon the earth, and arranged seats as if about to hold a royal sitting. And then they beheld the coming of a great king accompanied by diverse people who

---

*The author here follows the etymological tradition established by Hélinand.

made a marvelous great noise. And this king seated himself in the royal seat. . . . But all the knights of Duke Richard took so great an affright that they fled this way and that, and left the duke alone. . . . Then Duke Richard leaped upon the cloth with both his feet and adjured the king by the name of God to tell him who he was and who were the people with him and what he sought upon his land. "I am King Charles V of France, who died in this region, and I suffer penance for the sins that I wrought in this world. And these are the souls of my knights and others who served with me, who also suffer penance according to their sins." The duke then asked, "Whither go ye?" The king said, "We go to combat against the unbelieving Saracens and damned souls, to accomplish our penance." Then said Duke Richard, "And when will ye return?" The king said, "We shall return about the dawning of the day, and all the night we shall combat with them. Suffer us to go." "That will I not," said Duke Richard, "for I have a mind to go with you and help you in the combat." Then said the king, "Whatever thou seest, loose not thy hold on the piece of cloth on which thou art, but hold it fast." "So will I do," said Duke Richard, "and now let us go."

Then they set forth, making great tumult and storm.* The duke took the piece of cloth the king had given him, and entered the church.† And when he entered the chapel . . . he saw a knight, a kinsman of his own, who was within and serving for his livelihood, for he had been seven years a prisoner in the hands of the Saracens. . . . Then the duke told him that his wife was betrothed again and was to wed within three days. . . . Thereupon, the knight asked the duke to tell his wife that he was yet living.‡ After a time, the duke heard the king and his meiné arrive . . . and he sprang forth with them, and they went careening like wind and tempest.§24

---

*[Until they reached the Church of St. Catherine on Mount Sinai. —*Trans.*]
†And heard Mass.
‡And as proof gave him the half of a ring to show her.
§Richard woke up alone in the forest, went back to his castle, then on to Rouen to pass on the message to the wife of the knight he had met in Palestine.

The romance in verse comes in several variations.[25] When he is out riding, Richard spies a circle dance (carolle), and immediately, he thinks of the Mesgnée and spurs his horse in its direction, but then one of his squires, who had died an entire year earlier, plants himself before him and explains to him that he is paying penance (*je fais ma penance*) and that all those in the circle are under the orders of Helequin. Richard then rides on to demand an explanation of someone who "without my leave hunts in this forest." Helequin stands beneath a hawthorn and declares:

> *Dieu, qui est nostre maistre, nous a donné congé*
> *D'aller toute la nuict, puis le soleil couché*
> *Tant aurons cheminé, estans esmerueillés,*
> *Que trestons nous en sommes honny et traueillez*
> *Et si debuez scavoir, de ce que vous desplaisse,*
> *Que nous ne sommes pas du tout bien à notre aise,*
> *Si souffrons nous chascun tant d'angoisse et de peine*
> *Que pas ne le pourroit on dire en la sepmaine.*[26]

The two texts agree on the rest of the adventure.

In this legend the Mesnie Hellequin has become ornamental. Its use in a romance testifies to the theme's popularity and its ability to meld well with other themes. The magical transport provided by a cloth replaces that performed by a demon. It appears for the first time in Caesarius of Heisterbach's *Dialogus miraculorum* (VIII, 59),[27] before reappearing in the Middle High German *Lives of the Saints,* included in the *Song of the Noble Moringer* (fourteenth century), and in the texts just cited.

Significant in this literary adoption of the theme is that a fundamental change has taken place: the host of the dead no longer wander about aimlessly. Instead, it has the specific purpose of fighting the Saracens in the Holy Land as a form of penance imposed by God on these dead men. Furthermore, an apparently innocent detail is actually important: Charles Quint of France also plans to enter into combat against the *ames damnez* (damned souls), meaning the dead men who belong to another troop. In this we can recall Carlo Ginzburg's highlight about the Benandanti, individuals whose Doubles left at night to fight witches and wizards, who stole from humans the fertility of the soil.

We should hang on to the fact that the Mesnie Hellequin became synonymous with a great racket or din, a noise frequently compared to the tumult of a storm, and, according to Henry Guy, Gaston Raynaut, and Paul Sébillot, one is the personification of the other.[28] In both thirteenth-century France and Germany, the Wild Hunt no longer traveled in silence, which distinguished it from other throngs of the dead.

Angelic Hosts and Diabolical Hordes

Undeniable is the importance of the influence of the literature of revelations on the Wild Hunt. If we examine them extensively, visions and other related texts can deliver us one of the keys to the formation of the narratives that have been discovered up to the present time.

During the eighth century, a new theme appeared in the literature of revelations: angels and demons fought over the human soul when it left the sleeping body to visit the otherworld. Destined to enjoy a long and prosperous career, and highly illustrated with iconography, the theme first appears in the *Vision of Saint Fursy*.

> The angel standing at his right, told Fursey, "Fear nothing, you are protected." The angels bore him high up into the sky where he could see no roof or house. He could make out the howls and cries of demons, though. Then, while he was passing through their midst, he heard one say, "Let us make haste to wage war before his face" [*ante faciem illius bella commoueamus*]. At this moment, a black cloud formed on his left full of hellish shapes that marshaled their strength like an army [*bellicam aciem constituentem*]. The bodies of those demons he could see were deformed and black with long extended necks and their terrifying heads swollen to the size and shape of kettles [*capite in similitudinem caccabi intumescente*].[29]

The observation on the demons' heads recalls Orderic Vitalis's description of the tiny men carried in the coffins of the Mesnie Hellequin.

We find mention of the army of devils in the *Vision of Barontus,* that of Drythel, that of Wettin, and in those of countless others. "The Muspilli," an alliterative poem composed in Bavaria between 790 and 871 on the subject of the soul's fate after death, mentions the Last Judgment and the battle waged by angels and devils for possession of the soul.

> *enti si den lihhamun likkan lazit,*
> *so quimit ein heri fona himilzungalon,*
> *daz andar fona pehhe; dar pagant siu umpi,*
> *sorgen mac diu sela, unzi diu suona arget,*
> *za uuederemo herie si gihalot uuerde.**[30]

These battles between angels and demons seems to have popularized the idea of a celestial militia that comes in search of the righteous soul in order to bring it to God—a notion already firmly established in the Bible—and of a demonic horde that captures the soul of the impenitent sinner. Though this is clear in the literature of revelations, it is more ambiguous in the beliefs and texts they inspired, marked by a vacillation between the dead and angels, which results from a collision between a pre-Christian notion and that of the church.

According to the first notion, the deceased form a troop and often seek those condemned to accompany them. We encounter this belief in the work of Ralph Glaber (see page 41). We can also find it in Spain, where the Huestia and the Santa Campaña, Spanish names for the Wild Hunt, came in search of a dying person's spirit in order to merge it into the community of the dead of the parish.[31] The idea of the dead massing together into a group before the final transition is an extremely old one and is described by the historian Procopius:

---

*As soon as the soul begins its journey and abandons the body an army from celestial stars arrives and another from pitch (hell); they battle over it until Judgment begins, the soul needs to worry about which army will possess it.

They imagine that the souls of the dead are transported to that island. On the coast of the continent there dwell under Frankish sovereignty, but hitherto exempt from all taxation, fishers and farmers whose duty it is to ferry the souls to the other side. This duty they take in turn. Those to whom it falls on any night go to bed at dusk. At midnight, they hear a knocking at their door and muffled voices calling. Immediately they rise, go to the shore, and there see empty boats—not their own, but strange ones. They board the boats and seize the oars. When the boats are under way, they perceive that each is laden choke full, with her gunwales hardly a finger's breadth above water. Yet they see no one, and in an hour's time they touch land, which one of their own craft would take a day and a night to do. Arrived at Brittia, the boat speedily unloads, and becomes so light that that she dips only her keel in the wave. Neither on the voyage nor at landing do they see any one, but they hear a voice loudly asking each one his name and country. Women who have crossed give their husbands' names.[32]

In Brittany, the Bay of the Departed was regarded as the site from which these boats embarked. According to other traditions, between the moment of death and the time of the body's Christian burial, the soul undertakes a journey to the place of personal judgment, where its fate is determined while it awaits the Last Judgment. Quite often the writ is given to St. James of Compostela or involves passage over St. James's Bridge, because Santiago is associated with the Milky Way as the road of the dead. We should recall that the pilgrimage routes to Santiago de Compostela follow the Milky Way toward the Campus Stellae, the Star Field. In Ariège and Couserans, the Milky Way is called Path of Souls,* which we can view in light of an ancient belief, which maintained that souls transformed into stars after dying. In the Aran Valley, dying is the equivalent of taking the path of St. James (*eth camin de san Jacou*). We should also remember that from the Foix region to the Aran Valley, the

Camin de las amas.

passage to the otherworld is affected by a Cart of Souls.* On the eve of
a death, the devil comes to borrow oxen to pull this cart. In Andorra,
the Car dels difunts is almost identical to the cart of the Breton Ankou.
In other places, souls make a pilgrimage to Jerusalem, site of another
portal to the otherworld. Caesarius of Heisterbach tells how the soul of
a sleeping woman is transported to this city where, in the presence of
an entire heavenly host (*celestis exercitus*), she attends a Mass.[33] We find
some versions of the Infernal Hunt in this city.

The vacillation between the dead and angels is perceptible in the
gesta featuring the Crusades. During the second siege of Antioch (1098),
a spectral army came to the aid of the besieged Crusaders, which allowed
them to mount a victorious sortie.[34] In the *Chanson d'Antioche,* an Occi-
tain work by Grégoire Béchada (ca. 1120–1126), which is quite close to
that of Richard the Pilgrim, the ghostly army is made up of pilgrims
who died in battle. In the version reworked by Graindor of Douai, it is
formed by knights of a bygone age (*vieux homes d'aé*) who fought under
Roland, who wore white beards (*com flor des prés*), and who seem to
have descended from heaven (*avalés de paradis celestre*) and *faés*† (verse
8096). On two occasions, Graindor describes the members of this troop
(*compaigne*) as "feather-covered angels" (*angeles empenés,* verses 7720 and
9071). In a third text, Robert le Moine's *History* says, concerning the
same scene, that there appear celestial troops and saints (*numina coelestia
legiones sanctorum*). In her study of this passage, Suzanne Duparc-Quioc
points out that in around 1150, John, abbot of La Chaise-Marie in Italy,
wrote to St. Bernard about a vision he had in which dead Christians
became a multitude of angels (*multitudinem angelorum . . . de illis qui
ibi mortui sunt esse restauratam*).[35] Even if it is a compensatory belief
intended to support the idea of the Crusades, it was not spun from whole
cloth. It recycled the idea that the dead form themselves into a troop. In
the work of Conrad of Eberbach, we can see another army of the dead,
which bears white weapons and rides white horses.[36]

Car de las amnas, cart deras armas.
†[Enchanted. —*Trans.*]

Figure 10.1. St. Michael and the Prayer that Should Be Addressed to Him.
Ars moriendi (Bilder Ars) (Leipzig: Conrad Lachelofen, 1496)

The Lay of the Dream (Draumkvæd), a splendid Norwegian visionary poem, collected in the nineteenth century but going back to the
thirteenth century, presents two armies that come to receive judgment.

The army of the damned rides in from the north, making a great din. It is led by Grutte Graskeggie (Gráskeggi),* who wears a black hat and, depending on the version, rides a black steed* (*han reið pá svartan hest*). The other army, that of the blessed, comes from the south and is led by St. Michael of the Souls accompanied by Christ.[37] In Scandinavia, souls are thereby led by St. Michael, who has been granted the nickname "of the souls" (*sankte sale* Mikkjel). The saga bearing his name (*Michael's Saga*) presents a vision in which he appears to come out of the east at the head of an angelic host "more brilliant than the sun," which is then engaged in combat by a horde of demons that comes from the north.[38]

From the time the notion appeared of celestial or diabolical troops contending the possession of the soul and the good dead that transform into angels, we can see a similar evolution for the dead that are doomed to hell. The pseudo-Turpin relates these events: "A man failed to execute the instructions of his parent's will. The dead man appeared to him in a dream thirty days later and predicted his imminent demise. The next day, in front of the entire army, 'they suddenly heard in the air above him a commotion resembling the roar of lions, the howls of wolves, or the mooing of calves' [*in aere, quasi rugitus leonum, luporum, vitulorum*]. He was immediately abducted, while still living and healthy, by the howling demons [*a demonibus in ipsis ululatibus vivus ac sanus rapitur*]."[39]

The devil's hosts therefore seek the soul of the damned. The novelized story of Luque the witch is a good example, but this is likely a Christian interpretation of much older elements. If we refer to the *Saga of Snorri the Godi* (see page 40), the evil dead group to indulge in their crimes and other depredations. The Wild Hunt could easily be one of the forms they take, reinterpreted by Christianity and altered to serve as an example.

---

*Frye rei Grutte Graaskeggje [Grutte Greybeard —*Trans.*]
Alt moe sin svarte Hatt.

11
The Birth of New Legends

THE FOURTEENTH AND FIFTEENTH CENTURIES marked a new stage in the history of the Wild Hunt, which underscores its propensity to act as a magnet. Increasingly, numerous blends and contaminations profoundly transformed the belief. Yet we must examine them if we truly wish to understand the folk traditions surrounding the belief, examples of which were collected even into the dawn of the twentieth century.

We therefore focus our attention on the new motifs and figures that enter into the Wild Hunt. We will find ourselves in familiar territory: in most cases these figures are the same as those we met in chapter 1.

The Rope and the Cross

Born in Schaffhouse in 1445, a professor in Basel and Friburg, the Strasborg preacher Johann Geiler von Kaiserberg makes several observations about the Wild Hunt in his sermons. In a sermon he gave in the Alsatian capital in 1508 on the Thursday following Reminiscere, he borrows the story of Noel from Vincent de Beauvais, but uses it only to illustrate a short preamble.

> You ask, what shall you tell us about the Wild Army? But I cannot tell you very much, for you know much more of it than I. This is

what the common man says: those who die before the time God
has fixed for them, those who leave on a journey and are stabbed,
hanged, or drowned, must wander after death until there arrives
the date that God has set for them. Then God will do for them
what is in accordance with his divine will. Those who wander are
especially active during the Lenten days, and first and foremost
during the lean times before Christmas, which is a sacred time.
And each runs in the dress of their rank—a peasant in peasant
garb, a knight as a knight—and they race therefore bound to the
same rope [*lauffen also an einem seil*]. One holds a cross in front
of him, the other a head in his hand, "Make way, so God grant
you life!" This is the opinion of the common man about which I
know nothing, but the *Speculum historiae,* book XXX.c. speaks in
two places of Charles V, king of France, who, after his death, wan-
dered here and there with his army, paying penitence, but he found
redemption, thanks to the prayers of St. Denis, and his penitence
ended. The Furious Army is called Charlequint, but others call it
Quint.[1]

That souls must wait on earth for their leaving time set by destiny
is an ancient idea that found its way into medieval literature through
Tertullien (*De anima* 56). It would take too long to trace its long and
winding course through the texts of this period, but we know that
De Universo (III, 12), written between 1231 and 1236 by William of
Auvergne, makes use of it before speaking of the Mesnie Hellequin
(III, 14). Geiler explicitly states the date of the apparition, the Christmas season—that is, a period when spirits invade the earth because
the otherworld is open—and the Ember Days. The majority of the
appearances of the Furious Army are concentrated in these times of
the year.

This preacher, Johann Geiler von Kaiserberg, is the first to intro-
duce three important motifs: the rope, the bearer of the cross, and the
herald who warns the living to keep their distance.

The Rope

What does Geiler mean when he says *lauffen also an einem seil,* which, translated literally, means "running the length of a rope"? This rope probably served to bind to each other the members of the host. The rope (*seil*) undoubtedly comes from the Christian tradition of the "devil's bond" (*laqueus diaboli*), which spread parallel to the image of the devil huntsman we looked at earlier (pages 78–79). It could also go back to elements that predate Christianity. Lucan of Samosata depicts the god Ogmios, an infernal psychopomp, as pulling "a large number of men attached to each other by the ears with bonds of small gold chains and amber that resemble beautiful necklaces" (*Discourses, Hercules* 1–7).[2] In order to carry this interpretation further, we must access other testimonies, which, alas, we cannot. We do know though that the name of the Wild Hunt is sometimes Furious Bond in Swabia and Muetiseil in Switzerland, where the term has even entered the local lexicon and people sometimes still say "he acts as if he was in the Furious Bond" when they mean "he is unruly."[3]

The Bearer of the Cross

The bearer of the cross is completely unexpected and out of place in this procession of the damned or souls in purgatory. Of course, we can view him as a promise of redemption, but redemption that is valid only for the dead who atone for their sins in this host. The host, then, also requires a purpose and its members to be on pilgrimage to a holy site, which is the case for other troops.

The presence of the cross bearer becomes clearer if we refer to the Hispanic testimonies in which the Santa Campaña—also called Estadea, Güestia (Asturias), and Estantiga (deformation of the Latin *hostis antiquus,* the name of the devil)—is a host of the dead and a parallel version of the Infernal Hunt.[4] It is the procession of souls (*la procession de las animas*) that appears in October, from December to March, or even on certain days such as Saturday, between midnight and one o'clock in the morning. A figure carrying a cross precedes it and is accompanied by the tinkling of bells and lights, details to keep in mind. The procession follows the same route as burials, is visible or invisible, makes a noise like that of the wind, and gives off an odor of candles. Whoever hears its, sees it, or smells it is gripped by terror. In his study of the worship of the dead, Vincente Risco notes that the models for this troop are the procession of the Holy Sacrament and the burial ritual.[5]

Spanish traditions specify that the person bearing the cross is alive and cannot be released from this charge unless he encounters another living soul on the route of the Santa Campaña. Generally speaking, this is a man who possesses the gift of second sight and is thus able to know who is about to die. Geiler von Kaiserberg's sermon and these traditions from the Iberian Peninsula reflect the same ritual complex whose meaning we must clarify.

The person who gives the warning could be an extrapolation of the giant, who in the story by Orderic Vitalis warns Walchelin not to stir. His function is to forewarn people of the passage of the Wild Hunt in order to prevent them from being compelled to follow it. The figure who gives the warning is a helpful individual who tries to impede the dangers represented by the demonic phalanx. He therefore occupies a special place that, starting in the sixteenth century, prompted people to seek its explanation.

The Warning Figure

The Protestant theologian Johannes Agricola (1492–1566) is the first to name the person who preceded the Furious Army. He records what he has learned from a certain Johann Kennerer, the pastor of Mansfeld near Eisleben, who was more than eighty years old.

> I have heard . . . that the Furious Army—that is what it is called— has passed through Eisleben and the entire Mansfeld area every year on Lent Thursday—that is, the Thursday following Ash Wednesday. People hasten here and await its passage as we do when an emperor

or grand and powerful king comes to visit us. An old man who carries a white staff and is called the Loyal Eckhart precedes the troop. The old man commands people to move back and even suggests some return to their homes if they wish to avoid misfortune. Behind him followed riders and footmen, and among them we might see people who have recently died and even some yet living. One rides a two-legged horse, and a second is bound to a wheel that turns by its own volition. A third carries his leg over his shoulder yet still runs, another goes about without a head, and there are plenty of similar apparitions.[6]

The Loyal Eckhart is one of the oldest figures from German heroic legends, and in the *Song of the Nibelungenlied,* for example, he plays the role of the warning figure.[7]

The Mountain of Venus and the Loyal Eckhart

During the sixteenth century, Eckhart made his entrance into the legend of the Mountain of Venus,[8] known in France as *Paradis de la reine Sybylle,* the title of a romance by Antoine de la Sale.[9] He went on to become proverbial in this role.

The relationship of the Wild Hunt and the legend of the Mountain of Venus is specified by Martin Crusius (1526–1607), a professor of Greek and Latin in Tübingen. He does not cite Eckart, but he says that the Furious Army consists of all the infants who died unbaptixed, all who have fallen in battle, and all ecstatics—by which he means those "whose personality splits but whose traveling soul has not returned to the body."* This retinue appears during the Ember Days and during the Christmas season.[10]

The rapprochement of the two legends can be explained by a belief concerning the Hörselberg, a Thuringian mountain near Eisenach,

---

. . . vel exercitum furiosim, in quo essent omnes infantes non baptizati, omnes in pugnis caesi, omnes ecstatici, in quorum animae quae evolassent non redissent.

from which the Furious Army is reputed to emerge and which also houses the palace of Venus. Between 1607 and 1614, Henry Kornmann, placed purgatory in this mountain, which he called Horrisonus, because very often people could hear the many howls and lamentations of souls or spirits echoing from its depths.[11] Wolfgang Heider (1558–1626), a professor of morality and politics at University of Jena, speaks of apparitions occurring in the Thuringian forests around Christmas, when "specters, lemurs, larva, and empusae" appeared along with troops of horsemen and footmen, preceded by the Loyal Eckhart, who carried a staff and urged everyone to keep their distance.[12] The tone of this account is repeated by David Fechner (1594–1669), a Protestant theologian and rector of Görlitz (Silesia), whose account is also based on that of Agricola. Vechner and Heider provide the new, scholarly name for the Furious Army: the Bacchic Host,* which can fall into the notion of masquerade. Vechner made Eckhart the leader of the host (*agmen ducente*) and forged a link between this troop and the Brocken (Brockelsberg, Blocksbarch), "where gathered witches and magicians from all lands to hold their Sabbath."

We can be inerested in the testimony of Zuanne (Giovanni) della Piatte, an inhabitant of Anterivo, taken from his trial, which took place in Fié on the Sciliar around 1497. Zuanne speaks of journeys into the otherworld and abductions in the Mountain of Venus, where lives Dame Herodias (*el monte de Venus ubi habitat la donna Herodiades*), and he mentions the faithful Eckhart, "an old man with a white beard (*uno vecchio con la barba bianca che dize el fidel Eckart*), and even Tannhäuser. Beautiful women (*ragazze bellisime*) feast with Venus in this mountain, and sometimes men are invited. One day, around the Ember Days of Christmas (*una nocte Jovis quatuor temporum de Nadale*), the entire company leaves the mountain of Venus and travels in five hours all around the globe on a black horse.[13]

We must note one final testimony: that of Georg Michael Pfefferkorn (1646–1732), pastor of Friemar and later Gräfentonna. When he

---

*De cohorte refert illa Bacchante (vulgus appellabat das wüttende Heer).

lashes out at Catholics and the papacy, he feels obliged to mention the Hörselberg.

> I must now speak of Hörselberg, which stands between Gotha and Eisenach, on which monks of old confabulated and claimed, among other things, that this mountain was part of purgatory, for souls were tortured there. They thus gave this place the name Hear Souls (Hör-Seel) and also said that if we were at night to grade the sand in front of the mountain's large cave, on the morrow, we would find traces of much coming and going of both men and beast. They also say that the Loyal Eckhart, as the peasants call him, lives in this mountain and precedes the Furious Army and warns people of its danger. For this reason, it is said that the closest village, Settelstädt, should be called Satan-Städt (Satanville). It is possible that the prince of darkness often played his tricks during the time of the superstitious papacy.[14]

Dame Holle

In the middle of the seventeenth century, the Leipzig polygraph Johannes Prætorius identified the place where the Wild Hunt appeared as Schwarza, a Thuringian village near Suhl, on the southern slope of the massif of Thüringer Wald.

> It is also said . . . that at Christmas, Dame Holle passes through and that the Loyal Eckhart goes before her troop to warn any folk they encounter, asking them to remove themselves from its path so that no misfortune befalls them. Several lads of this village claimed to have seen it when they were on the way to the tavern in search of beer to bring back home. Because the ghosts were taking up almost the entire width of the road, they were pushed a little to the side with their jugs. Some of the women of this troop supposedly took the jugs and drank their contents. Struck with fear, the lads

kept their peace about this, overlooking how they would be greeted back home with their empty jugs. Finally, the Loyal Eckhart allegedly told them, "God inspired you to say nothing—otherwise they would have wrung your necks. Quick, return home and say nothing to anyone about what happened. Do this and your jugs will ever be full and you shall never want for beer." The story says that the lads kept their peace for three days. [. . .] Finally, they could not keep it to themselves anymore, and they told the story to their kinfolk. That brought an end to the horn of plenty [*cornu copiae*], and the source dried up.[15]

The troop described by Prætorius seems to be made up solely of women. Here, we find a new amalgam: the Furious Army conflated with the legend of Dame Holle, which is the German form of the belief in the Good Women and Dame Abundia, whom we looked at in chapter 2. The theme of the jugs whose contents can never be exhausted as long as the talking taboo is respected intersects with that of the female figures who dispense fertility and wealth. The further we find ourselves from the Middle Ages, the more opaque the tradition becomes and the more adulterated it is.

What should we retain from all these testimonies? First, the movement of the Wild Hunt is concentrated upon several dates, which are always the same. Second, that das wüttende Heer has become combined with other nocturnal troops and associated with sorcery. Finally, the Hunt has sunk deep roots into the local soil and been given a specific place where it sojourns. This place is selected with respect to its interpretation as a troop of souls in perdition. Interesting details emerge here and there: the folk that gather to watch the night host pass (Johannes Agricola), for instance, is a completely unexpected detail that suggests that the Hunt is a ritual procession, a kind of masquerade about which we will talk again with regard to the romance of *Fauvel*. The children who died unbaptized about whom Martin Crusius speaks are evidence of the rapprochement of beliefs that touch on the Wild Hunt and Percht

Iron Nose, an ambiguous figure who combines the features of a psychopomp and Mother Abundia.

Percht and the Host of Children

Though the medieval witnesses portray Percht (Bercht, Berchta) as equal to Mother Abundia and the fairy women who enter houses on certain nights to grant their inhabitants prosperity if they find a meal prepared for them,[16] folk traditions know her as the leader of dead children who had not been baptized. These women and their baby followers would enter houses and eat the food left out for them, most often on Christmas night or Epiphany. In the Eisack Valley in the Tyrol, Percht was accompanied by dogs that represented the souls of these children. This belief was widespread throughout Austria and Bavaria. In other regions of Germany, she was known as Dame Holle (Holl, Holla), and in Switzerland, she was Dame Selten.[17] In the Haut-Adige, the night troop was called Corteo della Berta and traveled on the night of Epiphany or

Figure 11.1. Percht of the long nose. Hans Vintler, *Pluemen der Tugent* (Augsburg: n.p., 1486).

St. Martin's Day.[18] In Cadorino and in the Belluno region of northern Italy, the Redodesa corresponded to Percht, and she passed through at midnight of Epiphany night, accompanied by her twelve children (*alora passa la* Redidesa *coi so dodese* Reodesegot).[19]

Contrary to the Wild Hunt, this troop had no reputation for causing any loud noise. It was possible for its members to be redeemed if someone gave them a name. Here we come across a legend motif we encountered earlier: the pitcher full of tears, for which the following text is a variation: "A person encountered Percht and her troop behind which was laboring a small child who was continuously tripped up by tails of the too-long shirt he wore, which was hampering his ability to keep up with them. On seeing this, the person cried out, 'Oh, the poor ragged urchin!' ['*O du arm's Zoadawascher!*'], which amounted to giving the child a name. In the South Tyrol, the spectator ties the child's dragging shirt tails for him while calling him *Zuserbeutlein*."*

The theme that being unbaptized is a cause of postmortem wandering overlays elements from a time that predates Christianity, especially those touching on the prematurely dead, *aori* and *immaturi*.

Around 1400, the anonymous English monk of Byland left us a story that illustrated the pagan background of the troop of children, which shows how it became disconnected from the Wild Hunt.

The story is told of a certain citizen of Cleveland called Richard Roundtree, who, leaving his wife pregnant, went on a pilgrimage to the tomb of St. James.† He and his companions spent a night in a forest near the royal road,‡ each of them keeping watch for a time

---

*[According to an Austrian correspondent who is very knowledgeable about all things Perchten, this is a made-up term of endearment that is possibly a compound word of *zuserl,* meaning "waxwing," which is considered a nuisance bird in Schwabia, and *beutlein,* meaning "little sack." The bird reference likely refers to the cries uttered by the child as it stumbles in his large shirt, falling farther and farther behind, and the little sack is likely his clothing. —*Trans.*]
†[At Santiago de Compostela. —*Trans.*]
‡[The *camino real,* across northern Spain. —*Trans.*]

while the others slept. When Richard's turn came to keep watch, he heard a great noise that came from the direction of the royal road. Then he saw several figures who sat astride the horses, sheep, oxen, and other animals, which had been used to pay their funeral expenses when they died. He noticed, in particular, what appeared to be a little child in swaddling clothes, and he asked who it was and what it might be seeking. It replied, "It is not appropriate for you to address me, for you were my father and I was your stillborn child, buried without being named and baptized." Hearing this, the pilgrim took off his own shirt and put it on the little child, naming it in the name of the Holy Trinity, and he took with him as proof the old swaddling cloth. With its name bestowed, the child went off exultantly, walking upright instead of floundering along, as before.[20]

Russian traditions are particularly interesting, for they have preserved beliefs and rites of great antiquity. These children had no right to be buried in the village cemetery or to receive the normal ceremonies. Because they did not live their full life (*svoj vek*), they were assimilated into the ranks of the unhappy dead who transformed into demonic spirits (*rusalka*). They were buried in either the vegetable or herb garden. To neutralize them, they were sometimes buried beneath the threshold of the *isba*,* which connected them to the household gods and spirits (*domovoj*), or at the village border or at a crossroads. In the Ukraine, poppy seeds were sprinkled over their graves, because of a widespread European belief that they could do the living no harm as long as they were kept busy counting these seeds. It was forbidden to mourn them, for it was believed that they were obliged to drag behind them pails full of their parents' tears. If they did not, these tears would drive them deeper into the ground, and they would not be able to resurrect. The stillborn child pursued his existence as an evil spirit who moved about in the form of a whirlwind.[21]

---

*[An isba is the traditional small wooden house found everywhere in the countryside of northern Russia. —*Trans.*]

Dame Abundia

More or less visible, depending upon the testimonies, the collusion between the night hosts of the Good Women and those of the Wild Hunt indicates that at the juncture of the fifteenth and sixteenth century, the contours of each became blurred. As their original meaning became lost, a new meaning was constructed.

We can find one of the first traces of a merger of the Mesnie Hellequin and the troop of Good Women in the work of Norman cleric Guillaume de Guillerville. In his *Poenitentiarus,* written between 1200 and 1255, Guillaume inserts in a chapter on gluttony a criticism of beliefs in witches, seers, unlucky days, New Year's Day, and the worship of trees and stones, and he notes: "I have seen many people fooled by Dame Aminda"—cacography of Abundia—"and the Mesnie Hellequin."[22] The *Roman de Confession,* dating from the second half of the thirteenth century, poses this question:

> *Ne lou ui tu ne la masnée*
> *Herrlequin, ne genes ne fees?**

In the literature of entertainment, the first traces of this rapprochement appear in the *Jeu de la feuillée* (1276), by Adam de la Halle, in which the Mesnie Hellequin heralds the coming of the fairies Morgue, Arsile, and Maglore,[23] who are regarded as representatives of supernatural beings who visit people's homes on certain dates. The Mesnie is preceded by Hellequin's messenger, Crokesou, whose wild and tangled mane of hair emphasizes her demonic character—and she is accompanied by the sound of small bells (verses 578*ff.*), perhaps those that were once affixed to the breasts of horses, and enjoyed great popularity up until the fourteenth century:

---

*[Don't listen to them, neither her nor the Mesnie
Herlequin nor evil nor good fairies? —*Trans.*]

J'oi le maisnie Hielekin
Mien ensïant, qui vient devant
Et mainte clokete sonant . . . *

We can note that in *Renard le novel* (1289), by Jacquemart Gielée, Hellequin is evoked by means of a comparison between the noise of the bells adorning the reins and saddle of Orgueil's saddle and the tumult that announces the arrival of the Wild Hunt.[24]

A sa siele et a ses lorains
Ot cinc cent cloketes au mains
Qui demenoisent tel tintin
Con li maisnie Hierlekin. †

Adam knew the exemplum of Étienne of Bourbon about the familia Hellequini as shown by the question of Crokesos, *Me siel-il bien, li hurepiaus?* (verse 590), which is an exact reproduction of a question posed by a member of the familia: *Sedet mihi bene capucium?* ‡ In other words, the hurepiaus or capuchon§ is a means by which we can recognize the Wild Hunt.[25] It is not rare to find alarming figures in folklore that wear headgear that conceals their faces and sometimes grants them invulnerability;[26] increased strength, as in the *Merveilles de Rigomer* (thirteenth century);[27] or invisibility, as the Tarnkappe of the dwarf Alberich. In one Icelandic tale, the hood belongs to a revenant.[28] In addition, there are those "hooded spirits" (*genii cucullati*) whose mystery remains to be penetrated.

---

*If I am not mistaken, I hear the Mesnie Hellequin approaching with the sound of many bells a'ringing . . . —*Trans.*]
†Verses 528–32, "On his saddle and harness
he had at least five hundred little bells
that made a din resembling
that of the Mesnie Hellequin."
‡[Does my *hurepiaus* (cap) sit on me well? —*Trans.*]
§[Hood. —*Trans.*]

Raoul de Presles (1316–1382), *maître de requêtes* (counsel) at the estate of Charles V, definitively confirms the rapprochement of the troops of Hellequin and those of Dame Abundia in his translation (1371–1375) of St. Augustine's *City of God*: *"La meignee de Hellequin, de dame Habonde et des esprits qu'ils appellent fees, qui apperent es estables et es arbres"* (XV, 23).

We can note the same evolution outside of France.

The Blessed and Music

The *Collections chronico-historiques* by Renward Cysat of Lucerne offers admirable documentation of this evolution, and it is worth paying particular attention to what he says about nocturnal apparitions.

> The common folk, especially old men and women, believed in what they called the Blessed Ones [Salige Lütt] and the Army of Good [Guottesheer]. These were supposed to be the souls of those who perished violently—by accident, war, or by the executioner's hand—before they finished the term set for their lives. Thus they were destined to wander until that time and act with friendship and charity toward men, entering, at night, the houses of those who spoke well of them. There they lingered, to light a fire, cook, and eat, and then they left, causing harm to none. People do not realize that the food had been eaten. Many wished to hear them and shared their company, and this folly reached such heights that many believed men and women still living wandered with this company for the sake of greater happiness. Wherever it was assumed that someone was a member of the troop, they were held in high regard and esteemed above all else. These people, it is said, were characterized by a pious integrity—in short, they were saints.
>
> I remember an elderly couple who lived here and had such a reputation and were held in great honor by fools. It was said they belonged to one of these blessed communities. I have also known

many people whose homes would be visited at night by these beings
[*diß wäsen*], but they did not move a muscle and were not seen.
Those who boasted knowing something about this subject say these
beings came in quite softly, making a pleasant noise, as if they had
all manner of stringed instruments. One being would precede the
rest in order to warn those present to stay away and many other stu-
pidities that I do not consider worth repeating. . . . But it is certain
that all this is deceit and illusion [*laruen und affenwerk*], and it is
said that the living cannot rove with the dead, unless in supernatural fashion, as is written about magicians and witches . . .

I knew a peasant whose farm was a two-hour walk from the city.
He did not live a long life. His wife let it be known that she would
go out at night to stroll with these dear souls or Blessed Ones. I
learned this, because she secretly confided it to an honorable inhabitant of the village, who divulged it to me. Among other idiocies, she
said that these folk that roam the night become irritated when the
kitchen has been left untidy. She often found herself transported in
an instant to Einsiedeln and other places that are far from here, and
she told how she had sometimes met dead people or those who had
died abroad, unknown to those in their homeland, and that they
had held their hands out to her, although they were deceased. As
this honorable individual professed his great amazement and asked
her how such things were possible and if her husband had known
or clearly perceived it, she answered no, because her body remained
lying in bed. Only her soul or spirit left. . . .

Reasonable people have never wished to acknowledge this troop
as a host of the Blessed or as an Army of Good nor name it as such.
They have called it a diabolical illusion (*ein Tüfflisch gespenst*), a
Furious Army, although others have replied to those who name it
this way by saying they are cursed and that evil spirits bore them off
[*der böss geist zerzeeren*], that they are an Army of Good, that they
honor God, and that it is specifically this army, this apparition, that
sometimes abducts people at night in the fields and streets and takes

them to remote lands in the blink of an eye. Those to whom this has happened acknowledge that a noisy wind approached, filled with a strange din, as if many stringed instruments were being played.[29]

This extract from Cysat's *Collections* is a true lode of common beliefs about the Wild Hunt. We can see from it that we are dealing with two different troops here: the Infernal Hunt—that is, the Furious Army—and the Blessed Host consisting in fact of ecstatics, meaning those who created a Double that is able to act independently of their bodies. This brings to mind the judgment that Burchard of Worms made about those people who went out at night to follow Diana and Herodias.

The theme of transport or abduction by the Blessed Ones carries no mortal danger—this host is made up not of the dead—and the different natures of the Furious Army and the Army of Good (Guottisheer) are revealed by the presence of music in the Guottisheer. We have moved beyond the jinglings mentioned by Adam de la Halle, Jacquemart Gielée, and the *Chronique de Zimmern* to the drums and fifes mentioned in Jacques Trausch's account and the violins mentioned by Cysat. We also have the earlier testimony from the Vosges region of France: in it the maisnieye Hennequin designated invisible nocturnal musicians. A certain confusion reigns in all the texts that note the presence of various noises. The nature of this music—martial, cacophonic, or sweet—in fact indicates that we are not always faced with the same nocturnal phalanx.

Klaus Beitl meticulously studied the People of the Night (Nachtvolk)—the dead, in other words—and he draws up a chart of these apparitions and their variants, noting that in the Voralberg in Austria, this name meant a troop of priests, black and horrific silhouettes that roamed the night where they could be either seen or heard, and that elsewhere this name was applied to the dead who sometimes were beneficent and sometimes were maleficent. When they were beneficent, the living person who encountered the dead was taught to play a musical instrument like a virtuoso. When they were maleficent, the living person was stricken with disease or blindness or was even carried off. Beitl notes that the appearance of this Night Host is wilder in the Swiss cantons of St. Gall, Glarus, and the Grisons, where it is not accompanied by music and its appearance heralds a death or an epidemic.[30] The element of music reappears in Antwerp legends in which the Wild Hunt is given the name Freemason (Framasson) and on one occasion is even called the Army of the Dead (Dodenheir), which travels, it is said, accompanied by singing, fanfares, and the sounding of trumpets and organs.[31]

In his study of the same theme, Arnold Büchli notes the last traces of a similar belief: a day laborer hears a troop he cannot see. It passes by, playing music, and it bears the name of Violin(s) of the Dead (Totägeigi).[32] In some places, it was believed that the coming year would be fertile if the Furious Army traveled through accompanied by sweet music.[33] The testimonies collected by ethnologists are often confused, because the night hosts and processions have been given a wide array of names that are taken as synonyms, whereas they can be applied to different realities. We should note that the People of the Night (Nachtvolk) is not identical to the Nocturnal Troop (Nachtschar) or to the Blessed Ones (Sälige Lütt), although all share common elements. The first is a troop of the dead, called *pievels da noatg* and *procesiung digls morts* in the Grisons. The second consists of the Doubles of living individuals, as shown by a declaration made by Chonrad Stoecklin (1549–1587), who was executed for witchcraft: "He had no choice about taking part in his trip with the phantoms of the night each Ember Week on Friday, and Saturday after Ember Wednesday, and mostly at night. Shortly before he was to travel, he was overcome by a lethargy, an unconsciousness. Then, as he thought, his soul would leave his body and travel thither, remaining separated for two or three hours. This would occur sometimes painlessly, but sometimes with pain. Nevertheless, his body would remain wherever the trip seized him.

And he confessed that whenever his soul was out on its travels, if his body was turned over on its other side, his soul could re-enter his body only with difficulty or with great pains."[34]

The Blessed Host corresponds to the troop of Dame Abundia; Bensozia; Bonae res; Percht; and, in Italy, Madonna Horiente, who, around 1380–1390, the Milanese Inquisitor Fra Beltramino de Cernuscullo identified as Diana and Herodias or the bona domina Richella whom Nicholas of Cusa (1401–1464) notes was one with Dame Fortune (Richella quasi Fortuna) and with Hulda, the Frau Holle of German traditions.

The Game of Diana

Fra Beltramino also mentions the Game of Diana (Ludus Dianae), which is nothing other than a trip taken by Doubles.

Petrina, from the time you were sixteen until the date of this confession, you have continually taken part in a certain game of Diana, whom you call Herodias [*fuisti ad ludum* Diane *quam vos apelatis* Herodiadem], and you have come before this mistress and have always given her your devotion, in the following manner: you have bowed down to her and spoken these words, "May you fare well, Lady Horiens" In answer to you, she herself has said, "May you fare well, good people." And you have said that they go to the game in the form of animals, or more exactly as a donkey, a fox, or as human beings, as living or dead people, and that those who were beheaded or hanged display a great sense of awe and do not dare to lift up their heads in that company. You also said that in that society they kill animals and eat their flesh, but that they place the bones back into the skin, and the mistress herself strikes the skin of the slaughtered animals with the staff that she holds in her hand with the apple [*cum bacheta quam portat in manu cum pomo percutit*], and these animals at once revive, but they are never much good for work thereafter. You said that they go with their mistress through the houses of various people, and they eat and drink there, and they rejoice [*ibi comedunt et bibunt et multum letantur*] in finding houses that are spacious and well ordered, and the mistress then gives her blessing to this house [*dat illa domina benedictionem dicte domui*].[35]

The Game of Diana is identified as a "good society," and its concerns mirror exactly those listed by Burchard of Worms in his *Decretales*. The resuscitated animals theme is new. Shamanic in origin, we can find this theme throughout the Middle Ages.[36] In the trial conducted by Fra Beltramino, Juliana Winkern, a native of Umes on the Schlern, tells of a meal at the Game of the Good Society in which a baby was cooked and eaten, but her friend Anna Jobstin gathered its bones and brought the child back to life.[37]

In 1457, Nicholas of Cusa, bishop of Bressanone (Brixen), conducted an investigation of two woman from the Val di Fassa who claimed to form part of the retinue of Mistress Richella, interpreted, and the two claimed this individual was the demon Diana from the *Canon Episcopi*,[38] but Richella means "she who presides over fortune."

The regions that sit in both Italy and Austria also have different troops that haunt the night. One is called Game of the Devil (Zogo del Diavolo), that of souls in perdition, and another is called della Signora, donna del Bon Zogo, Mistress of the Good Game.[39] We therefore have a diabolical and harmful troop in which we can find, according to Margherita Vanzina de Tesero (Val di Fiemme), "incubi, nightmares," and other spirits;[40] another, second society that performs good works; and, finally, the dead who we know form processions on certain dates. The Dominican Inquisitor Bernard of Como notes the existence of a *ludas bonae societatis*[41] in the trial he conducted in 1485 in Bormio (Val Tellina).

Requests and Gifts

The clerical accounts in Latin most often pivot around a request for suffrages: the dead individual reveals the nature of his or her sin and asks that reparation be made for it or asks for the living individual to pray or have Mass said for him or her as the sole means of being released from the Wild Hunt. The texts in the common tongue reveal two other motifs: a request for help and a gift sometimes offered in tandem with the first request. The *Chronicle* of the counts of Zimmern recounts the following event, which occurred in 1550.

> The same night, the Furious Army crossed through Veringen around midnight. At this time, a watchman named Hans Dröscher was walking through the streets to announce the hour. Jingling noises drew closer, coming from the old castle. Then someone shouted at him: "Mano, mano!" The good watchman grew scared, realizing that something odd was going on, but he had no wish to go nearer or respond. The other person continued shouting and calling to him for such a long time that eventually he went to see him. He found a terrifying man dressed in a soldier's garb. His head was cleft down to his neck, with one half hanging over his shoulder. The injured man or ghost implored the watchman to bandage his head so that he could continue to follow the troop, and he pulled a handkerchief from his sleeve or doublet, which he could use to dress the wound. In terror, the good watchman declined, saying he could not bandage him, for that was not his profession, but that he was more than ready to seek out a barber or surgeon to tend to him. He was fully purposed to get away from this apparition. The other refused his excuses and insisted so strongly that the watchman eventually bandaged his head. In the meantime, the other revealed that he was a native of Veringen and that his head had been cloven this way during the war. Now he was traveling with the Furious Army. He thanked the watchman for his care and added that the living man should not watch him leave, to avoid suffering. The two separated. I do not know if the watchman heeded him or not, because once he had returned home, he fell ill and remained in bed for sixteen weeks.[42]

This final detail clearly indicates that the members of the Wild Hunt did not wish to reveal either from where they came or where they were going. This is contrary to the exempla in which we are told where they come from, but the goal of their itinerary remains in the shadows.

For his part, the Strasborg chronicler Jacques Trausch (died 1610) notes this among the wonders of the year 1516:

> Not only this year but for many others, what is known as the Furious Army has been heard throughout all the lands, and especially in Alsace, Brisgivie, and elsewhere, at night as in the day, and in the forests and in the mountains. At night, the Army hastens through the fields, playing drums and fifes, and also it travels through the towns, its members carrying lights and making loud cries. Such ghosts number sometimes fifty or eighty and even one hundred or two hundred. One carries his head in his hands, another carries a cross or sometimes an arm or a leg, depending on the manner in which each found his death in battle. They carry candles that cast enough light so that it is possible to recognize who they are and if they died in war or elsewhere.
>
> A man always preceded them, ceaselessly shouting, "Make way, make way, lest you suffer!" In the common lands of Eygen . . . they roam through the fields. . . . In the towns they roam through the streets and the houses and over the thresholds, and nothing happens to anyone; but if they are encountered on the common lands, it is fatal.
>
> In Friburg, a woman saw that her husband, who had fallen in battle, accompanied this phalanx: his head was cleft in two. She raced to him and bandaged his wound with her veil. He asked her for many Masses to grant his soul rest. Another man emerged from the ghostly troop and gave her a large gold head from which she had to drink. She took it, and the troop moved on, and she kept it in her hand and nothing happened to her. Subsequently, it was seen that the gold head was real and not an illusion. The devil certainly had stolen it elsewhere.

These years, similar apparitions are constantly seen everywhere. They make their requests for help and assistance, so many, in fact, that it is thought that all the souls of purgatory seek succor.[43]

While the framework of this account still corresponds to the basic structure of clerical literature, we nonetheless find here some particularly interesting details. First, we can note that the dead carry lights—candles or torches—which reflect more the idea of a procession than a troop of fantastic riders and bring to mind the Spanish Santa Campaña. Next, we can note that the space is split in two: into the commonly held fields, a place of mortal danger, and the city where an individual is safe. We must understand here that the dead of the host entered the towns and lingered in its houses. Now, thanks to more recent traditions, we know that the dead gathered on certain dates, formed a procession, entered their former village, and returned to their houses to get warm or to eat. For this reason, into the nineteenth century, food, light, and a fire were left for this purpose. This belief and custom show that the troop of Dame Abundia, Satia, the Good Folk, or Percht all fell into the same domain: the cult of the dead.

Remaining is the motif of the gold head, which is inexplicable. J. Trausch explicitly states that the woman suffered no ill effects from drinking from it. He therefore is aware that tasting the food or drink of the otherworld is fatal. Perhaps this head, whose origin I do not know, is a substitute for the motif of the burn mark in the literature of revelations. It constitutes the indubitable proof of the reality of the encounter, like the horn in the story of the priest's housekeeper (see page 63). Nevertheless, this gold head could also replace a more sacred vessel that we have seen in the retinue of the Santa Campaña. This procession was preceded not only by a figure carrying the cross, but also by someone who carried a transportable font of holy water.

The Theme of Abduction

We have learned that encountering the Wild Hunt carried with it a risk of being kidnapped. In the tellings of Richard the Fearless, this opinion is made a fictional device. On two occasions, Renward Cysat tells of abductions. In the extract from his *Collections* (cited earlier), he attributes this kidnapping to evil spirits, but now he offers us a complete account of a "real" event.

On the fifteenth of November in 1572, a compatriot, Hans Buchmann, nicknamed Krissbüler, an inhabitant of Römerschwyl in the jurisdiction of Rothenburg, then aged fifty and someone I knew well, suddenly disappeared. This sparked keen agitation and to-do among the authorities. He had two grown sons. His wife knew their father was going to Sempach on that day, and she noted that he . . . was not back yet and that it was getting late. She sent their sons out to look for him and bring him home, fearing that he might have stopped too long to drink. Their sons went off and made their way to the forest, where the battle of Sempach had taken place. There they found scattered, on the edge of the path, here and there their father's hat, cloak, gloves, and sword and its scabbard, which frightened them. Their suspicions immediately turned to Claus Buchmann, their neighbor and their father's closest relative, who had been quarreling with him for years . . . as his possible murderer. They gathered their father's effects and brought them home, and their mother began to weep and moan. The neighbors began to do likewise, confirming this suspicion. The sons hastened to Claus's house, to find and kill him. They looked everywhere in his house, even in the smoke cellar, to see if he might not have buried the body somewhere, but they found nothing. They brought the affair to the authorities and demanded that Claus be arrested. . . . Nothing was discovered in his home, and as his reputation was spotless. . . . He was released. . . .

Four weeks later, it was learned that the missing man had been seen in Milan, but no more. Finally, on Candlemass of 1573, he returned home, bald, beardless, his eyebrows gone, and his face and head so swollen and puffed up and so dreadful to look upon that only those closest to him could recognize him. Once the authorities got wind of his return, they had him arrested and interrogated once or twice—I was present and recorded the course of these discussions in the register of the clerk's office. They scolded him for the trouble he had caused by vanishing in such a dangerous and wicked fashion. They told him that he had intentionally and hatefully caused his cousin to bear suspicions of being a murderer, which had caused him much suffering and placed him in a difficult position. This is how he responded.

He had taken sixteen florins the day of his disappearance, thinking to pay back a man he was not able to find. He had then gone to Sempach on business, lingered there into the evening, and had a little to drink. He then sought to return home, and he made his way back into the forest, where he had reached the spot mentioned above as night was falling, when he suddenly heard a stange noise, a tumult that in the beginning sounded like a swarm of bees, but as it drew closer, it resembled more the sound of many stringed instruments [*ein selßam gethöss und Susen, anfangs einen ganzen Imbd oder Bynenschwarm glych, darnach aber alls käment allerly seittenspil*]. This din so terrified him that he no longer knew where he was or what was happening. He then got a grip on himself, drew his sword, and began striking around him. At that moment, he was stripped of reason, sword, cloak, hat, and gloves, and he was carried off through the air into a foreign land [*jn Lüfften hinweg jn ein frömbd land getragen worden*], which he did not recognize, having never been there before. He did not know where he was. He felt pain, and his face and head had become swollen, and he had lost his hair and beard. Finally, fifteen days after his disappearance, on the eve of St. Andrew's Day, he found himself in Milan. He had no idea how he had arrived there, but had recovered some of his reason, although he had apparently gone some days with no food or drink and was now in a weakened and downtrodden state. He did not recognize the city, for he had never been there before, and because he did not know the language, he could not understand anyone. When he asked directions to Lucerne, people answered him, "Milano, Milano," meaning Milan, but he thought they said Vilana, a locale in the Piedmont where he had spent time many years before, when he was a soldier. He had promised to make a pilgrimage to Rome, Notre Dame de Lorette, and Einsiedeln in order to recover his reason completely, and then he returned to his homeland. In the meantime, he met a German guard who had spoken German with him, taken care of him, and given him German money—which he still had—and this guard helped him change it so he could feed himself on the road to Rome and to Lorette. . . . He reached Rome on Christmas Eve, and there he was recognized by a captain in the Swiss Guard who was a native of Lucerne and who knew him. When he sought to return home, the captain and other compatriots supplied him with written statements attesting to what had happened to him, and a venerable Agnus Dei, and plenty of crowns to provide him with food on his return trip. He also brought attestations of his passage through Lorette and Einsiedeln. He stuck to his statements every time he was interrogated.[44]

This account presents all for its credibility, and Cysat never questions its authenticity. He simply notes that nothing would have happened if Hans Buchmann had taken the precaution of making the sign of the cross. If we subject Cysat's testimony to close analysis, we see that the sole reference to the Furious Army is the noise that echoes through the forest. The site of the abduction—where the Night Host passes—is a battlefield where the Habsburg army met the Eternal League composed of the cantons of Schwytz, Uri, Unterwalden, Lucerne, Bern, and Zurich, in 1386. Therefore, we can recall the theme of phantom armies that return to the site of combat (see chapter 3). We should also note the dates of the assorted events for which Hans Bushmann is the protagonist. He vanishes on November 15 and found himself in Milan on St. Andrew's

Day—in other words, in November, at the beginning of Advent, a period marked by masquerades, and the onset of a time that is propitious for the return of the dead.

Cysat revisits the subject in the chapter he devotes to the Army of Good and to the Blessed Ones, and he clearly states that the abduction is their doing: "I have heard this told by people who have encountered this apparition and been transported in the blink of an eye to distant foreign lands."[45]

Defensive Measures

We can note that in Hans Buchmann's adventure the abduction takes place at the moment the man draws his sword from its scabbard and starts striking the air around him. All indicates that he thinks he can protect himself in this way against the horde of invisible spirits. This is a common reaction, for it was long believed throughout Europe that iron had the power to stop demons or send them fleeing. One night, while he travels along the banks of the Loire on the way to see his lady, Ronsard is intercepted by the Wild Hunt and by a skeleton riding a horse, but he escapes them.[46]

> *Stretching my hand to remount . . .*
> *Smothered suddenly by a pressing fear,*
> *Without God, who promptly gave me the thought*
> *To draw my sword and tightly slash*
> *The air all about me, with the naked iron:*
> *Which I did so swiftly and so suddenly they did not hear*
> *The whistle of the blade in the air, and all vanished*
> *With no more to be heard, no noise or marching . . .*

Thus, drawing a circle around yourself or making the sign of the cross allowed you to remain safe. A scrutiny of nineteenth-century folk traditions that casually commingled the Wild Hunt, diabolical huntsman, and wild hunter, provides us with additional methods: when the demonic horde is heard, an individual should lie beneath a harrow; cover himself with dirt; stand or lie in the righthand rut of the road; keep quiet; avoid joining in with the noises; avoid clicking his tongue; avoid saying the name of the Furious Army on Mondays, Wednesdays, or Fridays, or even speaking about it; fold his handkerchief into the shape of a cross; place his head in a cart wheel; lay down on the ground with his arms in the shape of a cross; and so on. We can note the amazing close kinship of the German and Spanish traditions on this point.[47] The Spanish tradition is identical to how the Wild Hunt in certain regions of Germany are said to cross through houses whose front and back doors are in a row in order to leave a blessed branch or bread crumbs on the table.[48]

New Assessment

This legend of the Wild Hunt has evolved ceaselessly. It is alive and blends with all others that offer a point of contact. One of the keys to its evolution is the belief that purgatory is inside a mountain. This belief has brought about the merger of this legend and that of the Mountain of Venus, characterized by the presence of the Loyal Eckhart as the figure who gives a warning and the localization of certain apparitions in Thuringia.

We can also note the theme of the spirits of the night who enter dwellings—spirits behind whom we can distinguish the dead in in medieval literature. The ritual banquet of the fairies is in reality a repast of the dead.

We can also note the idea that the departed form a community and celebrate a rite at certain dates on which they appear together in a procession. The entire legend revolves around the problem of our future in the otherworld or beyond the grave and what the fundamental implications of the unique status of the dead are for the living. Depending on the nature of the texts, we meet souls in perdition as well as individuals who have no connection to purgatory and who lead a life about which we know nothing, for they overtly seek to conceal the purpose of their wanderings.

Another detail we must keep in mind, because it literally recurs: the Wild Hunt is regarded as a company, a society. This is expressed with varying degrees of clarity depending upon the witnesses, but we can gain the impression that the Wild Hunt is a rite that both the living and the dead celebrate. This is a point that must be clarified.

One of the major obstacles we encounter is obviously the plethora of names for the various nightly hosts. The elements are tangled up to such an extent that it seems they were interchangeable in the minds of our ancestors. This suggests a loss of meaning that went hand in hand with the acquisition of new meanings. Two important turning points emerge here: the thirteenth and the sixteenth centuries. These are the times when we note that the degraded and blended forms appear most strongly.

Though we do not know the origin of the turning point for the evolution of the legend in the thirteenth century, it seems clearer in the Renaissance. This was the time when the Reformation took place east of the Rhine and Protestants refused to accept the idea of an itinerant purgatory. Jacques Trausch of Strasborg observes that it was nothing but deceit (*Betrug*) and superstition (*Aberglauben*), idolatry (*Abgöttery*) and blindness (*Blindtheit*), "for as soon as Doctor Martin Luther began writing against indulgences, idolatrous Masses, and his attack on the splendid hierarchy of the Roman church, all these ghosts and rapping spirits retreated and came to an end."[49] Of course, Trauch was himself mistaken on this point: Luther did believe in these manifestations, as shown in his *Table Talk!* We should remember that from the seventeenth to nineteenth centuries, the majority of folk traditions were nourished by these amalgams that were spread by sermons as much as by word of mouth. They then received a new lease on life, adapted to local conditions, and followed their own evolution. We should note, though, that the alpine regions preserved the tone of medieval beliefs better than anywhere else. The Swiss occupy a choice place here through the wealth of their accounts of what is practically unknown in France and elsewhere in Europe.

12

The Wild Hunt, Masked Men, and Bawdy Fellows

AMONG THE ACCOUNTS CITED up to this point, there are some that prompt doubts: Are we dealing with the dead or confronted by living men in disguise? Some texts are quite ambiguous—especially those of the late Middle Ages and the Renaissance in which everything plays out as if those who tell these tales and the authors who recorded them couldn't make up their minds, prisoners as they were of received ideas and beliefs. The least that we can say: they did not dispel the ambiguity and kept alive doubt.

Little aware of research conducted in Germany and Scandinavia— often for simple linguistic reasons—French and Italian researchers have pushed their investigations toward processions of masked living men that made plenty of noise. Carlo Ginzburg[1] has made a link between the Mesnie Hellequin and the Charivari and Henry Rey-Flaud[2] has studied the Mesnie Hellequin in its connections with fundamental rituals of sexuality. In general the interpretation of the Mesnie Hellequin as the Charivari is the result of a hypothesis of romance languages specialists (G. Paris), repeated by M. Debrouille[3] in his study of the connections between the Mesnie Hellequin and the legend of King Herla, and cited by Hans Flasdieck. Here, Herla, the name of the leader of the Herla-thingus, Walter Map's name for the Furious Army (thirteenth century) is linked to the old French *herler*, "make a racket," and *herle*, "tumult," "noise." We must note, however, that analysis of this Germanic name (Herla) has revealed that it means "war leader," "head of the army." The essential problem is knowing if the Charivari is a form of the Furious Army or is an independent entity. Our decision depends on the value we give to the scriptuary evidence and if *The Roman de Fauvel,* on which this interpretation is primarily based, is a later text. Should we give it priority over the evidence offered by the accounts of Walter Map and Orderic Vitalis?

The Romance of *Fauvel*

At the very beginning of the fourteenth century, Gervais du Bus finished his romance *Fauvel* in which, in 1316, Chaillou de Pestain inserted a long interpolation about a Charivari that takes place on the night of Fauvel's wedding. The miniatures depict this wedding as a man with a horse's head with his wife, Vaine Gloire. This poetic reportage describes how the ecstatic and unbridled retinue of the knight Hellequin comes to lead a wild Charivari beneath the castle windows. Following is the text, which I have divided into numbered paragraphs for convenience in the analysis.

1. Fauvel said to himself that it was now time to turn in, and imme-diately, he leaped in to bed next to his wife. Never, however, was such a Charivari made outside by coarse and bawdy men as was now to be heard in the crossroads of the city and in its streets. There is no man under heaven with the power to describe it, whatever mind he may possess. Those making this din were push-ing about everywhere, with no fear of Fauvel or his folk. So alert and on their guard were they that no enemy did they fear. On the manner and ways of this Charivari I note some splendid features in this story that I am setting down here for memory. Some had

donned their garments backward, while others wore large sacks or monks' robes. They were hardly recognizable beneath their paint and ill-fitting garb. All their thought went into making mischief. One held a large kettle; another a pan, hook, and grill; and another a copper pot; and yet another a tub. They all acted the drunkard—and all struck their instruments so forcefully that it stunned the town. Some wore cow udders sewn to their buttocks and thighs, and, over all, large bells, loudly tinkling and pealing, and others bore cymbals and drums and large, ugly, dirty instruments, rattles, and magic charms from which they drew such loud cries and high notes that none could describe. One pushed and the other pulled. Here is the foolish song of those making the Charivari in the streets: *En Hellequin le quin n'ele en hellequin.**

2. All the participants then led in a chariot on which was mounted a machine with wagon wheels, stout, strong, and well fashioned. In the midst of the wheels were attached six iron bars that struck each other as the wheels turned! When they struck each other, they made such a loud and varied noise so ugly and dreadful that it would drown out God's own thunder.

3. They made a tumult the likes of which was never before heard. One showed his bare ass, another snapped off awnings, one broke doors and windows, while another cast salt in wells, and another threw manure [*bren*] in people's faces. They wore false beards [*barboeres*] over their faces and carried two coffins in which rode those all too capable of singing the devil's song. One shouted baskets and bins, the other the place whence comes the wind.

4. A huge giant came before them, screaming. He was clad in good buskin, and I believe it was Hellequin and all the rest of his hunt.

5. His attendant followed him in a rage, mounted on a tall charger who was so thin that, by St. Quinaut, you could count its ribs and scale them like laths for covering tiles or shingles. He looked as if he were returning from exile.

---

*The only surviving verse of this song.

6. It was a thing most dreadful to see, I daresay. In all ways, in disguises, words, and deeds, never had any Charivari been as perfect as this one. Not a mouth was closed in this din of loud yelling and braying. Yet though it should have been most unpleasant, it seemed to cause Fauvel no suffering, who instead imagined the pleasures he would take with his wife whom he honored as his lady.[4]

This testimony has been often minutely studied as testimony on the Charivari,[5] so we too should revisit it and choose another angle with which to approach it. Chaillou du Pestain obviously knew the text of Orderic Vitalis, from which he borrowed coffins, the giant, the troop's name, and, undoubtedly, the idea of the domestic utensils carried by members of the cortege. The clothing worn backward refers to the reversal of values characteristic of Carnival, and the disguises, well depicted by the miniatures in the manuscripts, transform the participants into devils and demons. The musical cacophony already announced by Adam de la Halle and Jacquemart Gielée has nothing in common with the sound of violins that accompany the Wild Hunt in Germany and Switzerland, and emphasizes the demonic aspect of the troop, whose only thought is to misbehave. This commotion forms the very substance of the Charivari, and it certainly testifies to society's disapproval[6] and punishment of a breakdown of normal or ideal matrimonial unions—a dangerous destruction of order—but the date on which it takes place is significant. It corresponds to the liturgical *triduum*— that is, the Thursday to Saturday that precedes Easter, when the bells, the "good music," are prohibited from ringing and must remain mute. The din is a countermusic prompted by the "instruments of darkness." It evokes the diabolical powers and natural disorder that accompanied the death of Christ.[7] This countermusic makes itself heard during the twelve days of Christmas, Carnival, and St. John's festivals.

The great novelty here is the cartwheel machine, a true noise-making machine, a new kind of rattle whose sound is comparable to thunder. Patrice Uhl perspicaciously compares it to the Wheel of Fortune: "This complex mechanism of wheels turning in solidarity undoubtedly serves to transpose the allegorical representation of the book into the 'reality' of the street. For the Wheel of Fortune is composed not of a single piece, either. We must refer to the second book of Fauvel to learn this. When Fauvel goes to Macrocosmos, city of high fantasy, where Fortune resides (whose hand he hopes to win), he finds her sitting in front of her wheel or wheels, rather."[8] Quoting Gaston Paris, Patrice Uhl adds: "Before Fortune are two large wheels that turn without cease, one quickly, the other slowly. Within each are contrived two smaller wheels that move in the opposite direction. The wheels on which all humanity is laid out is the game with which Fortune ceaselessly amuses herself."[9]

It is important for us to recognize the close relationship that links Fortune and Hellequin. First, this linkage introduces us to a tradition whose first trace we can find in the work of Adam de la Halle. Next, Fortune is only one of the shapes adopted by the Good Woman called Abundia, Satia, Bensozia, or Percht. We therefore find in France the exact same shift of the legend: these hosts of women and the Mesnie Hellequin are brought together and made one.

In his study of the relationship among the dawn, fairies, and Fortune, J. H. Grisward[10] has shown that Morgue, Arsile, and Maglore, who emerge in Adam de la Halle's *Jeu de la feuillée,* and Fortune function as

Figure 12.1. *The Romance of Fauvel,*
Bibliothèque Nationale de France.

Figure 12.2. *The Romance of Fauvel.* Bibliothèque Nationale de France.

the two faces of fate: the first three reserve their gifts for those they have chosen, and the latter has been, since birth, blind, deaf, and dumb (verses 771*ff.*). They are inclined to favor those who honor them, which implies a rite. This rite happens to take place on the spring or autumn equinox, dates on which the Wild Hunt also appeared. We can accept that the rapproachment we have noted did take place, because the apparition of the Mesnie Hellequin and that of fairies that visit homes falls into the jurisdiction of the same liturgy, is based on the same belief, and shares a temporal kinship: all the dates denote a turning point and refer back to the notion of beginning.

Hellequin's appearance in the Charivari seems to indicate another shift.[11] Is it truly a shift, however, or does *Fauvel* retain features older

Figure 12.3. *The Romance of Fauvel.* Bibliothèque Nationale de France.

than the clerical accounts that are still available for reading? It is practically impossible to answer this question with any certainty. At most, we can see that the troops of true dead are mute (see the narrative by Walter Map, page 86), and what is said of the People of the Night—in fact, the new status of the deceased—normally involves the loss of body, shadow, and voice, whereas the living dead are instead noisy. There is a mystery here that we can explain only if we turn to the notion of alter ego, which justifies the corporeal nature of the dead and thus the noise they make. It is quite likely that ancient beliefs collide and telescope in our accounts. Some beliefs come from ecstatic and shamanic phenomena and others from religious thought.

Fauvel's Charivari is not the sole masquerade connected to the Infernal Hunt by one means or another.[12] In the Padstow tradition in Cornwall, still attested in the beginning of the twentieth century and called Hobby Horse, a man wore a demon mask over his head and held a wooden frame covered by dark cloth with a small horse head at one end. This Hobby Horse gathered his companions on the night of May 1. The next morning, the troop paraded through the village, with each companion wearing some sort of disguise, playing a musical instrument, and making a hellish din. Preceding the Hobby Horse and leading this procession was a man who wore a gnome mask and who was armed with a club. In the duchy of Kent, the troop was called Hooden Horse, and it paraded on Christmas night. Its members wore disguises and blackened their faces and carried small bells. They roamed the village, frightening the inhabitants and demanding beer. Here is an interesting detail: the Hooden Horse is represented by a man covered by dark sackcloth from which pokes the head of a horse fixed to a cane used by the man to prop himself up as he limps forward. The horse costume therefore represents the three-legged horse of death. In Westphalia the parades of horses on New Year's Day showed men wearing a horse costume and forming a horse with six or eight hooves. Richard Wolfram emphasizes its systematic connection to death—sometimes the processions ended in the cemetery—and to the Mesnie Hellequin. There is an undeniable kinship between these processions and the Charivari of the book of *Fauvel*. We can find in these traditions certain elements of the Wild Hunt: the bells and the leader armed with a club, for example. Even if it is hard precisely to identify the relationships between the Wild Hunt and these masquerades that use horse costumes, the parallel to *Fauvel* is worth noting.

Masks and the Dead

It has long been known that, depending on the circumstances, masks customarily represented the dead or demons: the same word in many languages was used to designate both the dead and masks—for example, the Latin *larva* and the Lithuanian *kaukas*. In ancient times commemorative feasts for the dead were accompanied by masquerades, and, if we refer to the customs of a country that was converted to Christianity quite late, such as Lithuania, we can see that the dead (*veles*) made up the troop of Veliona, god of the dead, and were represented by masks during solstice and Carnival celebrations. We also know that the masquerades took place on precise dates connected to the solstices and equinoxes and at the beginning of the year, which, depending on the era and the civilization, fell at different times.[13]

Before the reform of the Julian Calendar, the year began on March 1. In the Gregorian Calendar, it started on January 1.[14] Numbering 350 to 600 at the least, the New Year's Day celebration in the Roman world was marked by the appearance of masked processions that noisily roamed through the towns and cities.

In his study of the January New Year's Day,[15] Michel Meslin emphasizes that these masquerades inaugurated a new time, and that each act and object had a functional reason that was magical in nature. Each was for expelling the evil forces of the past and giving strength and vigor to the new time that the ritual invited. Early on, W. Mannhardt (1858),[16] then F. Liebrecht[17] aired the opinion that concealed behind the Wild Hunt was a set of beliefs connected to rituals for expelling winter.

In Switzerland, masquerades today still share a connection to the changing of the year. They are known as Chalandamarz in Engadine, and Colonda Mars, Calenda Mars, and Onda Marsa in the Grisons. We can recognize the old appelation Calends of March in these different names.

Additionally, we see the same in southern Germany and Austria, where the masquerades are connected to Percht. In Scandinavia, they are concentrated to the twelve days, the Christmas season, and the day of Santa Lucia. In Lombardy, Venice, and the Piedmont, people paraded to "burn the old one" (*brusar la veccia*), "one" meaning "year," which can be likened to the ancient Roman festival of Anna Perenna that fell during the Ides of March. Though the Roman New Year's Day celebration in

January was also that of the Lares, in Germany it was that of the dead, but we should not overlook the fact that the Lares—domestic spirits—are the good dead who have gained tutelary status. The Kalendae Ianuariae is therefore also a form of worship of the dead—at this time, a table of souls was set for the dead, who were given food offerings, a ritual also celebrated by the ancient Scandinavians. In France and the Germanic countries this setting took the form of the fairy feast, the table set for Dame Abundia, Percht, or the Parcae.[18] We find exactly this same table in Adam de la Halle's book in which the fairies are announced by the messenger of the Mesnie Hellequin, which underscores their collusion with the dead. We should not allow the blending of traditions to obscure their meaning: the dead ruled over fertility and fecundity of humans, livestock, and the earth. The fairies and the fates shared the same function.

The aim of the rituals that fall on the dates mentioned is therefore the expulsion of the harmful dead, who were perceived as demons, and to propitiate the other departed souls so that they contribute to the well-being of all over the course of the year that is just beginning. The superimposition of the Roman feasts of the dead—Dies Parentales, Caristia et Cara cognation (February), the feasts of the mother goddesses (Matronalia; March)—transformed into fairies, and masquerades is therefore not illogical.[19]

Fauvel's Charivari is therefore also a rite of the third function: the noisy masked cortege calls on the new couple's fecundity.[20] It is therefore usual that it brings onto the stage the reigning powers. The dead are represented by the coffins and the fates and are symbolized by the machine of wheels that refers to Fortune and her hypostases. The various utensils—kettles, hook, grill, pestles, pots, tubs—carried by the masked figures are household instruments connected to cooking and to the food that should not be lacking in the new home. Marriage is not only a rite of passage; it is also a new beginning. The Charivari therefore takes place in the liturgy of beginnings.

The presence of the Hellequin can be explained this way: he represents the dead connected to rites of the third function, but at the same time, he has been subjected to transformation into a figure of Carnival, as testified by the *Jeu de la feuillée* and *Fauvel*. This is the same process that turned Hellequin into the Arlecchino of Italian theater. Transformed into a figure of folklore, he found a place in the devilish mischief that accompanies performances of the mysteries, as clearly demonstrated by Otto Driesen, who performed a meticulous comparison of the mysteries with the Charivari.[21] This is why Arlecchino's coat designated the curtain that masked the entrance to hell or represented it on the medieval stage: a devil's head was painted on it.[22]

There is also strong evidence for the assimilation of the Mesnie Hellequin by Carnival in the regions east of the Rhine. We can see this in the Carnival procession that appears in a farce by Christian August Vulpias: "Behind the dragon's tale, the Furious Army ran riot. Its members were quite singular figures endowed with horns, beaks, tails, claws, humps, and long ears, and they made a large racket full of shouting, clapping, hissing, whistling, roaring, bleating, and growling. Behind them, riding on a wild black horse, was Dame Holda, the wild huntress, sounding her horn, cracking her whip, and shaking her unbound tresses."[23]

David Fechner (1594–1669) makes the troop led by the Loyal Eckhart a bacchanalia,[24] and many texts retain an ambiguity intended to allow us to contine to confuse the Wild Hunt and the masquerade. To distinguish one from the other, we must rely on a detail of the texts: the site of its passage. We can see that when the action takes place in town, we are dealing with a masquerade, but when the Furious Army emerges in the forest or open country, it is the Wild Hunt.

We should now revisit the meanings of Hellequin in an attempt to determine how this personage evolved.

The Semantic Field of Hellequin

In 1175, Pierre de Blois uses milites/familia Herlechini to designate individuals with a strong attachment to the vanities of this world and to the court of King Henry II that constantly moved from one place to another.

This metaphor primarily indicates that the name Hellequin was much older and that it fell into the public domain, so to speak. Under various spellings—Halegrin, Crenequin, Hennequin, Hanequin—it was applied to living people whose behavior the church desired to criticize.

It is undoubtedly these same courtiers that Chrétien de Troyes alludes to in his *Philomena,* concerning his heroine's talents for embroidery: "She could have painted foliage patterns and arabesesques on cloth, and even the Mesnie Hellequin" (verses 191–93).[25]

Toward 1263, the Chanson du Chevalier au Cygne et Godefroi de Bouillon says that the King of the Tafurs and his men were Hellequins:

> *et le rois des Taffurs o lui si halegrin*
> *Qui plus aiment bataille qui li glous ne faits vins.* *

The tafurs were the uncouth rogues of Hainaut and Brabant who formed part of the Crusades army and were regularly depicted as quarrelsome, gluttonous, and scruffy with little to recommend them. We can find this definition frequently in works dating from the thirteenth century on. In the *Actes des Apôtres* by the Brothers Gréban, dating from around 1250 (verses 8734*ff.*), we can read this:[26]

> *Desgoute, Rifflart et Briffault*
> *Tant plus y en a maint vault*
> *C'est le mesgnie Crenequin.*†

This expression became a proverb and Gabriel Murier's *Recueil des sentences,* published in Antwerp in 1568, notes it this way twice:

---

*[And the king of the Tafurs and his rowdy men
who loved battle more than gluttons love wine. —*Trans.*]
†[Disgust, Firebrand, and Gluttony
The more there are, the worse it is,
that's the Mesnie Hellequin. —*Trans.*]

The Hennequines, more madmen than scoundrels.
The Mesnie of the Hennequins, the more there are,
the less their worth.

In a sharp critique of lawyers, the thirteenth century text the *Marriage des filles au diable* (Marriage of the Devil's Daughters) notes the Hellequins's warlike nature by comparing them to mastiffs or guard dogs.[27]

It is the Mesnie Hellequin,
They are as unruly as mastiffs.

In the fourteenth century the *Songe doré de la pucelle* (The Maid's Golden Dream) likens allegorical figures to the spoken names of the members of Hellequin's troop.[28]

Dangier, Envie et Mal-Bouche
*Sont de faux helequins car ils valent pis que coquins.**

Jean Chartier, high chanter of St. Denis Abbey (d.1462) topped off the various meanings with that of "coward" in his *Chronique de Charles VII, roi de France.*

It is the Mesnie Hellequin
For you who lack all heart:
The more there are, the less their worth.[29]

In France, therefore, during the Middle Ages, Hennequin had come to mean "rogue," "madman," "fighter," "coward," "cur," "libertine," "ragamuffin." The name had come to mean people who banded together to form a troop that behaved in a reprehensible manner, which applies

---

*[Danger, Envy, and Slander
are false Hellequins because they are worth less than scoundrels. —*Trans.*]

perfectly to the men who performed masquerades, as we can see in the deeds performed by the masked individuals in *Fauvel.*

We can see that the historiography and the allegorical and entertainment literature no longer connects the Mesnie Hellequin to the dead, but the clerical literature remains captive to the old meaning, though it gives it devilish overtones. The *Second Lucidaire,* completed around 1312, explains it this way: "As I've told you, the Mesnie Hellequin is made up of devils who travel in the guise of folk on horseback who ride at a trot. This is what leap means when it says *Ab incursu,* etc. It is a manner of trotting." [30]

We find this repeated almost verbatim in the *Exposition of the Christian Doctrine* (fourteenth century).[31] These devilish overtones are fully expressed in the medieval theater, where the term Herlequin's Cope means, as noted earlier, a curtain on which has been painted a hideous, grimacing head, which represents hell.[32]

Herlewin/Hellequin followed the same evolution in Great Britain. In *Beryn's Tale,* also known as *The Merchant's Second Tale,* Geoffrey Chaucer (ca. 1340–1400) says that the mad, those who think only of joking and playing tricks, are devoid of wisdom and virtue and resemble the men of Hurlewayne (Hurlewaynes meyne). A poem attributed to William Langland ranks the comic oafs who were part of the retinue of King Richard II (Radeless) in the lineage of Hurlewayne (Hurlewaynes kinne).[33]

In more modern times, we may recall that a petulant child is called a *harlaque* in Wallonia, a *harlican* in Dorsetshire, and a *hannequin* in Normandy, but in Champagne *arlequin* still meant "will o' the wisp" in the nineteenth century.[34]

What connects the Mesnie Hellequin to the Charivari is a cluster of elements in which the notion of a noisy troop and a certain behavior regarded as mad and buffoonish occupy the main place. We could say that the name was secularized before going on to becoming a dual Carnival element. On the one hand are the processions of Charivari; on the other hand are those of the deviltries connected to the enactment of the *Mystery of Saint John.* Otto Driesen has shown that the people playing the devils on this occasion had eventually formed a society called Dev-iltry, which was provided with its own statutes.[35] It so happens that the Charivari possessed the same demon masks as indicated by the Synod of Langres held in 1404.[36]

A Parody of Burial?

Let us now return to *Fauvel*. What is the meaning of the coffins in the Charviari-like procession?[37] It seems that no one has yet noticed that the presence of coffins in Orderic's account and *Fauvel* indirectly suggests the notion of a funeral procession for which we can find a parallel in Switzerland: the Procession of the Dead formed by a parade of masked men who followed behind something that resembles a coffin.[38] What is being buried? Humorists would respond that Fauvel inters his boyhood life, which is an error, for he does not take part in the celebration. We can also view these biers as a simple means of transport, which com-pletely fits into the context of Carnival-like reversals in which objects are regularly diverted from their basic uses. It is also possible that we find here only a simple embellishment of the procession. The use of cof-

Figure 12.4. Miniature from the *Radziwill Chronicle*, fifteenth century.
In 1092 the inhabitants of Polotsk hid in their houses to escape
the spirits of the departed, who are depicted as monstrous creatures.

fins in this instance merely emphasizes the madness of the troop.

In combination with the devil masks and tumult, the coffins take on another meaning if we refer to the old significance of these masquerades: the evil forces are expelled to make way for the good forces. Generally speaking, loud noise sends demons fleeing, and it is possible that Chaillou de Pestain is unconsciously inspired by ancient rituals for expelling winter, such as mentioned earlier. Here, he departs from the coffins' meaning in Orderic's text, in which they are undoubtedly those of people who recently died and whom the Mesnie Hellequin seeks as suggested by the presence of large-headed dwarves.

An illustration from one of the manuscripts of *Fauvel* (see page 176) offers us an element worth noting.[39] In the top panel there appears a bearded figure who wears a hat and carries a basket from which emerges the curly-haired head of a child. In the middle panel, a bearded, hooded man pushes a small cart from which emerge two children's heads. We can recall that medieval iconography customarily depicted the soul leaving the corpse in the form of a newborn. We can therefore move beyond the simple notion of burial suggested by the coffins. These children/souls are either being carried into the otherworld or are being brought back from it. The Charivari description in *Fauvel* establishes a relationship to the Carnival, whose culminating point is, according to Claude Gaignebet, "the battle of the winds"[40] in which, in the beginning of February, the fart frees the breaths that are the souls of the dead. It so happens that the text mentions these winds twice.

The masquerade in *Fauvel* appears as a parody of a funeral procession, with demons that pull the dead (the men in the coffins) and souls (the children in the basket and little cart). Chaillou de Pestain picks up the theme of the Mesnie Hellequin, installs it within a Carnivalesque context, and, to describe the horde of the Charivari, may use a legend in preponderence throughout Europe: a man sees a burial cortege passing through a village at night. All the members of this procession are dead, save the last, who is the Double of the spectator and thus destined to die soon. This is a theme we will revisit later.

13

The Wild Hunt in Scandinavia

SCANDINAVIAN ACCOUNTS of the Wild Hunt are little known outside of that area, although their value is immense, because they provide us with archaic information. Furthermore, they document the evolution of the beliefs and help us to grasp better the alchemy of the texts.

Oskoreia

The northern countries, Norway in particular, offer a theme that seems to have come directly from the night hosts we have been examining. Here the Wild Hunt is known as Oskoreia, the Terrifying Ride.[1] This host is a troop of masked men or spirits* that ride horses (*ridende julevetter*) between Christmas and Epiphany or Santa Lucia Day,† hence another name for the Wild Hunt: Lussiferdi. In Scandinavia the twelve-day cycle can run from December 13 to Christmas or from Christmas to January 13.

We can note other names in evidence—Julereia, Trettenreia, Fossa-

---

*Confusion reigns on this point, and the accounts tend to commingle men and spirits, which suggests the masquerades are an imitation of a host of spirits, a point confirmed by the descriptions of the masks and attire.

†[Observed on December 13. —*Trans.*]

reia, and Imridn—all including the word *rei* or *reid,* meaning "to ride," "to go by horse," sometimes grafted on the determiners Jul/Jól (Christmas) or Imbre/Imbredagene. These terms designate the four days of Lent of the liturgical year (*ieiunia quatuor*) and Fosse (*name of a spirit*).[2] There is also another name for this time of the year: Trettenreia or Trettandreia, "the troop of horsemen of the thirteenth day (of winter)."

The host traveled through the air* or paraded over the ground and is characterized by two essential motifs: a connection to horses and an association with food and drink. The first motif brings to mind what we read in the accounts provided by thirteenth-century authors: during the cycle of the twelve days spirits slip into stables and abduct horses, returning them later covered with sweat, as if they had been galloping and ridden hard for a long time.[3] It is said that the members of Oskoreia or Lucy have ridden these horses (*at merri var* Lussi-*ridi*). This is what happened to Nils Taraldson Berge's (1769–1846) horse.† The second motif is the theft of food—especially drink. The Oskoreians slipped into houses and cellars and stole the food and emptied the kegs of beer, which they refilled with water.‡

Depending on the province, we may be dealing with spirits such as the Gulao or the Jula-gjeido or with men that rode with Oskoreia on these nights, which cannot help but bring to mind the Friulian Benandanti and the werewolves of the Baltic—a fraternity of men who work for the power of good[4]—as testified by Olaus Magnus, bishop of Uppsala: "In Prussia, Latvia, and Lithuania live a large number of these magicians. On Christmas night after leaving their human shape for that of a wolf, they gather in a place they have selected in the villages, where they then enter the cellars of the peasants and empty the casks of beer and wine [*cellaria cervisarum ingrediuntur, ac illac aliquot cervisiae, aut medonis tonnas epotant*] and strangle the livestock."[5]

One detail is important, for it reveals a link between these actions and

---

*For gjennen luften.
†*Hesten hans vart ridden av* Oskoreia.
‡*Drakk dei upp alt de øl der var, å fyllite vatn på tunnum.*

the deceased: "The place where they meet is held as sacred, and when an accident befalls someone there, an individual is convinced he or she will die that year [*eum isto anno moriturum*], for experience has long strengthened the belief of the inhabitants of these regions in that superstition."[6]

One story tells how a man met a stranger who told him he had taken his beer one night while he slept.[7] We can compare this account to an exemplum by Étienne of Bourbon.

> In the Cevennes diocese there was a man whom, it was said, spent the night in the company of women who the common folk called the Good Things (Bona res). . . . The priest promised to pester him no longer about this if he actually brought him along. On the advice of these creatures, the man came to summon him, telling him he had to rise immediately from his bed, naked as he was, and come with him and that a vehicle awaited them. Torn from his slumber in the most basic array, the priest found a piece of wood in front of his door, which on the man's command he straddled[8] as if it were a horse. The other cautioned him to avoid making the sign of the cross, because this sign would cause the women to blush.
>
> The priest then found himself suddenly transported into a very large cave, where he saw many women singing by torchlight and candlelight, as well as set tables covered with dishes.[9]

We should also note that Oskoreia carried off men, who then found themselves leagues from home, animals, and objects.[10]

The Phantom Cart

We can also note an apparition known in Denmark as *knarkevognen*. This was a ghost cart that could be heard in the sky, which appeared at the death of an individual. It is exactly reminiscent of the Breton Ankou.[11] In 1939, Julien Divivier shot a film on a very similar theme inspired by Selma Lagerlöf's novel *Cart Driver of the Dead* (Körkarlen),

Figure 13.1. Demons carry the dead away in their carriage.
Mural painting from Bagnot Church, fifteenth century.

based on Sicilian traditions, with Louis Jouvier as the ghost carter, and Viktor Sjøstrøm also made a film based on this theme. The cart has formed part of the Wild Hunt since the second half of the fifteenth century, but the origin of this addition can undoubtedly be traced back to the tradition of the death cart that we can sometimes see depicted in painted manuscripts and in a fresco in the church of Bagnot. On one of these we see a covered cart with windows, and from it heads appear and a devil is mounted on the horse that pulls it. The motif deserves a more detailed study than we can undertake here.

The Food of the Dead

It is impossible to know if the Scandinavian beliefs are direct or indirect borrowings from the medieval authors cited earlier. One element is certain, however: from the Middle Ages to the end of the nineteenth century it was believed throughout Europe that a troop roamed about in the winter that would enter houses for drink and sustenance. The deacon Christoph Arnold, born near Nuremberg in 1627 (died 1685), speaks of a Christmas custom of the Lapps: They would erect representations of the spirits of the dead, because during that time they believed that the majority of ghosts and spirits traveled through the air, and they wished to conciliate them through sacrifice: "They keep a piece of what they have eaten . . . placing it in a piece of birch bark, and, as if it were a small boat, they place a sail and oars on it. Then they pour in a little fatty broth, and then they hang the entire assemblage to a tree behind their house so that the Jól Army (Juhkafolker, Julheer) has something to eat."[12]

This nocturnal host has been incorporated into the Wild Hunt in more recent accounts. What clearly stands out: in all cases, the appearance of this host is linked to fertility rites, because the Christmas season is the time of omens, and the twelve days foreshadow what the twelve months of the year will be like.

Oskoreia and Guro Rysserova

Although akin to them in many ways, Norse traditions are distinct from those of their Germanic neighbors. The Norse claimed that a woman called Guro Rysserova (Gudrun Horsetail) led the Oskoreia, which matches what is said about Percht in southern Germany. Sometimes Guro was accompanied by Sigurd Svein, Sigurd the Young, whom everyone knows as Siegfried, hero of the *Nibelungenlied,* numerous poems in the *Edda,* and the *Saga of the Völsungs.* A ballad tells how Sigurd became part of the Wild Hunt.

> Sigurd the Young roughed up his gaming companions, who told him
> he would do better to be out looking for his father. His mother sent
> him to her brother Griep and gave him a horse, Grani. Sigurd left

and met an ogre, whom he permitted to mount up behind him, but Grani threw him to the ground. Greip told Sigurd that his father was dead, gave him a chest filled with gold, and urged him to go back home. Grani brought him to a swamp, but there the horse broke a shoe, and the hero dropped the chest. He then met the Wild Hunt led by Gudrun Horsetail, who asked him if he would prefer being the first in her troop or the last in heaven. Sigurd chose to follow her: *so rid eg med deg til oskor i dag.*[13]

The final sentence is not at all clear. Ronald Grambo says it means "then I will ride with you until *oskor*," a word that some have seen as a deformation of Ásgarðr, the realm of the gods. In this case we should take it to mean "so I will ride with you toward/in Oskoreia."[14]

In an extremely well-documented and meticulous study, Folke Ström has unearthed what Guro Rysserova[15] conceals. He starts with an analysis of the ancient accounts and highlights the fact that since the eighteenth century, it has been believed that Oskoreia was composed of a certain kind of dead person (drunks, homicides, and so on) who was doomed to wander until the Last Judgment. Next, relying on the work of H. Celander, he demonstrates that Guro is identical to Gudrun Gjuki Daughter (Gjukedotter), "reduced to the rank of a female troll (*trollkvinna* = witch) endowed with a horsetail." This Gudrun is a well-known figure from the legend of Sigurd/Siegfried, and she reappears in the thirteenth century in Snorri Sturluson's *Sturlunga Saga:* "Eyolf Thorsteinsson dreamed that a woman visited him riding a gray horse. She came from Náströnd, "Shore of Corpses," the empire of the dead. She appeared to him several times, eventually revealing that she was Gudrun Gjukedotter."[16]

F. Ström observes that this is the most important and the oldest testimony concerning Guro. We note its importance, because it creates a bridge between the Wild Hunt and the Dísir, female deities similar to the Valkyries, who are sometimes called "Odin's Dísir," the Norns (the Germanic Parcae), and the *fylgjur,* the tutelary spirits of men. According to Ström, Guro is "a Dís who has been demonized and debased."*[17]

It so happens that the Dísir were the object of a form of worship in which food offering played a large role and took place in ancient times at the beginning of winter, which places these women in the same sphere as the Matronae and Dame Abundia, Satia, and Percht to whom meals were offered at certain times of the year. Furthermore, the Dísir are regarded as the dead (*Atlamál*, strophe 28), or the souls of deceased women, a belief that is the foundation for their comparison to "the tutelary Dísir of the countryside," the Norse *landdísir*.

In other words, we see a kinship at the heart of the evolution of this complex—the same merging of beings that incarnate Dumézil's third function with the dead and the same rites at the same dates. That this kind of kinship appears from the northern to southern extremes of the Germanic area and poses a challenge to the law of ecotypes cannot be a coincidence. Instead it shows that what we find here are beliefs of a venerable antiquity, from a time before the various Germanic ethnic groups went their separate ways. What we have here supports the hypothesis of an Indo-European origin for the Wild Hunt.

En demoniserad och degradered digestalt.

14

The Passage of the
Wild Hunt

TO GRASP TRULY how the Wild Hunt is anchored in reality, we must analyze the motifs and themes that accompany it. Despite their contradictory nature, the texts provide information whose importance we should not overlook. First and foremost, they permit us to situate the facts in time and space.

The Dates of Its Passage

We can bring the appearance of the Wild Hunt down to three major time periods: winter—the duration of which varies depending on the latitudes and era of the narratives, Holy Week, and summer.[1] The dates in winter are staggered from St. Martin's Day (November 11) to the Chair of St. Peter (February 22), with two periods of high holy days, Advent and the twelve days, separating Christmas and Epiphany. In the Palatinate, for example, the Wild Hunt was abroad during Advent, but in Swabia it appeared precisely on the day of St. Thomas (December 21).

The most frequent date in Norway for the passage of the Wild Hunt, which is called Oskoreia, is the night of Santa Lucia (December 13), which means, according to some, twelve nights before Christmas or even "eleven nights before Christmas, while others maintained it was merely three."² Before the introduction of the Gregorian calendar, Santa Lucia Day was considered to be the shortest day of the year and was viewed as the beginning of winter, a time marked by masquerades and other rites. In Sweden, the spirits that formed part of this retinue were called Lussegubber, Lussen, and Lussiner.

We find the same rite in Switzerland at the beginning of the sixteenth century, three days before Christmas during what was called "noisy night" (*bolster nächt*) or "hunt of the *sträggele*."³ The *sträggele* was the equivalent of the Howler (Schrat), a kind of dwarf that was sometimes combined with a nightmare (*mar*). Today this name is used to designate the masks used in Carnival processions. On St. Crispin's Day (October 25) there emerges the Scälarageister, which can be translated as "souls of purgatory" insofar as the third site is called Scälaratobel in the Grisons,* and they ride horses whose nostrils spit fire. Another purgatory is located in the Lötschental.⁴ In Switzerland and Alsace, Hutata is on the move during the twelve days, and takes his name from the scream he unleashes.

In Lithuania, the autumn festivals (Ilges) that correspond almost exactly to All Saints' Day, last for ten days, three of which were dedicated entirely to worship of the dead. At this time, the dead were invited to leave their graves to bathe and feast,⁵ and the Wild Hunt was abroad.

There are a number of dates for other times of the year, among which we have: Easter, Pentecost, Walpurgis Night (April 30–May 1) St. John's Day (June 24), St. Peter's Day (June 29), and St. Bartholomew's Day (August 24).

Some of this troop's movements occur cyclically. It is said that the Wild Hunt appears during the meatless times of the Ember Days (first week of Lent, the week of Pentecost, third week of September, Advent),⁶ or that it returns every seven years.

All these dates are heavy with significance in the folk calendar, and many rites occur on them, but I cannot go into great detail on this subject, for this would require a huge tome! We should note, however, that

---

*It is called Bockitobel in Uri Canton.

St. Martin's Day marks the end of the old fiscal year and the beginning of the new one, as well as the beginning of winter. St. Bartholomew's Day performs the same offices for autumn, and St. John's Day is the Christian reinterpretation of the Janus bifrons, which, in antiquity, marked a pivotal point in the year. It so happens that a full set of rites take place on dates considered to be the ending and beginning of the year: purifications; purgings; removal of demons; expulsion of evil; the extinguishing and relighting of fires—see Cysat's text in the appendix; masked processions; a ceremonial reception of the dead, who are then led back outside of the village.[7]

All that we find here possesses its own internal logic, and these kinds of blended mixtures are not created by chance. We can clearly see this if we examine more closely the date of February 22.

Feast of the Chair of St. Peter

The Feast of the Chair of St. Peter (February 22) replaced the ancient ceremony of *di parentes* or *dies parentales,* an expression of ancestor worship. Furthermore, we have seen that one of the names of the Wild Hunt's leader is Goï (Westphalia). As it happens, Goï was the name of the fifth month of winter for the ancient Scandinavians, and it fell at the end of what is now February or the beginning of March. When the new year was still celebrated on March 1, Goï was marked by rites to expel winter, purification rituals, and commemorations of the dead. This corresponded almost exactly to the Greek Anthesteria, during which the dead were given free rein and permission to invade this world, and to the Roman Lupercalia whose purpose was to purify the city and drive away the demons responsible for sickness, sterility, and poor harvests.[8] In Sweden, the sacrifice of Goï was celebrated in the spring equinox. The Westphalian name for the Wild Hunt leader could quite conceivably be a recollection of the past. This would not be the first time that the name for an important festival was anthropomorphized—for example, the Befana is the personification of Epiphany and Perchta personifies Christmas.

The Day and the Hour of the Troop's Passage

The time is sometimes specified as being between eleven o'clock and midnight or between midnight and one in the morning. Nighttime hours predominate, with a strong concentration on midnight (Silesia), but we can also find in the Allgäu and Bavaria noon for the Hunt's passing. Latvian folk songs (*dainas*) offer us some invaluable information in this regard. The dead make their way to the otherworld successfully by being buried before noon, the hour that marks the beginning of the setting of the sun and the transition to twilight.[9]

> *Bury me before noon*
> *After noon do not bury me*
> *After noon the Children of God*
> *Have closed the gates of heaven.*

Another variant of this is:

> *After noon, the Children of the Spirits*
> *Have Closed the Gates of the Spirits.*

The day is rarely indicated, and when it is, it is Saturday—a day that conveys the idea of the Sabbath and attests to a connection between our theme and that of the flight of the witches.

Common Denominator

If we look for a denominator common to all these dates, we see that they all indicate key times of the year that involve changes, ends, or beginnings—in short, they are all transitional periods. Easter, for example, provides a key to the entire medieval calendar. Its French name, Pâques, comes from the low Latin *pascua* and the Greek *paskha*, derived

from the Hebrew *pesah,* "passage" or Passover. The English name Easter
is derived from the Old English *Eostre* and the Old High German *Ostara,*
who was a goddess of the dawn whose feasts were celebrated in April.
The holiday was an equinoctal spring rite, a lunar festival connected
to several seasonal myths. Even today it marks the transition from the
death of winter to vernal life, and the Christian celebration integrated
many pagan rites, such as the din intended to drive off the demons of
winter. Mircea Eliade cites an eighth-century text: "the Alamans sought
to expel winter during the month of February," and points out more
than one custom for expelling death.[10] All the year's transitional passages have the distinctive feature of permitting communication between
the otherworld and our world, evidence for which is provided by the
invasion of the undead and spirits during these times. We can find a
faint echo of this in the festival of Halloween (October 31), which corresponds to the Celtic Samhain (November 1)—a veritable November
Carnival and night of the devil, witchcraft, and the dead represented by
masks and popularized in countless movies. In ancient Ireland this was
the time when the Army of the Sidhe left the otherworld to roam the
earth. This account is the sole piece of evidence reminiscent of the Germanic Wild Hunt: "In the *Intoxication of the Ulstermen,* several festivals
were organized for Samhain. Following the feast arranged by Fintan,
all the nobles, who were already fairly intoxicated, engaged in a wild
race across Ireland, following Cuchulain, and at the passing of this furious troop, hills were flattened, trees were uprooted, and the fords and
streams were emptied of their water."[11]

We should also recall that there is a European corpus of ballads
on Hallewijn, which E. Smedes connects to Halloween and to the reli-
gious conceptions of the ancient Celts (*oud-Keltishe voorstellingen*).[12]
Hallewijn, whose name is quite close to Herlewin (seen the work by
Pierre de Blois) is sometimes regarded as the leader of the Wild Hunt.
We must further investigate this possibility.

Oracles, Taboos, and Hauntings

All the dates cited here are associated with oracular and soothsaying practices: in Silesia and in Austria, the twelve days that span the period from Santa Lucia's Day to Christmas prefigured what would take place in the twelve months of the new year, and numerous divinatory practices took place at this time. During Candlemass, servants exchanged positions and rites were performed that sought the blessing of the higher powers to protect houses and farms. In addition the weather of this period foreshadowed the weather of the coming year.

All of these days were marked by prohibitions that affected work, mainly spinning and even marriage. For instance, individuals had to avoid a marriage in May, because it entailed a risk of taking for a spouse a revenant or a woman from the otherworld.

Some experienced hauntings on all of these days. St. Martin's Day (November 11) was the occasion for the passage of the bird of St. Martin, a kind of fire dragon; the wild herdsman; and the Kasermandl (Alps), a kind of demon that took possession of chalets after the livestock had been taken down to the lower valleys for the winter and that often bore the features of dead cowherds who were condemned to return, because they abused the livestock in their keeping. In Burgenland, Austria, Lutzl (Lucy) passed at this time.[13] She was the woman of the solstice, who roamed with veiled face. She was also armed with a kitchen spoon that she used to beat people in their houses and a knife for opening their bellies (the gastrostomy motif, which is also common in traditions concerning Percht). Clad in black and white, she was accompanied by monstrous figures, and her trajectory was a quest in which she begged for the deceased foodstuffs, the "bread of all souls." In Norway, Lussi was also seen as Adam's first wife, which means she corresponds to Lilith or else to the mother of the race of Cthonian beings, which explains her relationship to the Wild Hunt.

Libations and Feasts

Another two major constants emerge here: libations, feasts, and other festive rituals, which seem to have a fundamental connection to the pre-Christian cycle of pagan festivals (Christmas, St. John's Day, and so on), and masquerades accompanied by noise—rattles, the cracking of whips. Feasts, the offering of food,[14] and the masks explain the convergence of the Good Dame and the Wild Hunt, which finds expression in the fairy feast in Adam de la Halle's book and in the romance of *Fauvel*.

The passage of the Wild Hunt, which, in the traditions after the Middle Ages, was closely connected to food and drink, is perfectly logical to us once we grasp the role played by the dead. They presided over the fertility of the soil and the fecundity of livestock. Thus it was necessary to propitiate them if they were regarded as neutral or well-intentioned or to drive them away and send them fleeing if they were seen as wicked. In one way or another, the Wild Hunt fell into the vast complex of ancestor worship, the cult of the dead, who are the go-betweens between men and the gods.

These dates also are connected to Carnival, and they stand out in the yearly calendar: they corresponded to a pre-Christian cycle of movable feasts, which depended on lunar phases. Furthermore, the Celtic and Germanic calendars were most likely superimposed on two ancient apportionments of the year: two large seasons—summer, which runs from May 1[15] to November 1, and winter, which runs from November 1 to May 1. Philippe Walter notes that these apportionments "have undergone a more or less marked Christianization by virtue of being fixed to specific periods in the calendar"—in other words, originally movable feasts became fixed when "integrated into the Christian calendar."[16] Certainly this recuperation explains the plethora of dates, often quite close to each other. Their vacillations are due to the superimposition of different calendars as much as, of course, to the difference of the latitudes of the countries that attested to a belief in the Wild Hunt and to the fixing of commemorations of the dead at different times depending

Figure 14.1. Revenant. Claude Nourry, *The Calendar of the Shepherds*
(Lyon: n.p., 1508).

on region. We should therefore collect those dates that fall close to each other, for they are a clue that the rites have changed by moving from one region to another and being integrated into other ritual groupings. It would undoubtedly be a better idea to work this out by using seasons as our reference. We should finally note that the moon, regularly mentioned by our witnesses, converges with the idea of Carnival. In fact, a new moon at Carnival time opens the door to the otherworld and allows the passage of souls to their earthly or celestial destinations.[17]

PART FOUR

Odin and the Wild Hunt

15

Scholars and the Tradition

Hlude wæran hy,
la, hlude ða hy ofer þone hlæw ridan
*wæran anmode, ða hy ofer land ridan.**

Although many German researchers have long shown that the incorporation of the leader of the Wild Hunt into Odin rests on flimsy foundations, these reasonable voices have gone unheard, because they contradict a general tendency to discover mythological survivals in folk traditions—cost what it may. Furthermore, a number of older studies are conducive to error, because they make no clear distinctions between the diabolical huntsman, the wild huntsman, the cursed huntsman, and the Furious Army. We begin by briefly retracing the development of these studies since the time of Jacob Grimm.

---

*Loud they were,
yes loud, when they rode over the mound,
they were fierce when they rode across the land.

This may be the oldest attestation of the Wild Hunt in Great Britain. For more, see Anne Berthoin-Mathieu, *Prescriptions magiques anglaises de X^e au XIIe siècle,* 2 volumes (Paris: Amaes, 1996), vol. 1, 132; vol. 2, 440.

On the Existing Research

In quest of a German mythology, Jacob Grimm[1] studied the theme of
the cursed huntsman, which he compares to the Mesnie Hellequin,
known as the Furious Army and the Wild Army in the regions east of
the Rhine River. Starting in 1835 he sees in its leader a form of Odin
that had been downgraded by Christianity to the rank of a ghostly figure. Following in his footsteps, J. W. Wolf recognizes features of Donar
(Thor) in this figure.[2] The conclusions of the Mythological School
enjoyed great success and were recycled by L. Weniger[3] in 1906 and still
feed some contemporary studies.

Julius Lippert (1881)[4] offers a new hypothesis: the fuel kernal of the
theme is the belief in the soul's survival after death, a proposition that
fits well with the fact that the dead make up the Furious Army, which
is repeated by W. Golther (1895),[5] although he refuses to make Odin
the leader of this nocturnal host.

In 1889, L. Laistner tackles the problem from another angle.[6] He
suggests that the Wild Hunt is the result of dreams condensed into a leg-
endlike form. In his thesis, published in Leipzig in 1914, Hans Plischke[7]
creates a kind of synthesis of his predecessors' theories without taking a
stand in favor of any one of them: the Furious Army is rooted in beliefs
concerning the soul, meteorological conditions, and dreams. In 1934, A.
Endter[8] develops an animist theory, underscoring the role played by the
dead in ancient and primitive beliefs. In 1937, Edmund Mudrak devotes
a highly documented study to this subject, referring primarily to recent
legends.[9] Geza Roheim ventures a psychoanalytical interpretation, and he
casually commingles traditions that have nothing in common.[10]

Taking a position at the antipodes of the mythological interpretations and undoubtedly in reaction to them, Karl Meisen's thesis is
simple: the Infernal Hunt "is the expression of the Christian dogma of
the punishment of the soul of the person who has committed reprehensible acts."[11] Within this punitive system, we can seek the origin of the
Infernal Ghost Army, this troop of the damned led by the devil and his

satellites.[12] Meisen acknowledges that the roots of this belief originate in ancestor worship in classical antiquity, but he does not deal with this matter with any greater precision.

All the researchers note that hiding behind the Helle of Hellequin is certainly the Herla of Herlethingus, Herlechinus, and Herlewinus,[13] but the interpretations of *thingus* and *quin* have given rise to the wildest hypotheses[14]—those evoking the word *king* and that are incompatible with philological laws, as clearly demonstrated by H. M. Flasdieck. People have tried to see in Hellekin the "king of hell" (hell king), the "child of Hell" (Höllenkind), and the "king of alders" (*Erlkönig*). Indeed, we can stumble upon this error in many French books.[15] It has been claimed to derive from Erenquin, the name of an earl of Boulogne, and so on.

This theme became the object of a completely new and appealing interpretation in 1934. Picking up on an idea of Lily Weiser-Aall (1927), Otto Höfler, student of R. Much, a fine representative of the Vienna Mythological School, postulates "the priority of the ecstatic worship over the mythic legend."[16] For him, the Furious Army complex "is the reflection of secret German ecstatic cults,"[17] the reflection of rites binding warriors within a brotherhood, placed beneath the aegis of Odin, whose recognition sign is the mask. It involved a warrior aristocracy that had social and religious duties closely connected to the dead, because its members were intiated by means of a mock death. These fraternities would have been mistaken for armies of the dead by the noninitiated who caught sight of them. This is what Höfler seeks to demonstrate, chiefly relying on a passage by Tacitus in which the Roman historian says that the Harii painted their bodies black in order to pass for an army of dead men (*Germania* 43). O. Höfler shows thirty points common to the Furious Army and to the masked processions that mark the winter equinox, some of which allowed the participants to go into a trance, leave their bodies, and transform into the entities whose masks they wore—in other words, the dead. According to Höfler, the myth of the Furious Army has its socio-religious counterpart in the "rite" of the warrior societies. Hence its root should be sought in their actions. Readers pressed for time can find a good summary of Höfler's involved and deeply detailed investigation in the study that H. M. Flasdieck devotes to Harlekin.[18]

Widely debated by many researchers, Höfler's thesis has made its presence felt, inspiring as much rejection as it does approval. For example, H. P. Hasenfratz, in 1982,[19] takes it up when he builds a case that relies on a corpus of Indo-European texts and emphasizes the close connection existing between masked fraternities and the dead, veritable tutelary spirits (*fravashay*) of the living. The passage of the Furious Army falls into the context of Dumézil's third function (fertility/fecundity), a point that has won a rather large consensus today. One aspect remains obscure, however: the relationship between warriors (second function) and fertility. Spanish traditions—the Galician Society of the Bone (Società do Oso), for example[20]—inform us that masked societies whose members were not soldiers but had a connection to the theme of this book did in fact exist.

In 1980 a disciple of Höfler, Christine N. F. Eike,[21] published an extensive study on the Oskoreia, the name for the Mesnie Hellequin in Norwegian folk traditions that picked up on the trance theory, noting that the manifestions of the winter-nights troop seem to reflect phenomena, such as forming Doubles, well known in shamanic traditions. This finally explains why it is logical for Odin to have been made the leader of the troop: he was considered the "god of ecstasy" (*ekstasegud*). She does not say explicitly just when this took place, so a major question is left hanging: Did Odin form part of this complex since its origins? Depending on the traditions they use for reference—Indo-European tradition, nineteenth-century folk legends, medieval texts—the researchers are not all of the same opinion.

Following in the footsteps of others before him, Friedrich Ranke delivered a concise critique of Höfler's theories. Supporting his case by citing the folk traditions reflecting the legends (*Sagen*), he refutes these theories point by point.[22] In fact, the major point of Höfler's argument is that we do not know whether or not such fraternities existed and if the rite predates the myth or legend. It is hardly possible to answer these questions, because the myth explains the rite and vice versa, but our texts allow us to state that the belief in the return of the dead on certain dates must have given concrete form to a ritual monopolized by a group. In France, the name Mesnie Hellequin gradually came to mean people who assembled to commit acts contrary to good character and morality—but this could be a clerical interpretation of a rite that had a whiff of paganism.

The theories of German scholars can be summed up in a few key words: beliefs connected to the soul and ancestor worship, to the elements, and to dreams are the source of what initially appeared as a myth, then as a legend (Sage). They were crystallized in the form of rites of which processions of masked men would be one form. Two essential elements emerge from all this: the importance of the dead for the well-being of human societies, and the role of ecstatic practices that carry with them vestiges of shamanism.

We should take into account these theories in order to see just how pertinent they may be. A myth is not a narrative *ne varietur* whose stable elements offer a canonical version. We must therefore abandon the illusion of a primordial text that spawned all others, for a myth is perpetually recrafted and can be given several different meanings. As we have seen, the medieval narrations are already the result of several rewritings and adaptations, so it is pointless to assume that we can draw from them a single interpretation. This inability provides this subject with its charm—and difficulty! We can first note the texts we cannot rely upon, then we must study the "La Procesiòn de las ànimas y las premoniciones de muerte," themes that have been used to attribute the Wild Hunt to Odin.

False Testimonies

Several German accounts from the Middle Ages collected by Karl Meisen in a very helpful anthology are quite dubious: some confuse the

Figure 15.1. Scandinavia according to Olaus Magnus, *Historia de gentibus septentrionalibus* (Rome: n.p., 1555)

Wild Hunt with hunters of all kinds, and the others, which are harder to identify, offer only vague pieces of information.

For example, we must consider the *Song of Roland* by the priest Conrad, which speaks only of an army gathered by the devil (verses 3909*ff.*; 5738*ff.*). The *Moritz von Craun,* written around 1210–1220, mentions a Furious Army à propos the nocturnal apparition of a wounded man who passes himself off as a dead man.[23] The poem titled *The Resurrection* (ca. 1230) mentions the Furious Army in connection with a commotion that accompanies the arrest of Christ.[24] Le Stricker calls the troops of the pharaoh who pursued the fleeing Hebrews the "furious army," and Rüdiger d'Ostermonra speaks of its involvement in a charm intended to restore reason to someone who has lost it.[25] Another charm from the beginning of the sixteenth century lists the spirits that roam the night and cites the Furious Army with its hanged men and men who have been broken on the wheel (see appendix 1).[26] I could continue this list, but all the texts say the same thing: the Furious Army is diabolical and synonymous with a noisy ruckus. Never do the German texts recorded in the vernacular name any leader, except for the devil, who is named in a German text recorded in the sixteenth century.

In short, once we have made all the necessary verifications, we are forced to see that we can find no connection between Odin and the Wild Hunt.

16

The Indo-European Roots of the Wild Hunt

The Tempest

One of the principal arguments made by scholars in favor of Odin as leader of the Wild Hunt is the motif of the storm. It opens the door to the Indo-European world. In the majority of post-medieval traditions, the passage of the Wild Hunt was connected to atmospheric conditions. This was also true of stories about ghosts or abnormal deaths,[1] which would be normal, for an extremely ancient notion linked the soul to the *pneuma,* the breath. Therefore, when souls moved on, the wind rose. This immediately caused a problem. The same was said of the passages of the cursed huntsman, the wild huntsman, animal ghosts, unbelievable packs of all kinds, the phantom coach (*Nachtgutsche,* in Switzerland), and the flights of witches. We must, therefore, treat the motif with caution, for we are unable to know in what sense the borrowings have been carried out or even if the motif is original. Furthermore, researchers have long felt that the Wild Hunt undoubtedly had an Indo-European origin, because in ancient India a we find a troop that was apparently akin to it.

All this raises some major questions whose resolutions are possible on condition that we place our trust in conjectures based on the earlier works in this text. Multidisciplinarity has its limits, and, in fact, this subject vastly overspills the field of our knowledge, so on certain points, we are compelled to go back to the studies performed by our predecessors. Let me be blunt: the terrain over which we are advancing is full of land mines and subject to scholarly controversies, therefore we should continue to apply our investigation methods. We must question the text and use the lessons it provides as a guardrail. When these do not correspond to the extrapolations made by scholars, our preference must be to follow the textual evidence.

In the *Atlas of Swiss Ethnology,* Elisabeth Liebl provides a synthesis of the relationships between the Wild Hunt and the weather.[2] The passage of souls in perdition heralded bad weather. The apparition of the Türschtegjeg was accompanied by the roar of thunder and bolts of lightning, and when a strong autumn gale blows or a heavy winter storm rages, people in Switzerland still say "the Türscht is on the hunt." People also say "it is as if the Türscht was hunting."[3] In the Thun region, the passage of the riders of the Furious Army is accompanied by rumblings. When the Waldhooli blows his horn, the weather is going to turn foul. On stormy nights, the grand duke (*der wilde Geissler*) leads the Wild Hunt.

The oldest accounts go back to the sixteenth century. Before this time, we find essentially the motif of noise, the tumult that undoubtedly may have inspired The Hunt's connection to that of the tempest. This is the case with *Luque la maudite* (Luque the Cursed) of Bourdet (thirteenth century), in which the random wandering of the devils of Hellequin across the Caux countryside recalls the passage of a tornado. Swirling about, the devils uproot trees and knock them down during the course of their frolics, cause the waves of the Bec to rise, pulverize a tower, and destroy the chimneys of the inhabitants of Rouen.[4] Describing a tournament, the anonymous author of *Reinfried von Braunschweig* (ca. 1300) talks of the rising clamor of shouts and screams. He compares them to the sound of thunder (*hört man in lüften schrîgen / sam unge-witers dunres krach*) and says that the din resembles that of the Furious Army.[5] The *Chronicle of Normandy* recounts the story of Richard the

Fearless, who leaves with the Mesnie Charles Quint: *Adonc partirent le dit Richard sans-paour, Charles Quint et sa mesgnie faisans grant noise et tempeste.*[6] The locution shows that we should take *tempeste* in the sense of "din." From the sixteenth century on, the terms regularly used to describe the nightly hosts were *gedöss* or "din"; *brausen*, "to howl, rumble, roar," "to breathe violently"; and *sûsen*, "howls," "makes a terrible din when passing by."[7] Renward Cysat first mentioned the wind when he told of the hauntings of Pilatus Lake.

> There are other spirits too up in these high and wild Alps. Some of them can be seen and heard only at night, sometimes riding horses and sometimes taking the shapes of real people whom we know to be living. Sometimes, they come up the mountain and through the forest near Lake Pilatus, riding and racing with a full charge of horses in such a mass as if they were several hundred horses and with such a loud rushing and with such force that the whole mountain seems to be shaken by them. It sounds like an earthquake and as if many cannons were being fired at once. Sometimes, it roars around the dairy huts at night, making such a wind and such a shaking [*und macht einen wind und zittern*] that it feels as if it is going to collapse.[8]

Cysat a second time mentions Lake Pilatus, whose surroundings abound in "evil and diabolical spirits" that are so numerous that they fill the night with their awful cries (*grusamen gschrey*) "like a strong squall (*ouch glychsam alls jn einer starcken windsbrut*), although the weather in the valley is beautifully still and clear."[9] These are the only old testimonies I have found. All the others merely go back to the nineteenth century and involve all nocturnal hosts, making no distinction between them.

The Troop of the Maruts

When exploring the relationships between folk beliefs and paganism, W. Schwartz observes that the theme of the cursed hunter existed among other Indo-European peoples and suggested we view natural phenomena—such as tempests and storms—as the root of the portrayal. On the basis of this study, some researchers have compared the Wild Hunt to the god Indra's companions, the troop of the Maruts, as Jan Gonda describes: "Large and powerfully strong and dreadful in appearance, they cleave the air over mountain and hill, armed with their glittering spears. Admirable and irresistible, they travel in their sparkling golden chariots pulled by red-roan horses or gazelles. All tremble before them, even the earth and the mountains. They cleave the rock and cause solid ground to tremble. Coming from heaven, they give birth to wind, lightning, and rain. The urine of their steeds is like the rain."[10]

We can note that in the *Lay of Helgi Hjörðvarðsson*, the Valkyrie Hrimgerd says this about horses and her companions:

> *Three times nine maidens, but one led them all*
> *White-skinned beneath her helmet*
> *When the horses lifted their heads, the dew fell*
>   *from their manes*
> *Into the deep valleys;*
> *Hail in the high forests*
> *Whence prosperity comes to men.*[11]

Georges Dumézil again takes up the work of Stig Wikander[12] and suggests that the Maruts be interpreted as "the atmospheric projection, with reference to the storm as a battle, of bands of young warriors, the *márya*, who were both dreadful and necessary, useful and excessive."[13]

The leader of the Maruts was Rudra, the patron of hunters and master of thieves and brigands. A wrathful archer, this dark, wild, and alarming figure dwelled in the mountains of the north.[14] From there he came to sow terror and violence. In short, it is a virtual certainty that this troop represented the Indo-European version of the Wild Hunt and that its chief was one of the archetypes for the leader of the Infernal Hunt. It is not thinkable, however, that an ancient Indian tradition could have maintained itself this way for millennia and suffered no modification when it traveled through other lands. It is probable that the Mesnie Hellequin was the medieval Western form of a historical-religious reality of Vedic India that was more or less transformed into myth. Up to now, the connections that have been discovered are typological in nature rather than genetic. We must therefore revisit the medieval case files.

There are some flaws in this theory that the Maruts are the ancestors of the Wild Hunt. Odin, the somber, binding magician god, did not correspond to Indra—counterpart of the god Tyr—but instead to Varuna, and the Romans identified him with Mercury. His connection to agrarian considerations is relatively recent, as clearly demonstrated by Jan de Vries.[15] In addition, thunder and lightning were attributes of the god Thor and his hammer, Mjöllnir. In the eleventh century Adam of Bremen writes: "He rules in the air, commanding lightning and thunder, and the wind and the rain, and sunshine and fruits. . . . When epidemics and famines threaten, sacrifices are made to the idol Thor."[16] In northern Sweden, the peasants called Thor "the good farmer; the good fellow of wheat and the fields" (*go-bonden; åkerbonden; korngubben*). Thor appears here as a god of the third function (fertility). In fact, in Vedic India, Vayu resembles the leader of the Wild Hunt most closely. He is the god of wind and storms, and leads a troop of the dead.[17]

Even taking into account all the slips and deviations, the substitutions of duties, the confusion of different gods, and the phenomena that mythologies give more than one god the same attribute, we still run headlong into a major obstacle: weather is connected to Thor and not to Odin. Nevertheless, Odin is a complex god who rebuts all simplistic definitions. He has appropriated to himself the attributes of the agrarian gods, the gods ruling fertility, and the gods of the dead, hence we can detect many overlaps. It is possible he belongs to the Wild Hunt, but it is impossible to say whether this has been the case since the beginning or if he entered this legend much later. In view of the texts and the most current research, we may be inclined to accept this second hypothesis.

Perhaps we can extricate ourselves from this impasse by recalling that there was not one but there were many nocturnal hosts—often confused for each other, as we have seen, and some with a pronounced martial character and some without. As mythic thought connects storms and combat, tempests and battles, the slippages that we detect are quite logical. To spell out precisely how something for which we have only the culmination is extremely delicate, but all will sense the inner structure of this complex.

The most solid argument in Odin's favor is undoubtedly the fact that the Infernal Throng sometimes consists of warriors and horsemen. As the god of war and the owner of the horse Sleìpnir, Odin is at home in this context. He also finds a place as master of Jöl (Jölnir), through his knowledge of necromancy and other magical practices that make him the god-shaman who has mastered the trance journey, and by his Einherjar, the dead warriors that make up the army with whom he will confront the powers of chaos during Ragnarök.

Mutilated and Monstrous Animals

We can note that the animals who are part of the Wild Hunt are mutilated: they do not possess a normal number of feet—generally, the horses, dogs, and hares have only three (see page 68)*—or else they are missing their heads,[18] which is a sign of their Chthonian nature. This detail has been compared to Sleipnir's eight hooves, but in the case of Odin's steed, the speed of his movement is evoked as well as his supernatural nature. Otto Höfler points to the existence of a two-legged horse (38) and another with eight legs (40) and compares them to the people disguised as horses in masked processions, but he neglects to mention that these people never disguised themselves as badgers,

---

*In Molina di Fiemme (Italy), Tatrico, or Patàu, the wild huntsman is a giant accompanied by four giant, six-legged hounds that have three legs under their bellies and three over the spine.

foxes, sheep, and so forth. Kurt Ranke notes that these animals smack primarily of popular belief and should be ranked alongside the lame or headless animals and men that haunt folklore and that we can find in stories concerning the diabolical huntsman, the cursed huntsman, and the wild huntsman.[19] Hans Peter Hasenfratz[20] reminds us, however, that the fraternities of ancient Iran were described as demon denigrators, as wolves, and even as two-legged wolves, and they were said to visit cemeteries at night, where they dug up cadavers, certain parts of which they cooked and ate. These individuals were either naked or clad in dark-colored garments topped by a pointed cap or hood, which recalls a phrase quoted by Étienne of Bourbon and Adam de la Halle: "Does this cap fit me well?"

We can thus ask ourselves if this image may have been contaminated by exterior motifs intended to strengthen the fantastic nature of the nightly hosts. This is quite likely the case, for this motif does not appear before the sixteenth century (Cysat), and it is the distinguishing feature of several legends concerning revenants.

The Pig and the Horse

Among the animals cited as having a connection to the Wild Hunt, it is quite startling to find the pig, Freyr's sacred animal (F III), but also a beast that plays a role in Celtic funerary gifts during the Hallstatt (1000–500 BCE) and the La Tene (500–300 BCE) eras. The pig is one of the most often cited ghost animals, and it appears most often around Christmas and during Advent, which is hardly surprising, for we know that the restless dead—sinners, suicides, the sacrilegious, the greedy, and the usurious—often appear in this form[21] and that women who slew their children emerged in the shape of a sow accompanied by her piglets. This shows that Gloso, the incandescent pig of Swedish tradition, is not the only example. Near Pfeiffikon in Switzerland, a sow and her young accompany the Türscht, which appears from the east with the bad weather.[22] In Adelboden, in the Bernese Alps, the Rochelmore travels through the air, and she sounds like a snuffling sow (*Färlimore*). In Grindelwald, the sow is a herald of bad weather. In Oberiberg, the priest's concubine crosses the Münsterbach Ravine in the company of a sow and her piglets.[23] Switzerland has other phantom creatures, such as the Tuutier, the Grägi, and the Fährlisau.[24] We can see how difficult it is to attribute to a specific god the phenomena connected to the passage of a nightly host. We have in fact too many putative patrons: Odin, Thor, Freyr! We should note that a detail from the painting by Lucas Cranach the Elder titled *Melancholy* (1532)[25] depicts a fantastic aerial ride in which appear a wild boar ridden by an emaciated naked woman who bears a spear, a ram mounted by a Landsknecht, and a cow that carries a naked man and woman. In addition, we can note P. N. Arbo, who painted a Wild Hunt (*Asgaardsreien*, 1872) led by a bearded king who brandishes a hammer, in other words the god Thor.

The animal that seems to be the oldest member of this complex is the horse, whose role as a psychopomp[26] clearly emerges in several accounts—namely, that concerning King Herla and the episode in the story recounted by Orderic Vitalis, when Walchelin seized the riderless steed and "felt a heat as hot as fire and an intense cold." When demons carry off the soul of a sinner, they arrive on horseback, and the Infernal Hunt often includes a mount for their intended victim. Theodoric the Great is carried into hell by a demonic horse. We should also recall that archaeology has unearthed evidence of men and horses buried together. In addition is the case involving Heremod, one of Odin's sons, who rode Sleìpnir into hell when he sought to rescue his brother Baldur.

In Gotland, the tombstones from the Germanic sepulchres of Ardre, Hablingbo, and Tjangvide confirm the horse's psychopomp role.[27] There is abundant testimony from the eleventh through fourteenth centuries telling us that the dead make their way to the otherworld bound to a horse.[28] In Denmark and in the regions east of the Rhine, a horse buried alive in the church would appear before the house on whose door the dead man would knock, and it had only three legs.

It was said that a horse was buried in all new cemeteries before the first deceased human being was buried there. The dictionary still reflects the horse's role in accompanying the dead: the litter, or mortuary stretcher, was called St. Michael's horse. When someone died suddenly, it was said that "the white horse had struck him with its shoe." In Denmark, someone recovering from a serious illness said, "I gave Death a bushel of oats" (*jeg gav Döden en skäppe havre*).[29]

In folk beliefs and popular legends the dead often appeared looking like horses, a motif Henrik Ibsen borrowed for *Rosmersholm* (1886). We have seen that in certain versions of the priest's mistress, the dead woman serves the devil as a mount,[30] and in the fifteenth century, an anonymous monk of Byland (Yorkshire) records two stories of similar revenants.

1. A man rode home on his horse, which was also carrying on its back a pannier of beans. Suddenly, the horse stumbled and fractured its foreleg, so that the man had to dismount and shoulder himself the sack of beans. As he went on his way, he saw what appeared to be the phantom shape of a horse rearing up on its hind legs (*vidit quasi equum stantem super pedes posteriors*) and striking the air with its front hooves. Terrified, the man invoked the name of Jesus Christ and forbade the horse to harm him in any way. Whereupon the phantom horse began to follow him, and after a while the ghost manifested itself in the form of a whirling heap of hay with a light shining in the middle of it. At this, the man said, "Begone, whatever or whoever you are that wishes me ill!" With these words, there appeared a figure in human shape, and this ghost addressed him with a solemn oath, giving its name and the reasons for its distress.

2. William of Bradeforth, or Birdforth, met a ghost in the shape of a gray horse (*pallidum equum*) between Ampleforth and Byland Abbey. He implored it to go away and stop blocking the road.[31]

L. Malten notes that in ancient times the dead individual was first transformed into a horse, then was reconceived and depicted next to a horse.[32]

We can note another detail: the Hörselberg, the mountain where the Wild Hunt resides, is clearly implied by its name, Horse Mountain, for two variations for horse in Germanic, *hros* and *hors,* establish a clear parallel.[33]

In addition to its bond with the departed, the horse also is connected to fertility. We see that several blades of wheat were left for Odin's horse to insure a good harvest the following year. We can also note that throughout the entire Germanic area, men offered sacrifices or offerings to horses. Alfred Eskeröd provides an excellent glimpse of this.[34] It would be helpful to have a study on the mythology of the horse, for it is an extremely rich subject.

The Wild Hunt and the Third Function

It is common knowledge that the dead have a connection to the third function (fertility/fecundity).[35] Mircea Eliade has written on this matter with great depth.

> Agriculture as a profane skill and as a cult touches the world of the dead on two quite different levels. The first is solidarity with the earth; the dead are buried like seeds and enter a dimension of the earth accessible to them alone. Then, too, agriculture is preeminently a handling of fertility, of life reproducing itself by growth. The dead are especially drawn to this mystery of rebirth, to the cycle of creation, and to inexhaustible fertility. Like seeds buried in the womb of the earth, the dead wait for their return to life in their new form. That is why they draw close to the living, particularly at those times when the vital tension of the whole community is at its height—that is, during the fertility festival, when the generative powers of nature and of mankind are evoked, unleashed, and stirred to frenzy by rites

and orgies. . . . As long as seeds remain buried, they also fall under the jurisdiction of the dead. The Earth Mother, or Great Goddess of Fertility governs the fate of seeds and that of the dead in the same way. But the dead are sometimes closer to man, and it is to them that the husbandman turns to bless and sustain his work.[36]

Among other things, fertility depends upon precipitation from the sky, hence the link among the Wild Hunt, storms, and the third function (F III). The dead have power over the elements—the Scandinavian case file we study in my book *Return of the Dead* leaves no doubt on that score. The passage of the Wild Hunt as a sign of fertility is rarely mentioned explicitly.

When Nicolas Gryse (1543–1614) cites a Mecklenburg custom intended to appease Odin, he relays the words of a peasant song.

> Wode, take now fodder for your horse
> 'Tis now thistles and brambles,
> Next year it shall be most excellent grain.[37]

When Martin Crusius (1526–1607) discusses "these peasants who believed they had gone into Venus Mountain," he informs us that they went there to speak certain words to forestall storms from striking the fruit (*non percuto grandine fruges*).[38] Because Venus Mountain is the home of the Wild Hunt, it is easy to guess to whom these words were addressed.

Speaking of the Christmastime perambulations of Dame Holle (Holla, Holda), Johannes Prætorius (1630–1680) writes: "People also say that Dame Holle begins to move about during the Christmas period. This is why serving women replenish their spindles or roll large amounts of yarn or fabric around them, and leave them there over night. They say if Dame Holla sees this she will say, 'For every thread there will be a good year.'"[39]

In fact, the reference to fertility is implicit most of the time as if its connection to the nightly hosts is obvious. Otto Höfler explains it by the fertilizing magic of the cultic course of demons roaming over the fields, a course imitated by processions of masked men on certain dates, but he goes too far, perhaps, when he starts talking about sexual orgies, which are entirely absent from the texts we have examined here.[40] Like the dead, demons govern storms, but their action is generally pernicious and devastating, because they seek only to harm human beings. Because they are frequently confused with the dangerous dead, those who came to a bad end or who are unhappy with their fate and desire to get revenge on the living, it is quite difficult to distinguish them, particularly as they designated by the words *devil* and *demon*. We can be sure of this: in the mentalities of our ancient ancestors, the third function was inseparable from the dead, however they appeared—whether alone or in a band.

The importance of fertility and abundance springs from two other themes formerly associated with the Wild Hunt:[41] that of the night

Figure 16.1. *The Romance of Fauvel.* Bibliothèque National de France.

Figure 16.2. The Wild Hunt (*Asgaardsreien*), Oslo: Peter Nicolai Arbo, 1872.

feast, about which we have already talked a great deal, and that of the resuscitated bull. During the cultic meals of these spirits, a bull was killed and eaten, then his hide was placed back over its correctly arranged bones, and the troop leader struck it with her wand, restoring the animal to life. Shamanic in origin, this rite is greatly attested in alpine legends outside those concerning the Wild Hunt. Another recurring motif reflects a third function context: that concerning the neat and tidy house and prohibitions on working. Here, the dead appear in the guise of the guarantors of a certain kind of order over which they keep watch. They never hesitate to reward or punish.

The relationship between the nocturnal hordes and the third function is very old, and this is what forms the connection among beliefs, rites—masquerades and ritual feasts—and legends. The dead are never impotent or powerless. They continue to meddle in human affairs and they remain a force with which to be reckoned. They customarily appear on certain dates when communication is established between this world and the next, when they have a decisive value in our lives. H.-P. Hasenfratz notes that the Festival of the Dead and Carnival were common to all Indo-European peoples before Christianization and that the ancient Iranians regarded the dead as tutelary spirits (fravashay) of the living. E. Mudrak reminds us of their kinship to the Valkyrie.[42] He also shows how the role of masquerades in which the dead are represented is a rite of the third function, which explains the family resemblance between the Mesnie Hellequin and the Charivari in *Fauvel*.

17

Two Hypotheses

The Wild Hunt's Attribution to Odin

In Norway, the first mention of Odin as the leader of a troop of the damned—which is not called anything close to the Furious Army or the Wild Hunt—appears in the *Dream Song* (Draumkvœðe), the narrative by the visionary Olaf Astesom (or Akneson, the name appearing most often), which we read earlier (page 148). Odin has a nickname in this text: Grutte Greybeard (Grutte Gráskeggi), which corresponds to one of this god's names—of which there are more than one hundred seventy!—Hárbarðr (Gray Beard) in the Eddas. In the collection compiled by Jørgen Moe around 1847, Grutte Gráskeggi wears a black hat (strophe 17), which corresponds to the god's other nicknames, "Hat" (Höttr) and "Long Hat" (Síðhöttr), which allude to Odin's habit of concealing his face beneath a hat or hood. The problem is that this is a later text, even if its origin quite likely goes back to the thirteenth century. This leader could well be a later interpretation that had simply replaced a devil.[1] It is common knowledge that Odin was regarded as a devil by clerics.

We can find the first instance of Odin's name in connection to the Wild Hunt in Nicolaus Gryse's (1543–1614) *Mirror of the Anti-Christian Papacy and Lutheran Christianity,* printed in Rostock in 1593—quite a bit later. Gryse criticizes ancient pagan rites that were intended to petition the "false god Odin" (*den Wodendüel*) for a good harvest in the coming year. Gryse adds: "This idolatry persisted under the papacy . . . among many peasants in the form of superstitious customs and invocations of Odin (*solcker auergelöuischer gebruk in der anropinge des Woden*) at harvesttime, for the pagans believed that this same diabolical huntsman (*dersülue hellsche Jeger*) made his presence known in the fields at the time of the harvest."[2]

The attribution of the Wild Hunt rests only on bringing together Wotan/Odin and the hellsche Jäger. The third-function rite described by Gryse has nothing to do with our phalanx of the condemned. We should note that after the oat harvest in the northern German town of Rodenberg, a staff was implanted in the ground to which was attached a straw figure with the help of a horse shoe. This effigy was called Waut or Waul.[3]

We owe Johannes Locenius (1597–1625), professor of history and jurisprudence at Uppsala University in Sweden for the second mention of Odin. In his *Suebo-Gotland Antiquities* (1654),[4] he tells how the Norse made Odin the god of war and that a persistent old superstition widespread among the common folk said that "if any specter shows itself at evening or in the night on horseback or armed and accompanied by a loud din [*cum magno strepitu*], people say that it is Odin passing through [Oden *istac transire dicant*]." We find repeated here the theme of the phantom army, and the basis for its comparison to the Wild Hunt rests on the terms *specter* and *din*.

What Locenius says is recycled by the philologist and archaeologist Johannes Scheffes, who was born in Strasborg in 1621 and died in Uppsala, where he taught.[5] The sole difference in the narratives by Locenius and Scheffes is that Scheffes adds more emphasis to the text (*strepitus nocturnes spectrum larvarumque*) and lists the phrases in which Odin appears: "*Far till* Odens," "Go to the devil, and live with Orcus;" "Oden *eiga dig*," "May Odin carry you off!"*

Vade ad Odinum, pro quo latine: Abi ad rem malam, ad Orcum. Odin te possident.

As an enthusiastic philologist, Scheffes points out that Odin means "tumult" or "din" (*quis iste Odini strepitusve significet*) and that the Germans today call this fracas the Furious Army, which amounts to Wodan/Odin and his minions. In fact, Wodan/Odin does not mean "tumult" or "din" but "fury." Yet the attribution of the Wild Hunt to Odin/Wotan stems from this error. The identification of this god with the leader of the phalanx of the night rests on erroneous philological deductions—the work of scholars reinterpreting certain pagan customs.

Locenius and Scheffes give impetus to a movement that keeps growing and a scholarly tradition, which, over the course of time, merges back into oral tradition. Christoph Arnold (1627–1685), deacon of St. Mary's Church in Nuremberg, represents an important milestone in this scholarly tradition.[6] Attacking the idols of the ancient Saxons and Germans, he pens a lengthy examination of Odin, pointing out that his name shared the same root as the German *wüten* (inspires rage) and the English *wood,* as well as the Danish and runic *vode,* meaning "destruction," "danger," "threat of war," and mentioning that the Icelanders called the devil Odin and used the expressions *Oden eige dig* (May Odin take hold of you), *far du til Odens* (Go to the devil), and *huada Odens latum* (What is this deviltry?). He cites Locenius, then describes Lapp rites that took place during Christmas, when spirits called Juhlavolker (People of Jöl) traveled through the air. Small statues, similar to those erected for the spirits of the dead, were raised to them.

A book by Johann Peter Schmitt appeared in 1742 in the Baltic port of Rostock and established a bridge between the traditions of northern Germany.

It is said in particular that this younger Odin [*dieser jüngere Othin*] was an archmagician and had no peer in the arts of making war. This is why some people have sought to see his name Woden as a derivitave of "to rage" (*wüten*). Further, no one is unaware of the senseless belief held by countless folk, especially some hunters, that the time around Christmas and on the eve of Carnaval (Fastel-Abend) is when the one called Woor or the Goor or the wild hunts-man passes. They say that the devil organizes a hunt with a troop of rapping spirits (*mit einem hauffen Polter-Geister*). If we get to the bottom of this superstition, we see that it emerged from the story of this younger Odin, and that the common man thinks that Odin/Wotan passes. This is why a company of ghosts like this is called the Furious Army, Wotan's/Odin's Army, Gooden's Army, or the Army of Odin.[7]

Schmitt therefore hunts in folk beliefs for what he needs to support his investigation of the vestiges of paganism, and he makes some bold comparisons by using the various spellings of the name Odin in the Germanic countries: Òðinn, Oden, Goden, Woden, Wodan, Wotan. He is not even aware that he includes a woman in these comparisons: Goor, a name that in fact is very likely a deformation of Woor.

In Denmark, Odin was incorporated into the wild huntsman around the eighteenth century and appeared for the first time in the writings of the priest Frederik Monrad (1702–1758).[8]

The transmission of scholarly concerns to the common man was carried out by, among others, the press. Here is what a certain Flörke, a Rostock professor, writes in the *Freimuthiges Abendblatt* on May 18, 1832:

When I speak about those apparitions and phenomena that are entirely based on the natural order but are attributed to supernatu-ral causes, I immediately think of the Wild Hunt, also called the Furious Army and the Wohl in Mecklenburg, about which I heard so many terrifying things in my youth and later.

Our agrarian laborers, who seek to profit from the cool of the evening air to bind the rye, were so terrified by the Wild Hunt they would barely dare go into the fields, shivering all the while. First, they heard the baying of hounds, which then mingled with the fairly harsh voices of men and others that were fairly sweet. They saw fires that passed rapidly through the air, then, if they did not flee, the entire army paraded before them in a terrifying din made up of barking, instruments that sounded like hunting horns, and panting.

In my childhood, it was self-evident that these were ancient brigand knights who had found no rest in the grave and who, to amuse themselves, went hunting with their dogs in the world aboveground, as they were accustomed to doing while alive. A pious preacher has since told me that this was nothing other than the devil himself accompanied by several fallen angels, who took pleasure in frightening people. The devil, he said, took the form of Wotan, the old pagan idol, in which guise he had been worshipped in earlier times. The name Wohl comes from him. It is a deformation of Wotan.[9]

This last assertion has no philological basis.

The same Schwerin newspaper published another article on October 25, 1832, in which F. G. C. Pogge, an inhabitant of Ziesdorf, a village of Mecklenburg, reports a similar event. The farm workers had already loaded several carts with rye, when they suddenly heard, "Here comes the Waur." All the binders dropped their tools and hid inside the haystacks, but several old laborers did not budge. Grabbing hold of his courage with both hands, Pogge remained with them. Here is his story:

The noise was still far away and resembled that made by a baying pack on the hunt in a forest at a fair distance. The phenomenon gradually drew closer, and we could clearly hear galloping and a commotion quite similar to that made by the impetuous charge of many dogs, perhaps more than a hundred, with voices that were both rough and sweet. The company slowly passed by, high in the air, making quite a racket just a short distance from where we were. Although the moon was shining with a sharp clarity, we could see nothing, yet we could distinctly make out the different voices of the dogs . . . that were moving past us, it seemed, in the upper layers of the air. Little by little, the binders and their children came out of the haystacks. Some of them held their hands over their ears and pressed their faces into the straw, and thus saw and heard nothing. Others claimed they had seen fiery blocks in the sky, and, according to the testimony of some old people, things like that were seen during such manifestations. This time, however, it was simply an illusion, for none of those who had followed the phenomenon from beginning to end had seen anything other than what I saw. The troop traveled from east to west, and the folk stated that it was the devil of the east with his hunt.[10]

This description recalls a flock of migrating birds reinterpreted in accordance with a belief: reality is perceived through the distorting prism of existing tradition, a phenomenon for which Mircea Eliade has provided some good examples. A person who believes in the Wild Hunt is capable of hearing and seeing it, thus living his belief, which is why the majority of our testimonies fall into the category of "lived legends" (*Erlebnissagen*). Pogge's story is reminiscent of what is said in France about the Chasselquin and the Menée Ankine.* It is obvious that birds played an important role in the history of the Wild Hunt,† because even if this has been forgotten in modern times, the souls of the dead often took the form of a winged creature—black for a damned soul and white for a redeemed one. We can note that only Flörke's witnesses connect the phenomenon to the dead, providing a naïve explanation for it.

When we examine the sources, we cannot overlook an important issue: scholars connect the Furious Army to Odin, essentially relying on etymology and shoring up their investigation by materials pulled from

---

*In Brittany the Menée Ankine is considered to be a flock of birds of prey who are pursued by Jeanne Malobe, the night spinner. In the Lower Maine region the Chasselquin or Chassennquin is a term used to describe birds that make noise at night.

†In England the Wild Hunt is the name given to the Gabriel Ratchets or Gabriel Hounds, migrating birds whose calls are said to resemble the voices of spirits.

the beliefs—but just how much of this is pertinent? In other words, does the evolution we have detected go uniquely from the scholars to the people, or are the scholars put on the trail of their comparisons because the people had already been using them? The truth most likely sits midway between these conjectures. In fact, the study of the early mythology has taught us that the interactions between the scholarly community and the populace are decisive, although we can practically never know for certain, which, in the beginning, is the donating party and which is the receiving party who then returns it.

Fraternities and Societies

Otto Höfler, as we have seen earlier, believed that the Wild Hunt was possibly the image of brotherhoods that consisted of masked warriors. The mask permitted them to be identified with the dead. The festivals of this fraternity coincided with those on which commemoration of the dead was celebrated—in short, with ancestor worship.

Perhaps we can hypothesize, *cum grano salis,* that an evolution occurred that was comparable to the one Vincente Risco illustrates in the traditions of the Iberian Peninsula. In Spain we move from the Procession of Souls to the Società do Oso, formed by living people. Risco writes: "This gathering of souls into a group, often the dead of a parish, ancestors, and relatives, transformed into a secret society made up of living individuals, a society whose functions appear to be similar to that of any other pious fraternity or brotherhood. . . . All the members of this society possess the ability to foresee the death of individuals and announce them with certainty. This death premonition seems to be the privilege of those who are members of the Società do Oso."[11] These people also enjoyed the ability temporarily to leave their bodies—that is, they created a Double. When they marched in procession, they could cross through physical objects effortlessly, as an astral body would (see appendix 3). The Procession of Souls was akin to the Chasse Annequin that came in search of those on death's doorway.

The matter is extremely complex. It is not one I can resolve here, for it would require a long investigation that would prolong our research. Yet we can easily indicate the most important points, especially those that speak in favor of Höfler's theories. If we meticulously compare the Procession of Souls and that of the Società do Oso, we can see that the Società is an identical copy of the Procession. The most striking features of the Procession of Souls are these: it started from the parish church or its surrounding cemetery; it proceeded in silence, accompanied by the tinkling of small bells; and it followed the same route as funeral processions. Its members formed two rows and were dressed in white, they walked barefoot and carried candles that give off a bluish light. These dead people were guided by two living individuals who carried a cross and a holy water stoup. We can note another important detail: in this Procession were the souls of those slated to die soon. The passage of this troop was the herald of an imminent death. German folk traditions include two similar corteges, which speaks in favor of the great antiquity of the belief.

1. A troop of dead souls that encounter a living individual who was destined to die in the near future. The troop traveled through the streets of the village where this person lived, accompanied by a vague rumbling that caught the attention of this individual. Several variations on this theme come into play here. The living individual did not recognize the dead person at once, but soon, thanks to a detail in clothing, he discovered that this ded person was none other than himself.

2. A procession of living people whose members were those destined to die over the coming year. The oldest testimony of the troop can be found in the *Zimmern Chronicle* (sixteenth century): "Near Gernsbach (near Baden-Baden) there lived a chef named Marcel. One night, while the moon shone, he awoke and looked out his window in the direction of Quail Fountain toward Gernsbach. He caught sight of many people, both men

and women, holding hands and forming a circle. They danced forward along the path leading from the fountain to the castle. When they reached the castle, he recognized many of the people among this company, and, most especially, he saw himself in his regular attire, which caused him quite a shock. He watched them dance around the castle before disappearing he knew not where. That same year, all those taking part in this dance died, including the chef."[12]

Sometimes, the living members that appear in these corteges are not the future dead.[13]

One theme recurs: one night a man attends his own burial. He knows everyone in the procession, except for one person. He becomes acquainted with this person, and later, when he dies, this individual accompanies him with the other villagers to his final resting place.[14] Certain details anchor the events in reality—for example, the spectator sees a man who is moving forward while constantly slipping. At his death, it is icy, and one of the people following the burial procession has a hard time keeping his balance.

Other more recent texts allow us to form a synthesis of the events. In a span of several days to an entire year before the death, Doubles of the living form a funeral procession and cross through the village, following the customary burial route. One of the future dead individuals hears the noise of the procession, sees what's going on, and sometimes recognizes himself in the cortege. Sometimes, however, only clairvoyants, people gifted with second sight because they were born on a specific date, can perceive processions such as the Procession of Souls.[15] The members of the procession have physical consistency—that is, they appear to be living human beings, proof that they are Doubles. One detail recalls for us the romance *Fauvel:* sometimes, the deceased individual is seated on his coffin,[16] which appears at the head of the procession.

The implicit reference in Germany as well as Spain to the Double speaks in favor of ecstatic phenomena and makes it possible to draw up this kind of outline: a sleeper emitted his Double, which joined with a procession of the dead and gained knowledge of his imminent death. On waking, he believed that he had really seen this procession and accredits its passage as such.

Let us go back a bit. The possible confusion of corteges of masked men with the Wild Hunt emerges not only from *The Romance of Fauvel* but also from the testimony of Étienne of Bourbon in which one of the Hunt's members asks his neighbor, "Does my cap fit me well?" and that of Adam de la Halle, "Does my hurepiaus* suit me well?" As Phillipe Ménard notes, "the question posed on the subject of the cap should be attributed not to misplaced coquettishness. It means that the cap is not the normal headgear of this troop."[17] For us, it means that this headgear is donned in a specific circumstance: during the celebration of a rite.

This confusion also stands out in the narrative by Renward Cysat on the passage of a "truly strange and terrifying procession, whose members were horrible and hideous" (see page 246); in that of Jakob Trausch (page 162); in that of Johannes Agricola, who shows us the inhabitants of Eisleben waiting for the passage of the Furious Army on Lent Thursday (pages 145–46); and in that of Christian Vulpius, who teaches us that the Furious Army is represented in the Carnival procession (pages 181–82). In the Norwegian traditions, on Oskoreia, the confusion between the dead and masked men was permanent, a point that Christine Eike[18] has illuminated fully.

If we attempt a hypothetical timeline of the facts, we end up with this:

1. According to an ancestral belief, the dead roamed the earth on certain dates and played an important role in the happiness of the living, because they governed fertility and prosperity.

2. To honor them, propitiate them, or protect ourselves from them,

---

*[Hat. —*Trans.*]

we formed societies (brotherhoods, fraternities, and so forth) that depicted them or mimed them by means of masks and disguises. This action derived from ancestor worship and held an important social function.

3. Distinct entities—originally, these two troops, one of the departed, the other of disguised living men—became confused with each other, and people no longer drew any distinction between them, instead regarding each as the other and vice versa. See Cysat's testimony.

4. The fraternity of the living was thus cultish in nature, and its members, as much as we can deduce from the traditions examined, were a kind of elect who possessed the gift of being able to divide into Doubles, which allowed them, among other things, to foresee death and to move quite quickly, like the wind.

5. This company, more or less Christianized over the course of its historical evolution, lost its ties to Dumézil's third function and became purely funerary in nature. It took responsibility for burying the dead it sought. Here, elements are far from clear, because, according to Vincente Risco's investigation, the burial seemed virtual. The brotherhood did not abduct the true corpse, but instead it took its Double.

Let us revisit the fourth point: how members are selected for this society. It is likely that this changed over the years and bowed to the laws of ecotypes. The texts cited by Vincente Risco show that the living who accompanied the Societá do Oso were predestined by a gift, but the texts also reveal that their duties were transferable. In "La Procesión de las animas en pena," the bearer of the cross and the bearer of the holy water stoup can become freed of their obligation. They need only meet a living human being on their path. The bearer of the cross then hands over his burden, and the other is obliged to take it. The bearer of the font does the same, saying *Tócache a ti*.[19] All things considered, this transfer of power was strangely reminiscent of that of the Latvian werewolves,

Figure 17.1. Death scything in a cemetery, Jacques Wimpheling, *Adolescentia*
(Strasbourg: J. Grüninger, 1505).

the name of a secret fraternity of men who could cast Doubles who
would fight the wizards who had stolen the seeds. Here, we can take a
short digression to refer to my study of the Double in which we can find
the translation of the minutes of the trial of one such werewolf.[20] We
can note that these particular werewolves were active on Santa Lucia's
Day, St. John's Day, and Pentecost—dates that witnessed the passage of
the Wild Hunt. Otto Höfler has used this testimony to demonstrate
the existence of secret societies in Latvia. There is no involvement of the
dead, which makes the scope of the comparison relative.

It is possible that membership in these societies was reserved for a
particular social group that acted as a kind of mediater between the liv-

ing and the dead, but it might also have involved men capable of releasing their Doubles: shamans, experts on relations between this world and the otherworld. Höfler regards the members of these brotherhoods as soldiers, and we can find confirmation from our medieval narratives, which often depict armed men. Ronald Grambo believes that we have here the vestiges of an elitist cult of dead warriors.*

The different theories for which I have provided a glimpse disentangle the skein of beliefs and traditions. It is more than a certainty that ecstatic phenomena hid behind this legend complex, and it is more than sure that at its center were worship of the dead and fertility concerns. The church, it seems, adulterated the facts but simultaneously did some very creative work. It is possible that fraternities were involved with the worship of the dead and that masquerades and other Charivaris recuperated all or part of their activity.

---

*From a communication February 6, 1996.

18

Concluding Thoughts

Med lätta fötter gånga vi,
med kalla tungor sjunga vi.
Hur långt det är til dometag,
Det frågar vi.*

As you will have guessed, an investigation such as ours here is an attempt at discovery. We cannot reach a conclusion, and to reach one would be presumptuous as long as so many texts remain to be exhumed, so many testimonies remain to be pulled from unpublished archives that are piled on library shelves. The fruits of the field investigations performed by nineteenth-century ethnologists remain to be crosschecked, and bridges must be built toward other civilizations. So many points remain to be explored more deeply. In this sense, an investigation like the one we have engaged in is revealing, because it makes us conscious of the limits of our knowledge. Nevertheless, perhaps this investigation will inspire further research on the trails I have indicated, and one day, perhaps, we will have answers to all the questions left hanging.

---

*We are going on light foot
we are singing, our tongues cold.
How much longer will it be until Judgment Day?
We are wondering.

This was the song of the dead heard in the Swedish province of Värmland on December 24, when the dead celebrated their own Mass.

236

What is most striking in the history of the Wild Hunt is its variability, its ability to meld with other beliefs, to draw elements from them and to combine them. The narratives we have read here allow us to see two large vectors. First is the ancestor worship that encourages the merger of the theme and the table of souls, the fairy repast. Next is the cult rituals that culminate in masquerades and Carnival-like processions. Grafted upon this trunk are motifs taken from the legend of the wild huntsman and, when the clerics had taken possession of the Wild Hunt and adopted it in accordance with Christian dogma and other elements of medieval creation, the legend of a cursed hunter, which is nothing but a miniature version of the Infernal Hunt that has been reduced to its simplest expression. In turn, this edifying legend evolved over the course of the ages to produce that of the wandering Jew and the ghost ship. This permeability of traditions rests on a common reserve, a common vision of the universe, and the intellectual approach that permitted this glimpse is an attempt at explanation and mastery of the world in which lived our ancestors.

In the Middle Ages the Infernal Hunt was a Christian legend that borrowed ancient traditions. It was directly inspired by a mythic phenomenon, the passage of the Wild Hunt, whose origin is Indo-European if we accept that the troop of Maruts led by Rudra clearly represents the archetype.

It is undeniable that Orderic Vitalis was the initiator of a movement: by creating a Christian legend out of preexisting elements and then diffusing them, he inspired other clerics to do likewise, *ad majorem gloriam Dei,* and these clerics reutilized the traditions with which they were familiar, hence the numerous variations we have encountered. We could say that Orderic served as a kind of catalyst that gave an impressive narrative shape to elements that were in the air of his time. He was likely the first to grasp the benefits the church could wrest from beliefs concerning the dead and their return. By transposing events from the context of a vision into that of an actual encounter, he reconnected with popular beliefs and anchored his narrative in everyday reality. The sole distortion he made to earlier traditions was to transform this host of revenants into sinners and to have them describe their fate—in short, to transform a belief into an edifying exemplum. Simultaneously, the recycling of the theme of the Wild Hunt by the clerics allowed pre-Christian traditions to survive and evolve parallel to those spread by the church. Meisen is correct on the importance of Christianity's role in the development of the legend.

The leader of the Wild Hunt was certainly a psychopomp deity before he was recast as a demon. The last traces of his former identity are his gigantic size and club (Orderic). It is not obligatory for this deity to be a composite figure, for we can understand the cock and the dog as attributes rather than as a reference to his morphology. It is worth

Figure 18.1. The Horsemen of the Apocalypse (Strasbourg: n.p., 1485).
We can note the presence of death on horseback.

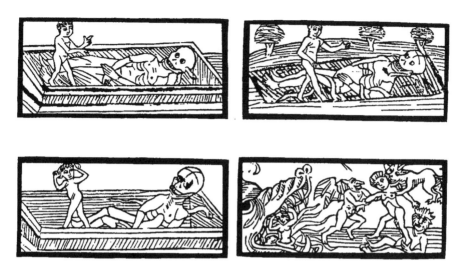

Figure 18.2. The soul returns to scold the body, whose sins have condemned it to damnation, *Visto lamentabilis*, Martin Flach (Basel: fifteenth century).

being cautious on this point, however, for the cock and the dog may well have been separated from this morphology in an anthropomorphic transformation of the deity.

The cyclical return of the dead to the earth retains a good part of its mystery. Exactly what is its reason for existing? Its explanation by the generative function of the departed is undoubtedly only part of the answer, and we must continue to look into it more deeply. Perhaps we must reassert the importance of ancestors and an unconscious refusal of their definitive confinement to the otherworld, the reiteration of a mental refusing of the finality of death and an understanding of life and death as to places on a cycle marked by an eternal return.

Roaming by day or night; visible or invisible; formed by horsemen, people on foot, or both; consisting of members who bear their normal appearance or that of their final hour; accompanied by animals or not; accompanied by a cart or chariot—the Wild Hunt has remained over the centuries one of the most singular legends of the Middle Ages, a model for the interaction of clerical traditions and popular mythology. It opens to us the doors to an imaginal realm that never rests, that works through associations. It represents a veritable quest for the knowledge of the universe taken in its totality, where this world and the next constantly interact, where we are thus never alone and we escape existential anguish only because we know that we are bound to the past and to the future. We know where we are going and what we will become, whom we will meet again when we quit this sublunary world, and what we will be doing in the world to come. The Wild Hunt thus also smacks of religion, whether pagan or Christian, and invites us to meditate upon a message that has survived centuries upon centuries.

For Protection against Spirits of the Night

A CHARM FROM THE fourteenth or fifteenth century jumbles all the creatures that roam the night into a kind of synthesis. It contains specific mention of the Wild Hunt and may well be the first evidence of the Hunt's connection to Odin. The language of the text is so inaccurate that is impossible to know with any certainty whether Wutanes Her should be translated as Furious Army or Wotan's Army.

> May the supreme *Numen divinium,*
> may the holy *sanctus spiritus,*
> may the sacred *sanctus dominus,*
> again protect me this night
> from the evil creatures that roam the darkness
> and I sign myself
> against the black ones and the white ones
> whom people call the Good ones*
> and who leave from Brockelsberg,†
> against the bilwizze,[1]

---

*As a euphemism.
†Name for Brocken Mountain, the highest in the Harz range.

against the moon eaters,*
against those who walk outside the paths,
against the hedge riders,†
against resounding incantations,
against all the evil spirits!
Glôzan and Lodevan,‡
Trutan and Wodan, Wodan's Army and all its members
Who bear wheels and rags,
Dead broken on the wheel and hung,§
Go far from me!
Elf and small elf,
Do not tarry long here!
Sister and father of elf
leave by the gate!
Mother of elves, (night)mare
Go out by the roof!¶
May the (night)mare not crush me,
May the (night)mare not pull me,
May the (night)mare not ride me.
Hooked-nose elf,
I forbid you to blow,
hairy elf, I forbid you
to scale me and blow your breath in my face!
And you, Weeper,**
muse well on me!
Herbrot and Herebrand,

---

*And not poppy eaters, as was formerly believed. This most likely means "those who have the power to make the moon disappear."
†Witches.
‡We do not know if these are the names for gods or for the spirits of illness.
§This is the Wild Hunt.
¶The house forms a sealed and sacred space that theoretically provides its occupants protection. The gate may refer to that of the garden.
**Klagemutter, a wood spirit that resembles the White Lady.

go to another land!
And you, infamous milk thief,*
avoid my door!
May fever and cramp†
stay outside with you!
Don't touch me,
nor lead me astray
nor carry me off,
do not cut the foot from the living
nor suck in his heart
and slip straw there in its stead!
I forbid you today and everyday,
I prefer to trample you, not carry you.
Go away, foul spirit,
There is nothing for you to do here!
I implore you, monster,
by water and fire,
you and your companions,
by the great name
of the fish called zelebrand
in the Mass.‡
I implore you with all my strength
by the Miserere,
by the *Laudem Deo*,[2]
by the *Voce mea*,[3]
by the *De profundis*,[4]
by the psalm *Coheuntes*,[5]
by the *Nunc dimittis*,[6]

---

*The name of witches who draw milk from the uprights of the door to the house or steal it from cows at a distance.
†Illnesses are personified.
‡The great name is, in fact, that of Christ as spoken by the priest performing the holy service.

by the Benedictus,[7]
by the Magnificat,
by the ancient Trinity,
by the noble psalms,
to go off beyond the sea
and touch me nevermore.
Amen.

The Wild Hunt in Constance

On the strange apparition that circulates at night and the common troop people call Guott jns Heer or die Säligen Lütt, although it would be better called Wuott jns Heer.[1]

I could have a great deal to say and write on this subject, but because time and other matters do not permit it, I shall be as brief as possible.

I recall treating this subject in my other chronicles or histories and citing many examples, especially those I have been given by several honorable people among my contemporaries who live in Lucern and whom I knew well. They themselves told me how they were transported in an instant to faraway foreign lands.

Today, this apparition enjoys high esteem among our old folk and especially among the common people. Those who belong to this company, as well as the living that accompany them in their travels . . . are regarded as saints and are blessed, whereas those who have called this company Wuott jns Heer have been abused and punished, because the blessed ones response to them is, "May you be rent apart by the devil!"

It was thought that they were the souls of those who had died before their foredestined day and hour, those who had not found a natural death and had thus had been compelled to wander the earth after their deaths until the advent of that time. They went about this way in procession, from one place to the next. All those who had perished by arms bore a sign that indicated how they left this life, and the other dead had to do the same.

The troop was preceded by a man who shouted, "Make way, make way! Here come the blessed." Accompanying them was sweet stringed music, not very loud but rather muted, just as was heard before, as I heard in my youthful years by those who claimed to have seen and heard this same procession pass through the streets of our city in 1568.

The living exhibited particular devotion and friendship to them.* Sometimes, they accompanied them on their travels, but at other times, they received them as visitors to their homes, as was the case with one individual who acknowledged it and testified about it before me and other honorable people. In her youth, in around 1530, this individual had been the servant of a very old city counselor, a man who, with his wife, had a reputation as being a member of this company, where she had heard and seen what follows. One winter night, while the two old people were asleep in the heated room. They had asked the servant to leave, but she had instead hidden behind the stove. She heard a tumult, as if a crowd of people had come through the door into the room. It was these said spirits. She spied a large number of heads in the moonlight gathered around the old couple's bed and heard them murmuring and whispering something in secret—she could not make it out. They then made their way to the kitchen, where they made a fire—cooking, steaming, roasting, and drinking without any noticeable reduction or change in the foodstuffs the next day. The old married couple was held in even greater esteem in the village, where they were regarded as saints, as I heard personally when I was young. Yet since the time our zealous

---

*The members of the troop.

spiritual guides and especially since the Jesuit priests, worthy and erudite spiritual fathers, settled among us in 1574 and have striven since in confession and from the pulpit to extirpate such superstitions and other things of which the world is full, we no longer hear talk of this apparition, which has not appeared, or let itself be heard or seen in our land. . . .

While writing this, I recalled that in my youth, when I was twelve years old and was going to school, I read something on this subject in the *Historial Mirror* by Vincent, bishop of Beauvais in France, in the chapter entitled Women Who Roam the Night with Diana and So Forth, which could be quite useful [for interpreting] something to which other times and long afterward I paid no attention until I began writing on the matter.

On this occasion, however, I could not resist introducing the marvelous example of this apparition as recounted to me by a distinguished and trustworthy legate of the highly esteemed bishop of Constance . . . in the presence of their lordships the ediles and other members of the council, in the year 1608. On Lent of that year, in a small village on Lake Constance and above the town of the same name, one evening, late after supper, when the wintry weather was rainy, gray and gloomy and all the doors were shut, there was heard coming from one place and crossing the village to a second place, the sound of a strange procession, like that of people accompanied by a sweet music from stringed instruments. Because the people in their houses were astonished by this, they lit their lamps and brandished them out their windows to see what was going on. They saw an extremely strange and terrifying procession whose members were horrible and hideous. None of them moved normally—some limped, some dragged, one was on crutches, another was humpbacked, and a third was on stilts, and all did different things.

An old woman preceded them. She bore something that burned in her open hand and that lit their way. When they came to a puddle of water, as a whim she cast the light into it, where it was extinguished. There, they performed strange feats before picking it up again. They then placed it back in her hands and relit it by blowing on it* before heading toward the upper gate, where they called the boatman or ferryman in his house at the edge of the lake so that he might give them transport. When he realized they were ghosts, he was terrified and did not wish to come out. They then placed the ferry in the water, climbed aboard, and set sail and, in the blink of an eye, as the ferryman who witnessed this attested, they made their way to the other shore, although it was a great distance away.

---

*This is a rite of commencement. The extinguishing and relighting of the fire generally marks a transition, the end and/or the beginning of a year.

No One Escapes His Fate[1]

*Here is how our theme combines with
other elements to create a legend.*

Sage

Encounters such as this with the Furious Army often took place
once upon a time in the Christian world, many years ago, and several times it appeared in Messkirch. Yet because of the time that has
passed and the negligence of our ancestors, all this has been forgotten. A similar Furious Army appeared and was seen not only during
the night, but also was seen more than once at morning, evening,
and sunset. We have a trustworthy account of one of them, which,
in our memory, took place in Franconia near Maulbronn Cloister.

Two nobles lived in Franconia. One was the lord of Seckendorf,
the other that of Erlikom. They detested each other and did as much
harm possible to each other, even wishing each other's death. It is
even said that one secretly enjoyed the friendship of the other's wife.
Once, however, when each was striving to ambush the other, Seckendorf and his squire rode through a forest at dusk, arms and bow
at the ready. Following the path through the wood, they reached a
chapel at its border and spent the night there. They woke early at
daybreak and continued their journey in the direction of where they

planned to set their ambush. In his haste, however, the county lord forgot his gloves, which he left on a stretcher in the chapel.

Once there, he realized he had forgotten them and sent his squire to get them. When the squire reached the chapel, it was already getting dark and no longer was truly day. He found a fiery phantom sitting on the stretcher. The phantom had put on the gloves and clapped his hands. A chill ran up the squire's back, and he could not force himself to stay a minute longer. He turned back and reported what happened to his master, who was quite vexed and scolded him for his cowardice and then went back to retrieve his gloves personally.

In the meantime, day was beginning to break. At that moment, while he followed a forest path, he heard a strange sound, shouts, a din, the blare of horns, and groans accompanied by a large fracas as if all the trees in the forest were cloven in two and were crashing to the ground. Seckendorff became acutely alarmed at not knowing the cause for this, left the path, and hid in the trees. He then saw, parading before his eyes, a strange, mounted procession: there were headless horsemen, and others with only one arm. Some horses had only two legs, and others were missing their heads. A number of people on foot accompanied them. Some of these footmen had only one leg or hand, and naked blades transfixed the bodies of others. In short, it was a strange and fantastic collection of people, and Seckendorf had never seen anything similar in his life, not to mention the din and tumult that accompanied the troop and filled the air. Nothing amazed him more in this troop than a gigantic man [*ainem raisigen man*] who led them on a gaunt white horse that limped. He wore ragged clothing and was so grievously wounded that his entrails spilled from his body, overflowing his clothing and hanging down to the ground along his mount.

When the procession had vanished from sight, leaving him unharmed—people claim that the Furious Army will cause no wrong to anyone who gets out of their way [*wie man dann sagt, das niemands vom wueteshere was nachthails begegne, so man user dem weg thue scheiden*]—he returned to the path where he met another knight of this company riding a gigantic horse [*uf em raisigen pferdt*]. Because he was alone, Seckendorf grew bold and questioned him to learn the identity of this company that had just passed a moment previous. The other answered that it was the Furious Army. He then asked the identity of the man in the front who rode the gaunt horse and whose entrails hung down over his mount. "That's Seckendorf," he responded and he called him by his baptized name. "In one year, to the very day, he will be slain by his enemy, the lord of Erlikom, when he will be riding a white beast like that, and his entrails will spill from his body and clothing to hang down over his horse." When the lord of Seckendorf heard himself named and learned he would be pitiably struck down in this way by his mortal enemy, his fear grew greatly, and although he would have gladly posed more questions, the other did not wish to stay any longer and followed the troop.

His stomach twisting with anguish, Seckendorf returned home, contemplated, and took this adventure so to heart that he strove to come up with a means that permitted him to escape such a miserable death and, especially, his mortal enemy. He gave away all he owned to his closest friends except for a little money and entered the Maulbronn Cloister as a convert or novice, as they were called, abandoning his former identity, and no one knew what had become of him. He remained at the cloister for a long time, and he never showed his face when strangers visited.

One year later, the lord of Erlikom came across Seckendorf outside the cloister.

Seckendorf fled toward the cloister. On his way, he stole a peasant's horse that was white and extremely thin, quickly leaped on its back, and tried to escape. Seeing this was futile, he turned back and seized a staff, thinking this would be his best chance to ward off Erlikom's attack and save his life. In the meantime, though, Erlikom had strung his bow and loosed an arrow that struck Seckendorf in the belly so hard that it caused his entrails to spill out over his robe and his horse's back, just as had been foretold. Seckendorf's strength deserted him, and he fell from the horse and died. He was buried at Maulbronn. The lord of Erlikom escaped, but no one knew where he went or what subsequently became of him. Yet it is not hard to guess his fate. Luck was no longer in his favor, and he came to a bad end.

The Society of the Bone

WE CAN SOMEWHAT CLARIFY the confused mingling of several beliefs, which is undoubtedly the root of the Wild Hunt, when we realize the importance of ecstatic phenomena connected to the Double and the gathering together of people prone to trances in brotherhoods. The passage here, translated from the article by Vincente Risco,[1] confirms that Otto Höfler's fundamental notion is right on the mark, even if his demonstration sins through excess extrapolation, and reveals that there is only a small step toward ending with societies of masked men.

One of the odd derivations of the Procession of Souls is the Society of the Bone, whose existence in Verán has been strongly substantiated. This society is made up of living inhabitants, but we do not know who the members are. Here is what information we do have about it:

In Verán there is a Society of the Bone. When one of its members suffers from a nonlife-threatening illness, if the doctor wishes to pay him a visit, a society member will contact him to tell him it is not worth his coming there, because the patient will not be leaving [dying] this time.

If one of the members dies, that eve or even on that same day, all the society's members, accompanied by their own priest [*con su cura*], come for him at his house. They hold bones in their hands that are lit [*huesos encendidos*] as if they were candles. This is what gives this society its name. They proceed without running into any other person [*sin tropezar con nadie*]. Other times, we might see a crowd of vague shapes, and no one knows what is going on. These, however, are living people, not ghosts. When they reach the church, they celebrate the burial and inter the dead person, and this all takes place that night, although the corpse of the deceased remains at his home.

Once, a woman arrived in Verán on the eve of a festival, very early in the morning before the sun had risen. She saw the open church, entered, and saw people there who were attending a funeral service. She approached them, and she was given a lit candle that she held in her hand through the entire ceremony. When [the ceremony] was over, she put it out and stowed it in a basket she had over her arm. Yet when she looked at it again after the sun had risen, she saw that what she held was in reality the bone of a dead man [*un hueso de muerte*].

The gathering of souls, quite often the dead of one parish—in other words, deceased ancestors [*los antepasados, los progenitors*]— has been transformed here into a secret society formed by living people. Its functions seem identical to that of any other religious fraternity or brotherhood [*hermandad o cofradía*]. This society does appear to have a certain spirit of secession toward the parish, which is manifested by the fact that it has its own separate religious service and its own priest who works independently of the parish. . . .

As we can see, all the members of the Society of the Bone have the ability to foresee individual deaths and announce them with great assurance. Death premonitions seem to be a privilege of the people who make up this organization. They also have the ability to leave their bodies temporarily [*la facultad du abandonar temporalmente su cuerpo*], and when they march in procession, they cross through all physical obstacles as if they were not there [*atraviesan todos los obstáculos físicos sin tropezar con elles*], passing through them like subtle bodies [*como cuerpos sutiles*]. It is said that they are living and not ghosts [*fantasmas*]. In fact, they are living beings [*seres vivientes*] and not dead men. Furthermore, we are assured that when these individuals bury a fellow society member, they do not transport the actual corpse, which remains at its owner's home. What they carry must therefore be something like his disembodied shadow or phantom [*ser algo asi common su sombra o fantasmas desencarnados*]. They inhabit this world and the next one at the same time.

APPENDIX 5

The Coach of the Diabolical Hunstman

By way of an illustration of the law of ecotypes, here is an extract from a Gaelic legend, *The Old Woman of Beare*,[1] collected in County Mayo, Ireland, by Douglas Hyde from the mouth of Michael Mac Ruaidhrigh. We find here all the principal elements of the old legend of the priest's mistress: the fleeing woman (who is dead); the hell hounds, the *infernalis venator;* the sin—but the cultural factors are a little different, and the devil no longer rides a horse, but instead rides in a coach.

> One day, my girl and I were out milking the cows. It was a fine, beautiful day, and after milking one of the cows, and when I raised my head, I looked around to my left and I saw a great darkness coming over my head in the sky.* "Make haste," says I to the girl, "till we get the cows milked quickly, or we will be wet through with the rain before we reach home."
>
> My girl and I were in a great hurry to milk the cows before we would get the rain, for I thought that it was rain coming. But on raising my head again, I looked about and I saw coming a woman, as white as a swan on the crest of the wave.† She went past like the

---

*Clouds are a means of transport for demons, and when the clouds come from the left, it is reflective of their demonic nature.

†The woman's color indicates that she is a ghost. She is obviously dead.

whirling of the wind, and the wind that was before her, she outstripped it, and the wind that was behind her could not come up with her. It was not long till I saw behind the woman two mastiffs and two yards of their tongues wound round their necks and fiery balls out of their mouths. And I wondered greatly at that. And behind the dogs I saw a black coach and a team of horses drawing it, and there were fiery balls at each side of the coach. And as the coach went by, the beasts stood up, and something made a sound or clamor out of the coach that frightened me, and faintness fell on me. On coming out of the faint, I noticed the sound in the coach asking me did I see anything at all going by since I came here, and I told him as I am telling you, and I asked him who he was himself, or what was the meaning of the woman and the two mastiffs who went by.

"I am the devil and those are two mastiffs that I sent after that soul."

"And is it any harm to ask," says I, "what evil did that woman commit when she was alive?"

"That woman," said the devil, "put a scandal on a priest,* and she died in a state of mortal sin, and she made no repentance. And if the mastiffs do not come up with her before she reaches the gates of heaven, the glorious Virgin will come and beseech her only son to forgive her sins, and she will obtain pardon for her, and I shall lose her. But if the mastiffs get up to her before she reaches heaven, she is mine."

The great devil drove his beasts, and away with him out of my sight. I and my girl came home, and I was heavy, weary, sorrowful, remembering the vision I saw, and I wondered greatly at that marvel, and for three days I went to my bed, and on the fourth day I arose, worn out and feeble,† and not without cause, for any woman who would see the vision that I saw, she would be gray a hundred years before her age would be spent.

---

*The motif is out of place here, for the devil generally makes fun of what may befall a priest. Because God has given him the authority to pursue this soul, it is a form of penitence if she can find redemption if the hounds do not catch her first.

†This is a recurring motif in these kinds of stories. The encounter makes the person ill and can be fatal.

APPENDIX 6

The Names of the Wild Hunt and Its Leader

WE CAN DIVIDE INTO three main groups the names of the Wild Hunt: those that derive, either directly or indirectly, from the name Hellequin; those from the names of other leaders condemned by Christianity; and those that express a value judgment or take a position on the belief or legend. These permit us to better appreciate how widespread is the theme.

The Hellequin Derivatives

France is particularly wealthy in confirmations of this legend.[1] Even if its original meaning has gone missing, the presence of each name testifies to the popularity of this legend complex.

In the Touraine region is the Chasse Arquin, in Anjou is the Chasse Hennequin or Helkin, and in Burgundy is the Mesnie Herlequin. In Normandy is the Chasse Hennequin, the Chéserquine (Equine Hunt), and the Chasse Hêle-tchien (in the area bordering the English Channel). The Maisnieye Hellequin is used in the Vosges to describe invisible musicians who perform at night.

We can note that the forms in /nn/Hennequin and in /ll/ Hellequin alternate, which already was the case in the Middle Ages,

258

when, however, the first forms were more recent. As for the forms containing /r/ or /rl/ that are initially found in Pierre of Blois's Herlewin or Walter Map's Herla, it is extremely difficult to say whether they are original.

Anathematized Leaders

A large number of the leaders of the Wild Hunt shared the common feature of being demonized by the church, and their names sometimes rested on traditions that still remain unknown. We must make a clear distinction between the anthroponyms, which reflect the legend of the cursed huntsman or the wild hunter. We should remain wary of the simple lists that appear in the ancient studies, because they quite often jumble different legends. It is therefore important to verify the text every time if we want to avoid maintaining the confusion that has reigned up until now. I cannot claim to offer an exhaustive examination here. The various French hunts deserve their own monograph that goes beyond the framework of this investigation. I cite only the examples I have verified. Interested readers can refer to the *Guides de la France mystérieuse*[2] and to *Mythologie française*[3] for additional information. Let us begin by looking at the names that are clear and that come from the Bible.

In Bresse is the Flying Hunt of King Herod, who was famous for slaying Jewish children, and in Normandy is the Cain Hunt—undoubtedly, Cain is a homophone of *–quin*. In the Franche-Comté is the Oliferne Hunt—the same Holofernes who was slain by Judith when his army laid siege to Bethulia. Meanwhile, the names King Solomon's Hunt (the Basque region), who was a fratricide and keeper of a harem, and David's Cart (Savoy), a king punished for his pride who also ranked among the cursed hunters, can allow no doubt to linger about the church's opinion of them.

Borrowed from Roman mythology, the goddess of the dead emerges in the name Proserpine (or Proserpina) Hunt, but again, this is most

likely based on homophony (see *Erkine*) and falls under the name
Chasse Harpine, a gathering of demons who were thought to feed on
cadavers they have dug up and carried off. This narrative tradition is
marked by the theme of a share of the hunt. Chasse Annequin is a
troop that comes seeking those on their deathbeds. In the Berry region
the Chasse Bodet is a host led by the devil that brings the souls of the
damned to hell. The Chasse Galière in the Creuse region is a group of
children who died without receiving baptism. This same hunt is called
the Chasse Galopine in the Poitou region, where the children are pursued by the devil. Galopine refers to the rapid galloping pace of this
hunt. The Chasse Ankin designates a gathering of souls in perdition
who return to their former homes to request that prayers be said for
them, which is reminiscent of one of Cysat's testimonies. The Chasse
Gayère (Bourbonnais) is an invisible troop consisting of the devil and
his pack who pursue the souls of the dying. Some names are clear and
require no explanation: the Chasse maligne* (Forez, Bourbonnais) and
the Chasse du diable† (Côte-d'Or, Normandy).

We can also see that the king of France Charles V (Carolus quinus)
was condemned to punishment in purgatory, according to Hélinand of
Froidmont, and gave his name to an Infernal Hunt.

In the Germanic regions, the Wild Hunt bears the names wilde
Jagd; wildes Gloat; hellsche Jagd; wütendes Heer; Muetesheer; Muetes-
seil; würtige Fahrt (a company of black birds‡ in a chariot); wilde
Hejagd; Gutis-Ee (Muri in Aargau Canton), Temper (Bavaria, Tyrol),
which refers to Quatember, the Ember Days; Wodesheer (Eifel); Odens
jagt (Denmark); Dürsten jegg (Switzerland); and so forth. We can note
that several traditions in one single region is a regular occurrence. The
leader is dubbed Rodes or Herod, the infernal huntsman (hellscher
jäger), Berndietrich, alias Dietrich von Bern[4]—in other words, Theodoric of Verona, whom the church condemned for his Arianism.

---

*[Wicked Hunt. —*Trans.*]
†[Devil's Hunt. —*Trans.*]
‡[Souls. —*Trans.*]

Dietrich was carried off to hell by a black horse, according to Caesarius von Heisterbach, or, according to other legends, was abducted to the Rumenia Desert, where he must fight dragons for eternity, or it is told that he followed a dwarf one day, never to be seen again. We note that certain individuals who disappeared under strange circumstances had a tendency to enter the Wild Hunt or to become cursed hunters. The theme of the psychopomp animal or entity, which can be found as early as King Herla's tale, seems to have been incorporated into this legend at a very early date, but it also continued a separate life, evidence of which we can find in this exemplum from the *Gesta Romanorum* (chapter 190):

> A king coveted the lands of one of his vassals and commanded him, on pain of forfeiture of his estate, to procure and bring to him within eight days a black dog, a black horse, a black falcon, and a black horn. The vassal was in despair, but met an old man who gave him counsel, thanks to which he successfully passed this test. A short time later, the king heard barking and was told that his hounds flushed a stag in the forest but were unable to catch him. The king mounted his black steed, hung the black horn around his neck, and followed after his dogs. When he saw the stag, he sounded his horn and spurred on his horse. The stag immediately took the direct path to hell [*cervus vero recto tramite ad infernum cucurrit*]. The king followed him, and was never seen again [*umquam amplius visus est*].[5]

Jacob Grimm's hypothesis that Berchtholde (Berchtold), once vouched for as leader of the Wild Hunt, was the devil or Odin, is no longer considered valid. The name is the result of the combination of Bercht(a) and Holda, one of whom led a troop of children who died without being baptized. The other led a band of witches.

This is what we can establish in the German language traditions: we have apparently neutral names that seek only to give a handle to the phenomena without casting judgment. The core idea that emerges from all the various phrasings is that of a procession of the dead: Totenzug, Totenprozession, Totuchrizgang, and so forth. There also appears the Night Troop, Nachtschar, the latter part of which, -schar, refers to a military unit, which, as Jean Carles notes, clearly describes the aggressive nature of the apparition. The Night Troop describes crude, rough spirits who are dangerous. The People of the Night, Nachtvolk, are akin to the Good Folk, because of their openly benevolent character, as revealed by the harmonious music that accompanies this group's passage. The two most common names, Wild Hunt (*wilde Jagd*) and Furious Army (*wütendes Heer*) emphasize several notions: danger, fury, the speed with which the troop moves, and its unruly and ungovernable nature, which can be found in the names forged with *wild* or *wut/mut*. We can easily imagine the hypothesis in which certain names for the Wild Hunt perform a normative function and eliminate other local names that could be quite old, some of which I have cited earlier. A giant, the Türst/Dürst, possibly the final vestige of the psychopomp deity of the original myth, appears in these traditions. The culmination of the evolution of norms undoubtedly testifies to a reduction in their number as well as to their normalization, but we can see over the centuries the distinction between troops of peaceful or dangerous dead.

We should not confuse the Wild Hunts with those of the cursed huntsman—with St. Hubert's Hunt (Normandy, Morvan); St. Eustache's Hunt (Normandy); Macchabee's Hunt (Orleans region); Herod's Hunt (Bresse, Perigord); the Chasse Galery/Galerie (Vendée, Saintonge); Valory's Hunt (Bas-Maine); Briquet's Hunt (bords du Loire); the Chasse Malé/Mare/Malo (Maine); the Chasse Artu/Artui (Normandy, Gascony, Upper Brittany, Guyenne, the Fougères region, and the Foix Earldom); the Chasse à Rigaud/à Ribaut (Berry); ewiger Jäger (Eternal Huntsman), wilder Jäger, Hochjäger, Goï and De Jon Hunter (Westphalia); Waldemar, Wode, and Wohljäger (Schleswig-Holstein)—or with that of the wild huntsman that can be found in Ille-et-Vilains (the Human Hunt), in Alsace and Franche-Comté; Wor of Rügen Island; Fru Gode (Mecklenberg); Hackelberg/Hackelblock (Thuringia); Nimrod (Upper Hessia); and Roods/Röds (Hanover), another name for Herod. In addition, we must not confuse the night hunter (*Nachtjäger*), who is invisible or headless and rides a white horse that spits fire from its nostrils. In the old duchy of Berg, the sheet metal hunter (*der blecherne Jäger*) carries a staff and wears a metal hat.

Vincente Risco summarizes the Spanish phenomena and analyzes the various names for the Infernal Hunt.[6] In the Iberian Peninsulan is Hoste (Hueste, Güestia), which was attested as early as 1469 in the form of Exercitus Antiquus, Huesta Antigua. This is an army of souls (*ejercito de las almas*). Estantiga/Estandiga is derived from the Latin *hostis antiqua,* which designates the devil. Other troops are more or less akin to the Wild Hunt, but they attest to a shift toward witchcraft, such as Hostilla, a cortege of witches; and Antaruxada, a troop that announces the death of an individual or a throng of witches or a host connected with Carnival. There has been some contamination from the Castilian *antruejo.* Estadea alludes to the candles in the procession of the dead, and to the "statue" (*estadea*) and the Santa Compaña.

We can note that practically there exist no witnesses free of any influence, hence the difficulty of classification. What are we to do, for example, about the Flying Hunt (Perigord), which is a hunt led by a white lady? What of King Herod who, in the French Alps, rides headless steeds or large goats with his companions? What of the Cavalry of Pilate (Savoy), which consists of men who ride horses that are all on fire? The testimonies collected in western Europe during the nineteenth century commingle everything and have helped obscure all the data.

Notes

Introduction

1. From "Aasgaardsreien" (1844), a poem by J. M. Welhaven. In 1872 a painting by the same name was created by P. N. Arbo, and another was created in 1877 by W. Trübner. In addition, the bas-relief *The Storm Ride* was created around 1900 by G. Bayes; *Atta Troll* was created by Heinrich Heine (1797–1856); *Valdemar Atterdag* was created by A. G. Oehlenschläger (1779–1850); *Kong Valdemars Jagt* was created by B. S. Ingermann (1789–1862); "Der wilde Jäger," the poem was written by G. A. Bürger (1747–1794); *Melancholy* was painted in 1532 by Lucas Cranach; *Wilde Jagd* was created by the painter Franz von Stuck; and *Chasse Sauvage* was written by the composer César Franck. [Other composers who adopted this theme include Franz Lizst and Karl Maria von Weber as well as many modern metal groups, such as Bathory and Aes Dana. William Butler Yeats, John Masefield, J. R. R. Tolkien, Simon Green, and Jim Butcher are a few of the many recent authors who have drawn inspiration from this theme. —*Trans.*]

2. Walter von Wartburg, *Französisches etymologisches Wörterbuch* XVI (Bonn: F. Klopp Verlag, 1928), 200.

Chapter 1. The Good Women Who Roam the Night

1. See D. Lesourd, "Diane et les sorciers. Etude sur les survivances de Dianes dans les langues romanes," *Anagrom* (1972): 55–74.

2. Burchard of Worms, *Decretum* XIX. See also John of Salisbury (ca. 1115–1180), *Polycraticus* II, 17, in *Mondes parallèles: l'univers des croyances du Moyen Age*, trans. Claude Lecouteux, (Paris: Honoré Champion, 2007), 51.

3. William of Auvergne, *De universo* II, 3, 24, in *Mondes parallèles,* Claude Lecouteux, trans., 56–63.

4. For more, see the fourteenth-century German nightly benediction *(Nachtsegen)* that lists the number of beings abroad in the night. Claude Lecouteux, *Geschichte der Gespenster und Wiedergänger im Mittelalter* (Cologne and Vienna: Böhlau Verlag, 1987), 39.

5. See D. Harmening, *Superstitio* (Berlin: E. Schmidt Verlag, 1979), 97.

6. For the texts of Burchard, see Claude Lecouteux and Philippe Marcq, *Les esprits et les morts* (Paris: Honoré Champion, 1990), essays 13, 15.

7. Carlo Ginzburg, *Les batailles nocturnes* (Paris: Flammarion, 1993), translated into English as *The Night Battles: Witchcraft and Agrarian Cults in the Sixteenth & Seventeenth Centuries* (Baltimore: Johns Hopkins University Press, 1992).

8. Burchard de Worms, *Decretum.*

9. See Claude Lecouteux, *Witches, Werewolves, and Fairies: Shapeshifters and Astral Doubles in the Middle Ages* (Rochester, Vt.: Inner Traditions, 2003).

10. Lecouteux, trans., *Mondes parallèles,* 17.

11. For more, see Julio Caro Baroja, *Les Sorcières et leur monde* (Paris: Gallimard, 1972), 85, note 2.

12. E. Voigt, *Ysengrimus* (Halle: n.p., 1884), Book II, v 71–94. I have used E. Charbonnier's translation from *Le Roman de Ysengrin* (Paris: Les Belles Lettres, 1991), 91. I have put the most relevant sentences in italics.

13. See also J. Grimm, *Deutsche Mythologie,* 3 volumes (Darmstadt: Wissenschaftliche Buchgesellschaft, 1965), vol. 3, 282. For more on Herodias in the mysteries, see J. Koopman, *Le Théâtre des exclus* (Paris: Éditions Imago, 1994), 120.

14. E. Charbonnier, *Le Roman de Ysengrin,* 256ff.

15. *Le Rommant de la Rose* (Paris: Jehan Longus, 1538), fol. 344r°–345r°.

16. J. Klapper, *Exempla aus Handschriften des Mittelalters* (Heidelberg: Carl Winter, 1911), Sammlung mitellat Text 2, no. 30.

17. See Claude Lecouteux, "Lamia," *Enzyklopädie des Märchens* (Berlin, New York: Walter de Gruyter, 1995), vol. 8, col. 738–40; Claude Lecouteux, "Lamia, holzmuowa, holzfrowe, lamîch," *Euphorion* 75 (1981): 360–65.

18. Lecouteux and Marcq, *Les esprits et les morts,* 27; Lecouteux, trans., *Mondes parallèles,* 60.

19. William of Auvergne, *De Universo,* 2 volumes (Paris: Operaomania, 1674), vol. 1, 1036. Further on, William revisits this subject by discussing the illusions of demons, fairies, and goblins: "You shall have the feeling that it involves nothing

other than these manifestations that haunt homes and are called night ladies, and the one among them to enter first is called Dame Abundia, because it is thought she bestows an abundance of temporal goods upon the houses she visits. . . . The foolishness of men and the folly of old women are in such agreement on this point that they leave uncovered the dishes holding food and drink, and cork nothing up because of these ladies of the night on the nights it is believed they visit homes."

20. Ibid., 1068.
21. A. Schönbach, "Studien zur altdeutschen Predigt II: Zeugnisse Bertholds von Regensburg zur Volkskunde," *Sitzungsberichte der phil-hist. Classe d. Kaiser. Akademie der Wissenschaften* 142 (1900): 1–156. I have provided the names used by Berthold to designate the spirits in parentheses. See also Claude Lecouteux and Phillipe Marcq, *Berthold de Ratisbonne: péchés et vertus, scenes de la vie du XIIIᵉ siècle* (Paris: Desjonquères, 1992).
22. Ibid., 21.
23. See J. Grimm, *Deutsche Mythologie,* vol. 2, 882.
24. See *De decem praeceptis,* ms. 578 (fifteenth century), fol. 149v°b (Graz Library): *Tercio videbant qui in certis noctibus, ut Epiphanye, Perchte. Vulgariter Phinzen, aut sabbato alias domine Habundie ponunt cibos etpotus et sal ut sit isto anno huic domui propicia et largiatur satietatem et habundanciam vel Sacia vocantur, videant quibus et cui offerant, utique sunt demons in specie mulierum apparentes et non boni angeli.*
25. See J. Schmelles, *Bayerisches Wïrterbuch,* 2 volumes (Munich: Cotta, 1827–37), vol. 1, 271.
26. Ms Clm. 1438, fol. 203v° in the Munich National Library.
27. *Vas quod habuerit operculum nec ligaturam desuper, immundum erit,* numbers 15 and 19.
28. Johannes Praetorius, *Saturnalia* (Leipzig: n.p., 1663), 395 and 403.
29. M. P. Nilson, "Studien zur Vorgeschichte des Weihnachtsfestes," *Archiv für Religionswissenschaft* 19 (1916): 50–150; F. Schneider, "Über die Kalendae Ianuariae und Martiae im Mittelalter," *Archiv für Religionswissenschaft* 20 (1920/21): 82–134, 360–410, especially 370.
30. See Lecouteux, "Romanisch-germanische," *Mediaevistik* vol. 1., (1988): 94.
31. Ms Clm. 2714, fol. 75 r°.
32. For more, see Lecouteux, *Les Nains et les Elfes au Moyen Age* (Paris: Editions Imago, 1988), 2nd edition, 1997; Lecouteux, *The Return of the Dead.*
33. See J. H. Grisward, "Les Fées, l'Aurore et la Fortune. Mythologie indo-euro-

péenne et *Jeu de la feuillée*," in André Lanly, *Mélanges* (Nancy: University of Nancy, 1980), 121–36.

34. See Claude Lecouteux, *Mélusine et le Chevalier au cygne* (Paris: Eds. Imago, 1997).

35. G. W. Dasent, trans., "The Lay of the Lance," in *The Saga of Burnt Njal* (chapter 157).

36. Prose after strophes 4 and 13.

37. *Flateyarbók* (Akraness: n.p., 1944), vol. 1, 465–68.

38. P. Jouet, *L'Aurore celtique. Fonctions du héros dans la religion cosmique* (Paris: Porte-glaive, 1993), 41.

39. See, J. Koopman, *Le Théâtre des exclus*, 118.

40. Jacques Sprenger and Henrich Kramer, *Le Marteau des Sorcières*, Armand Danet, trans. (Paris: Plon, 1973) 141, 240.

41. K. Meisen, *Die Sagen vom Wütenden Heer und wilden Jäger* (Münster: Aschendorffsche Verlagsbuchhandlung, 1935), 111.

42. J. Mathesius, *Auslegung der Fest-Evangelien* (Nuremberg: n.p., 1571), 22.

Chapter 2. The Phalanxes of Demons

1. The same idea can be seen in a hymn of St. Ambrose of Milan, *Pat. Lat.*, 16, col. 1410. This translation is by Martin R. Pope (1865–1944) (London: J. M. Dent and Co., 1905).

2. Texts from K. Meisen, *Die Sagen vom Wütenden Heer und wilden Jäger*, 24*ff.*

3. J. Fontaine, ed. and trans., 2 volumes, *Sources chrétiennes* (Paris: Cerf, 1967), 133–34, vol. 1, 304–5.

4. *Quomodo corporaliter maligni spiritus ad portas inferni illum asportaverunt.*

5. B. Colgrave, *Felix's Life of Saint Guthlac* (Cambridge: Cambridge University Press, 1956), chapter 31.

6. William of Newburgh, *Historia rerum Anglicarum*, II, 21, Joseph Stevenson, trans. (London: Seeley, 1861).

7. *De Universo* III, 24, 2 volumes (Paris: n.p., 1674), vol. 1, 61.

8. Texts from K. Meisen, *Die Sagen vom Wütenden Heer und wilden Jäger*, 61.

9. J. Gobi, n° 953.

10. Étienne of Bourbon, *Anecdotes historiques*, A. Lecoy de la Marche, ed. (Paris: n.p., 1877), n° 37. The story can be found in Jean Gobi's *Scala coeli*, n° 929, 560–62.

11. Text from K. Meisen, *Die Sagen vom Wütenden Heer und wilden Jäger*.

12. Ibid., 83.

13. Ibid., 84, strophe 66.

14. Gilles Roussineau, *Perceforest,* 2 volumes (Paris, Geneva: Droz, 1987), vol. 2, 740–45.

15. Thomas de Cantimpré, *Apiarius* II, 57, 449.

16. See A. Franz, *Die Kirchlichen Benediktionen im Mittelalter,* 2 volumes (Freiburg, Graz: n.p., 1909), vol. 2, 2 and 22.

17. I thank J. P. Sémon (Paris: Sorbonne) who gave this text to me, and who translated and provided a philological analysis of it.

18. See H. Celander, "Gravso och Gloso," *Arv* 8 (1952). A map of the phenomenon can be found in A. Eskeröd, *Årets äring. Ethnologiska studier i skördens och julens tro och sed* (Stockholm: Nordiska Museet, 1947), 115–17.

19. See H. F. Feilberg, "Der Kobold in nordischer überlieferung," *Zeitschrift des Vereins für Volkskunde* 8 (1898): 1–20; 130–46; 264–77, page 141 here.

20. Eike, "Oskoreia og ekstaseriter," *Norveg* 23 (1980): 256.

21. *S macht, wie wenn der Türscht jadti,* see Elisabeth Liebl, "Geisterheere und ähnliche Erscheinungen," in P. Geiger, R. Weiss, *Atlas der schweizerischen Volkskunde,* Kommentar, 2nd part (Basel: Schweizerische Gesellschaft für Volkskunde, 1971), 768–84, page 773 here.

22. A. Joisten, C. Abry, *Etres fantastiques des Alpes* (Paris: Éditions Entente, 1995), 168.

Chapter 3. The Troops of the Dead

1. Harold Edgeworth Butler, trans., *Propertius* (New York: G. P. Putnam, 1916), 313.

2. K. Meisen, *Die Sagen vom Wütenden Heer und wilden Jäger,* 27.

3. J. Duvernoy, *La Registre d'inquisition de Jacques Fournier* (Paris: Privat, 1965), vol. 1, 137.

4. *Acta Sanctorum, Apr.* 2, 648. Sur Wipert, in M. Manitius, *Geschichte der lateranischen Literatur der Mittelalters,* 3 volumes (Munich: C. H. Beck, 1923), vol. 2, 382–86.

5. Complete translation of this text can be found in Lecouteux and Marcq, *Les esprits et les morts,* 113.

6. Ekkehard of Aura, *Chronicles,* 1123.

7. Motif E, 492, in S. Thompson's nomenclature and N, 3, of Ingeborg Müller and Lutz Röhrich's catalog of legends about the dead: Röhrich Müller, "Der Tod und die Toten," *Deutsches Jahrbuch für Volkskunde* 13 (1967): 346–97.

8. See B. Deneke, *Legende und Volkssage, Untersuchungen zur Erzählung vom Geistergottesdienst,* dissertation (Frankfurt: 1958); B. Alver, "Dauinggudstenesta

ein europeisk førestellingskrins i norsk tradisjon," *Arv* 6 (1950): 145–65. For Norway, we have some thirty witnesses, the oldest dating back to July 6, 1786. The event almost always took place on Christmas Day.

9. *MGH rerum gemanicarum nova series,* volume IX (Berlin: Ed. R. Holtzemann, 1935).

10. Íslendingasagnaútgáfan, 1948), chapter 49, 1–77, here 70*ff.*

11. J. Grimm, *Deutsche Sagen* (Darmstadt: Wissenschaftliche Buchgesellschaft, 1974), n° 176, 198–200.

12. Pierre de Cluny, *De Miraculis,* I, 23, *Corpus Christianorum continuatio mediaealis,* D. Boutheillier, ed. (Turnhout: Brepols, 1988), 69–72, 83.

13. J. M. Lacarra, "Una aparición de ultratumba en Estella," *Principe de Viana* 15 (1944): 173–84.

14. O. Holder-Egger, ed., *De fundatione monasterii s. Fidis Sletstatensis* (Hanover: n.p., 1888), MGH, SS XV.2, 996–1000.

15. *Exordium magnam Cisterciense sive narratio de mitro Cisterciensis ordinis,* B. Griesser, ed., (Rome: Editiones Cistercienses, 1961), Series Script. S. Ordinis Cisterciensis II, 208.

16. E. Kleinschmidt, "Die Colmarer Dominikaner Geschichtsschreibung im 13. und 14. Jahrhundert," *Deutsches Archiv* 28 (1972): 447–49.

17. K. Ranke, *Indogermanische Totenverehrung I: Der dreissigste und vierzigste Tag im Totenkult der Germanen* (Helsinki: FFC 140, 1951), FFC 140, 290*ff,* 313–27.

18. G. Durand, *Rational* VII, 38, ed. G.H. Buijssen, 4 volumes (Assen: n.p., 1966–83), vol. 4, 261.

19. See Jean Gobi, *Scala coeli,* Marie-Anne Polo de Beaulieu, ed., (Paris: Édition du Centre National de la Recherche Scientifique, 1991); (*Sources d'Histoire médiévale*), n°649, 441; *Mariale magnum,* II, 37: Vincent de Beauvais, *Speculum historiale,* VI, 109.

20. Lecouteux, *Return of the Dead,* 92.

21. Ibid., 104.

22. G. Duby, *L'An mil* (Paris: Julliard, 1967), 77. Translation here by J. France from *The Five Books of Histories of Rodulfus Glaber* (Oxford: Oxford University Press, 1989).

23. Röhrich Müller, N 6.

24. See Cabal, *La Mitología asturiana* (Oviedo, 1983), 21–24; 35–44. Marianne Mesnil, "Chemin des morts, chemin des âmes: deux représentations d'une même typologie mythico-rituelle en Europe," *Mythologie française* 147–49 (1987): 127–33.

25. Text and translation from A. Micha, *Lais féeriques des XIIe et XIIIe siècles* (Paris: Flammarion, 1992), GF 672, 313–31.

26. Lecouteux, *The Return of the Dead,* 121 *ff.*

27. Röhrich Müller, N 1. Numerous examples of the dead dancing can be found in F. Karlinger, J. Pögl, *Totentanz und Fronleichnamsspiel: Farsa llamada dança de la muerte von Juan de Pedraza* (Salzburg: Lib. Hispano-Lusa 1, 1992).

28. E 374; Röhrich Müller, F 29.

29. E 481.3

30. In the Valais, St. Hilaire is the day of the *Commemoratio minor fidelium defunctorum.*

31. See Elisabeth Liebl, "Totenzug," in P. Geiger, R. Weiss, *Atlas der schweizerischen Volkskunde. Kommentar,* part 2 (Basel: Schweizerische Gesellschaft für Volkskunde, 1971), 753–67.

32. See A. Büchli, "Wilde Jagd und Nachtvolk," *Schweizerische Volkskunde* 37 (1947): 65–69.

33. See Folke Ström, "Tidrandes död. Till fragon om makternas demonisering," *Arv* 7 (1952): 77–119, here 104.

Chapter 4. The Phantom Armies

1. Motif E, 500l, Röhrich Müller, E 3.

2. Motifs E, 502, and D, 1960.2, in the nomenclature of S. Thompson and N, 18, in that of Röhrich Müller.

3. Motif E, 500.

4. *Geography,* I, 32, 4.

5. *Historia Langobardorum* II, 4, MGH SS *Rerum germanicarum in usum scholarum* (Hanover: Hahn, 1987), 87.

6. Richard Vaughn, ed. and trans., *The Illustrated Chronicles of Matthew Paris: Observations of Thirteenth-Century Life* vol. 2 (Cambridge: Alan Sutton Publishing, 1993), 91.

7. K. Meisen, *Die Sagen vom Wütenden Heer und wilden Jäger,* 132.

8. Snorri Sturluson, *Skáparmál* (Treatise on Poetry from *The Prose Edda*), 108.

9. *Fourth Continuation of the Story of the Grail,* 2 volumes, Mary Williams, ed., (Paris: Honoré Champion, 1922–1925) Verse 5066*ff.*, CFMA 28 and 50, vol. 3, Marguerite Oswald, ed. (Paris: Honoré Champion, 1975), CFMA 101. For *Perlesvaus,* see F. Dubost (Aix-en-Provence: n.p., 1994).

11. Virgil, *Georgics,* I, 466. See also Tibullus, *Elegies* II, 573.

12. Pliny the Elder, *Natural History, A Selection,* John F. Healy, trans., (London and New York: Penguin Books, 1991), 28, (II, 148).

13. *Pharsalia* I, 578*ff.*

14. See Rudulfus Glaber, *The Five Books of Histories of Rodulfus Glaber,* book 5, chapter 1.

15. Giraldus Cambrensis, *Expugnatio Hibernica* I, 4, ed. J. F. Dimock (London: n.p.,1867), 235. Translation here by T. Wright from *The Conquest of Ireland* in *The Historical Works of Giraldus Cambrensis* (London: George Ball, 1863).

16. K. Meisen, *Die Sagen vom Wütenden Heer und wilden Jäger,* 125.

17. U. Müller, *Sagen aus Uri,* volume 2 (Basel: n.p., 1929), 190.

18. All these testimonies appear in texts collected by I. Petzold.

19. For the French traditions, see Paul Sébillot, *Le Folklore de France,* 4 volumes (Paris: Arthaud, 1968), 2nd edition, vol. 4, 309.

20. William of Auvergne, *De universo* II, 3, 24, 2 volumes (Paris: n.p., 1674), vol. 2, 1066.

21. Lecouteux, trans., *Mondes parallèles,* 56–63.

22. George Johnston, tran., *Viga Glum's Saga,* chapter 21 [The Schemers and Viga Glum] (Erin, Ontario: Porcupine's Quill, 1997).

Chapter 5. The Diabolical Huntsman

1. Cesarius of Heisterbach, Henry V. Scott, and C. C. Swinton Bland, *The Dialogue on Miracles* (London: Routledge, 1929). Analysis in Lecouteux and Marcq, *Les esprits et les morts,* 149–51.

2. For more on the relationship between souls and the moon, see Porphyry, *On the Cave of the Nymphs in the Thirteenth Book of the Odyssey,* Thomas Taylor, trans., (London: Watkins, 1917).

3. Frederic C. Tubach, *Index Exemplorum: A Handbook of Medieval Religious Tales* (Helsinki: Suomalainen Tiedakatemia, 1969), TU 2542.

4. This is listed by Tubach under the shelf mark TU 4696. *De cognitione sui* XII, cf. *Pat. Lat.* CCXII, col. 731–36. Helinand provides two additional stories, one of which is that of the Mesnie Hellequin.

5. C. Ribaucourt, ed., 3rd cycle thesis (Paris: X, 1985).

6. John Bromyard, *Summa predicantium* XVII, 2 (Nuremburg: n.p., 1485).

7. Hermann Oesterly, ed., *Johannes Pauli's Schimpf und Ernst,* CCXXVIII (Stuttgart: n.p., 1866)

8. See V. von Geramb, "Die verwunschene Pfarrerköchin," *Blätter f. Heimatkunde*

22 (1948): 20–29; similarly: "Zum Sagenmotiv von Hufbeschlag," in *Beiträge zur sprachlichen Volksüberlieferung* (Berlin: n.p., 1953), 78–88.

9. See G. de Luca, *Scrittori di religione del Tricento* (Turin: Einaudi, 1977), Classici Ricciardi, 84.

10. L. Du Bois, *Préjugés et Superstitions en Normandie* (Paris: n.p., 1843), 310. The testimonies collected by Louis Du Bois are valuable, because they provide us with three local names for the Wild Hunt: Mère Harpine [Mother Harpine], Chasse Artus [Artus Hunt], and Chasse Hennequin [Hennequin Hunt], 309.

11. Text from K. Meisen, *Die Sagen von wütenden Heer und wilden Jäger,* 106.

Chapter 6. The Wild Huntsman

1. L. Fassung, *Eckenlied,* ed. M. Wierschin (Tübingen: Niemeyer, 1974), ATB 78, strophes 151, 5–170; the quotes can be found on pages 162 (12) and 167 (2).

2. See Claude Lecouteux, *Démons et Génies du terroir au Moyen Age* (Paris: Imago, 1995).

3. See L. Rörich, "Herr der Tiere," in K. Ranke et. al., *Enzyklopädie des Märchens,* (Berlin: Walter de Gruyter, 1990), vol., 6, cols. 866–79.

4. The Wunderer, G. Zink, ed. (Paris: n.p., 1949), BPhG XIV.

5. Texts from K. Meisen, *Die Sagen vom Wütenden Heer und wilden Jäger,* 115–119.

6. Ibid., 120.

7. Norse *Þurs,* Middle High German *türs.*

8. Hans Ellekilde, "Odinsjægeren paa Møn," in *Nordiskt Folkminne Studier tillägnade C.W. von Sydow* (Stockholm: C. E. Fritz, 1928), 85–116.

9. Ibid., 96.

10. Ibid., 96.

11. Ibid., 96, 98.

12. Ibid., 99.

13. L. Rörich, "Die frauenjagdsage," *Laographia* 22 (1965): 408–23.

14. L. Martinet, *Le Berry préhistorique* (Paris: n.p., 1878), 112.

15. Renward Cysart, DS n°47.

16. *Rüttelweiber,* DS n°271.

17. J. Berlioz, trans., and N. Zorzetti, ed., *Premier Mythographe du Vatican* (Paris: Collection des Universités de France, 1995). See also Charles David, "Le Grand Veneur ou le Chasseur Noir," *Bulletin de liaison des Associés franciliens de la Société de Mythologie française* 15 (1996): 3–6.

18. Philippe Walter, *Le Mythe de la Chasse sauvage dans l'Europe medievale* (Paris: Honoré Champion, 1997), 33–72.

19. See Philippe Walter, *Christianity: The Origins of a Pagan Religion* (Rochester, Vt.: Inner Traditions, 2006), 89.

20. *Das Wallis vor der Geschichte. 14000 v. Chr.–47 n. Chr* Sitten: Kantonsmuseen, 1986), 228.

21. Personal communication by Bronislawa Kerbelyte.

22. *Das Wallis,* 267.

23. See E. Schmid, *Steinkultur im Wallis* (Brig: Rotten-Verlag, 1986), 96.

24. See Paul Sébillot, *Le Folklore de France* (Paris: Imago, 1988), 2nd ed., vol. 1, 173.

25. DS n°48.

26. Fraysse, "La Chasse Hennequin au pays de Baugé," *Revue des traditions populaires* 20 (1905): 163. This theme is quite widespread. To read more on it from the Dauphin and Savoy regions, see Alice Joisten and C. Abry, *Êtres fantastiques des Alpes françaises* (Paris: Entente, 1995), 164.

27. Mackensen, *Niedersächsische Sagen* (Leipzig–Gohlis: Teil 2, 1925), n°118.

28. Zingerle, *Innsbruck: Sagen, Märchen, und Gebräuche aus Tirol,* n°32.

29. Ibid., n°30.

30. Gervase of Tilbury, *Otia Imperialia,* III, 70.

Chapter 7. The Cursed Hunter

1. Michael Beheim, "Von dem van Wirtenperg," *Die Gedichte des Michel Beheim,* H. Gille and Ingeborg Spriewald, eds. (Berlin: Akademie Verlag, 1968), DTM 60, 366.

2. P. Sébillot, *Le Folklore de France,* vol. 1, 164–78, 274–80.

3. L. Sainéan, "La Mesnie Hellequin," *Revue des traditions populaires* 20 (1905): 163.

4. Pierre Matthieu, *Histoire de France et des choses mémorables* (Paris: n.p., 1605), folio 75.

5. A. Gölnitz, *Ulysses Belgico-Gallicus* (Leyden: n.p., 1631), 164.

6. O. de Marliave, *Petit dictionnaire de mythologie basque et pyrénéenne* (Paris: Entente, 1993), 160.

7. See, for example, R. J. Menner, "The Man in the Moon and Hedging," *Journal of English and German Philology* 48 (1949): 1–14.

8. Legend listed under n°AaTh 777. See also *Enzyklopädie des Märchens* IV, col. 577–88, texts in L. Petzold, *Hitorische Sagen* (Munich: n.p., 1977), vol. 2, 1–4, commentary on page 272.

9. Ibid., vol. 2, 25 and 277.

10. P. G. Schmitt, ed., *Ludis nostris theatralibus vacare nos oportes* (Leipzig: n.p., 1978).

11. See C. Luttrell, "Folk Legend as Source for Arthurian Romance: the Wild Hunt," in *Mélanges L. Thorpe* (Glasgow: University of Scotland, 1981), 83–100. On another future for King Arthur, see A. Graf, *Miti, legende e superstizioni nel Medio Evo* (Hildesheim: n.p., 1985), 303–59. Reprinted *Artù nell'Etna.*

12. Gervase of Tilbury, *Otia Imperiala* II, 12.

13. A. Micha, ed., *Voyages dans l'au-delà d'après les texts médiévaux (IVe–XIIIe siècle)* (Paris: n.p., 1992), vol. 1, 151.

14. See *Poètes et Romanciers du Moyen Age* (Paris: Gallimard, 1954), Bibliothèque de la Pléiade, 424.

15. Brother Boissen, *Schleswig Chronicle.*

16. St. Augustine, *Totium mundi pessimum venatorem: De concordantia Matthaei et Lucae,* sermon 51.

17. Hélinand of Froidmont, *Verses on Death,* M. Boyer and M. Santucc, trans. (Paris: Honoré Champion, 1983), O, 4, XXII, 7*ff.*

18. William Shakespeare, *The Merry Wives of Windsor,* IV, 4, 28–38.

19. See A. Joisten, C. Abry, *Êtres fantastiques,* 166*ff.*

20. There are numerous variations. See Charles Joisten, C. Abry, "Du Roi chasseran au Récheran scieur des têtes: un avatar de la Chasse sauvage en Savoie," in *Mélanges Ernest Schille* (Bern,: n.p., 1983), 286–328.

Chapter 8. The Legend of King Herla

1. Walter Map, *De nugis curialium,* ed. Montague Rhodes James (Oxford: Oxford University Press, 1914), I, 11.

2. See, for example, Bartholomew the Englishman, *De proprietatibus rerum* XVIII, 58: *hircus est animal petulum et laciuum, semper feruens ad coitum.* On the legend, Ibid., XVIII, 84.

3. Map, *De nugis curialium.*

4. Lecouteux, *Les Nains et les Elfes au Moyen Age,* 105.

5. Story type AsTh 470, friends in life and death. See, G. Peschel, "Freunde im Lieben und Tod," in K. Ranke et. al., *Enzyklopädie des Märchens* (Berlin: Walter de Gruyter, 1987), vol. 5, col. 282–87. Peschel points out that this type is often combined with motif M, 252 (the message from the beyond). For more on this point, see the important study by L. Petzold, "Die Botschaft aus der

Anderswelt," in *Märchen, Mythos, Sage, Beiträge zur Literatur und Volksdichtung* (Marburg: n.p., 1989), 101–44.

6. Indexed by F. C. Tubach under n°780 (bridegroom absent three hundred years).

7. Map, *De nugis curialium.*

8. Lecouteux, *Les Nains,* 124–28.

9. Map, *De nugis curialium.*

10. Lecouteux and Marcq, *Les esprits et les morts,* 68–71.

11. Map, *De nugis curialium.*

12. For more, see E. S. Hartland, *The Science of Fairy Tales* (London: C. W. Daniels, 1925), 161–254.

13. Motif E, 481.3.

14. Lecouteux, *The Return of the Dead,* 149, 160–61.

15. Map, *De nugis curialum.*

16. Lecouteux, *The Return of the Dead,* 58–59.

17. Map, *De nugis curialium.*

18. Jean-Claude Schmitt, "Temps, folklore et politique au XIIᵉ siècle. A propos de deux récits de Walter Map," in *Le Temps chrétien de la fin de l'Antiquité au Moyen Age* (Paris: CNRS, 1984), 604, 489–515.

19. Map, *De nugis curialium,* IV, 13.

20. See the German romance *Friedrich von Schwaben,* 1300.

21. Lecouteux, *The Return of the Dead,* 204–5.

22. Ruodlieb V, 451, ed. W. Haug, B. K. Vollmann (Frankfurt: Deutscher Klassiker-Verlag, 1991). Also see *Zeitschrift f. romanische Philologie* 11 (1897): 353, and B. Sergent, *Les Indo-Européens. Histoire, langues, mythes* (Paris: Payot, 1995), 438.

23. Lecouteux, *Les Nains.*

24. Examples in Lecouteux, *The Return of the Dead,* 204–205.

25. See Edmund Mudrak, "Das wütende Heer und der wilde Jäger," *Bausteine zur Geschichte der Volkskunde und Mythenkunde* 6 (1937): 3–42, page 11ff. Here, Westphalia Legend on Purgatory in the Lutterberg.

26. See E. Mudrak, "Die Herkunft vom wütenden Heer und vom wilden Jäger," *Laographia* 4 (1965): 302–23, page 317 here.

27. Motif D, 2011.

28. A belief perfectly illustrated by the *Lay of Guingamor.*

29. Kuno Meyer, trans., *The Voyage of Bran* (London: David Nutt, 1895).

30. Felix Karlinger, *Zauberschlaf und Entrückung. Zur Problematik der Jenseitszeit in der Volkserzählung* (Vienna: n.p., 1936), 31.

31. See P. Gallais, *La Fée à la fontaine et à l'arbre: un archétype du conte merveilleux et du récit courtois* (Amsterdam: Rondopi, 1992), CERMEIL 1, 234, 254, 257, 274.

32. See Claude Lecouteux, *Dictionnaire de Mythologie Germanique* (Paris: Ed. Imago, 2006), "Garmr" and "Hel."

33. See *Das Wallis vor der Geschichte: 14000 v. Chr.-47 nach Chr.* (Sitten: Kanton-museum, 1986), 228.

34. Lecouteux, *The Return of the Dead,* 147–48.

35. See P. Alphandéry, "Notes sur le messianisme mediéval latin," *Annuaire E.P.H.E., Sciences religieuse* (1912): 2–26; J. Grimm, *Deutsche Mythologie,* vol. 2, 704; Ronald Grambo, "Balladen om Hakje og bergermannen," *Arv* 28 (1972): 55–81.

36. Jean-Claude Schmitt, "Temps, folklore et politique."

37. C. Plummer, ed., "The Land Chronicle," in *Two of the Saxon Chronicles Parallels,* 2 volumes (Oxford: Oxford University Press, 1892), 258; W. T. Mellows, ed., *The Chronicle of Hugh Candidus* (Oxford: Oxford University Press, 1949), 76.

Chapter 9. The Mesnie Hellequin

1. Motif E, 501.

2. Orderic Vitalis, *Historia ecclesiastica,* ed. Marjorie Chibnall (Oxford: Oxford University Press, 1973), 236–50. [This version includes certain corrections and additional details supplied by the author. —*Trans.*]

3. Vitalis, *Ecclesiastical History.*

4. Ibid.

5. Ibid.

6. Ibid.

7. For example, Gilbert de Nogent, *Autobiographie* I, 16, E. R. Labande, ed., (Paris: Les Belles Lettres, 1981), CHFMA 34, 128.

8. Vitalis, *Ecclesiastical History.*

9. Lecouteux and Marcq, *Les esprits et,* 201, a devil places a witch on a saddle covered with iron spikes.

10. Lecouteux, *Witches, Werewolves, and Fairies,* 48.

11. Shorthand for the inexpressible. By using it after citing known names, Orderic anchors his story in reality.

12. Lecouteux, *The Return of the Dead*, 120; Lecouteux and Marcq, *Les esprits et,* 137; Pierre de Cluny, *De Miraculis* I, 25, CCM 83, 77.

13. Vitalis, *Ecclesiastical History.*

14. Ibid.

15. Ibid.

16. J. Klapper, *Exempla*, n°34: *a mortuo tactus in brachio perforatus est cutis et caro usque ad os in signum, ut memorium haberet promissionis.*

17. The depiction of the mark imprinted by a dead person's burning hand can be found in L. Petzold, *Märchen*, 115.

18. Röhrich Müller, 62.

19. Vitalis, *Ecclesiastical History.*

20. For example, see Jacobus de Voraginem *Legende aurea* (Golden Legend), chapter CLXIII, "This cope weigheth on me more than a mill stone or a tower."

21. Vitalis, *Ecclesiastical History.*

22. Lecouteux, *The Return of the Dead*, 116.

23. Recorded in 1563 in *Wendunmuth*, see K. Meisen, *Die Sagen vom Wütenden Heer und wilden Jäger*, 106.

24. AaTh 769; Röhrich Müller, F, 41.

25. Story type AaTh 769. It can be found in the work of Thomas of Cantimpré (Thomas Cantipratensis).

26. E, 324; Röhrich Müller, F, 42.

27. See J. Bolte and G. Polivka, *Anmerkungen zu den Kinder und Hausmärchen der Brüder Grimm* (Leipzig: Dieterich, 1915), vol. 2, 485–90.

28. Lecouteux and Marcq, *Les esprits et les morts*, 110. Readers will find a complete translation in French and commentary here.

29. Vitalis, *Ecclesiastical History.*

30. Migne, *Pat. Lat.*, 87, col. 433–35.

31. Ibid., 164, col. 1287*ff.* English translation, Eileen Gardiner, *Visions of Heaven and Hell Before Dante* (New York: Italica Press, 1989), 131.

32. J. Klapper, *Exempla*, n°38.

33. See A. Micha, *Voyages dans l'au-delà d'après les texts médiévaux (IVe–XIIIe siècle)* (Paris: Klincksieck, 1992), 127.

34. Lecouteux, trans., *Mondes parallèles*, essays 14, 73, and 84.

35. Text in K. Meisen, *Die Sagen vom Wütenden Heer und wilden Jäger*, 80.

36. F. von Schönwerth, *Aus der Oberpfalz, Sitten und Sagen* I (Augsburg: n.p., 1857), 25.

Chapter 10. The Evolution of the Legend

1. William of Malmesbury, *Gesta Anglorum* II, 205, 2 volumes, W. Stubbs, ed. (London: n.p., 1887–1889). For more on the legend, see G. Huet, "La Légende

de la statue de Vénus," *Revue de l'histoire des religions* 68 (1913): 193–217; P. F. Baum, "The Young Man Betrothed to a Statue," PMLA 34 (1919): 523–79.

2. See Charles David, "Le Grand Veneur ou le Chasseur noir."

3. See M. Petry, *Herne the Hunter* (Reading: William Smith, 1972), 70–72, including references.

4. See H. M. Flasdieck, "Harlekin."

5. Virgil, *The Aeneid*, VI, 653–55.

6. Hélinand of Froidmont.

7. Ibid.

8. See Lecouteux and Marcq, *Les esprits et les morts*, 195 for a complete translation of this text.

9. Ibid., 57–60.

10. Rev. James Kirkwood, *A Collection of Highland Rites and Customes Copied by E. Lhuyd from the Manuscript of the Reverent J. Kirkwood (1600–1709)* (Cambridge: Cambridge University Press, 1975), 35.

11. See F. Alonso Romero, "Los Origines del mito de la Santa Campaña de las isles de Ons u Salvatora," *Cuadernos de Estudios Gallegos* 32 (1981): 285–305, 293 here. I thank F. Delpech (CNRS) for transmitting this article to me.

12. See Claude Lecouteux, "Geiler de Kaisersberg et Das wütende Heer," *Etudes germaniques* 50 (1995): 367–76.

13. *La Relation de Rein.*

14. Ibid.

15. Herbert of Clairvaux, "He Who Saw the Mesnie Hellequin," in *The Book of Miracles.*

16. See Otto Höfler, *Kultische Geheimbünde der Germanen* (Frankfurt: M. Diesterweg, 1934), 296.

17. *Liber certarum historium* VI, 12, F. Schneider, ed., in MGH, Script. Rer. Germ. 36 (Hanover: n.p., 1909–1910).

18. Lecouteux, *Witches, Werewolves, and Fairies;* Carlo Ginzberg, *Night Battles.*

19. Text in K. Meisen, *Die Sagen vom Wütenden Heer und wilden Jäger*, 101–3.

20. From F. Villon, "The Ballad of the Hanged Men."

21. J. Nider, *Formicarius* V, 1, Douai, 1602, 355*ff;* text in K. Meisen, *Die Sagen vom Wütenden Heer und wilden Jäger*, 81 *ff.*

22. L. Rörich, *Sage* (Stuttgart: J. B. Metzler,1971), 51.

23. W. Baumann, *Die Sage von Heinrich dem Löwen bei den Slaven* (Munich: n.p., 1975), Slavistische Beiträge 83. For more on magical transportation, see 144–63.

24. Michael Wyssenherre, *The Pilgrimage of the Lord of Brunswick* (n.pl., n.p., n.d.), 67, 3–68, 7.

25. The two texts summarized and cited appear in K. Meisen, *Die Sagen vom Wütenden Heer und wilden Jäger*, 77–79 and 85–94. The English translation of the first can be found in the *Sewanee Review,* in an article by William Hand Browne: "Harlequin and Hurly Burly" (New York: Longmans, Green and Co., 1910). [Helequin / Hellequin's speech in the second version describes how they have been given leave by God to travel the roads at night as penitence for their sins and how the anguish and pain this causes them would take more than a week's time to describe. —*Trans.*]

26. For more on this motif, see P. Walter, "L'Épine ou l'arbre fée," PRISMA 7 (1989): 95–108.

27. F. Schanze, "Moringer," in L. Ruh et al., *Die Deutsche Literatur des Mittelalters. Verfasserlexikon,* volume 6 (Berlin: Walter de Gruyter, 1987), cols. 688–92.

28. H. Guy, *Essai sur la vie et les oeuvres littéraires du trouvère Adam de la Halle* (Paris: n.p., 1898), 401–7; G. Raynant in *Études littéraires dédiées à G. Paris* (Paris: n.p., 1891), 51; P. Sebillot, *Le Folklore de France,* vol. 1, 164.

29. Claude Carozzi, ed., *Le Voyage de l'âme dans l'au-delà d'après la literattéure latine (Ve–XIIe siècles)* (Rome: 1994), collection de l'École française de Rome 189, I, 679–92, 681 here.

30. W. Braune, *Althochdeutsches Lesebuch,* 16th ed. (Tübingen: n.p., 1979), 86, verses 3–7.

31. See J. L. Perez de Castro, "El Origien de la animas y su presencia en la etnografia del Eo," *Revista* 34 (1978): 273–89.

32. "The Gothic Wars" IV, 48–57, in Jan de Vries, *La Religion des Celtes* (Paris: Payot, 1963), 264.

33. Caesarius of Heisterbach, *Dialogus miraculorum* VII, 20. This theme was indexed by F. C. Tubach under n°4519, soul carried to Mass.

34. See S. Duparc-Quioc, *La Chanson d'Antioche,* 2 volumes (Paris: Librairie Orientaliste, 1978), vol. 2, 188–90.

35. Ibid., 184.

36. Conrad of Eberbach, *Exhordium magnum,* 358. This same chapter suggests that a group of dead people protect a living person who customarily prays for them, 356.

37. *Fyri reid sante sake Mikkjel og noeste Jesum Krist.* See Knut Liestøl, *Draumkvedet, A Norwegian Visionary Poem from the Middle Ages* (Oslo: Samlaget, 1946), 136, strophe 16*ff;* 140, strophe 23–25. The English translation provided

by Liestøl cannot be used, because it condenses several versions and does not correspond to the original texts reproduced on pages 124–41.

38. Cited by K, Liestøl, Ibid., 80.

39. *Gesta beati Karoli in Hispania,* I, 7, ed. A. Hämel, A. von Mandach, *Der Pseudo-Turpin von Compostela* (Munich: Verlag der Bayerischen Akademie er Wissenchafter, 1965).

Chapter 11. The Birth of New Legends

1. Lecouteux, "Geiler de Kaiserberg et Das wütende Heer," *Etudes germaniques* 50, 367–76.

2. In his *Kunstbuch* of 1514, Albrecht Dürer made a sketch of the allegory of eloquence as follows: the god Hermes pulls humans by chains that connect his tongue to the ears of his captives.

3. Friedrich Ranke, "Das wilde Heer und die Kultbünde der Germanen," *Kleinere Schriften,* ed. by H. Rupp and E. Studer (Bern, Munich: Library Germanica, 1971), 12, 380–408, here 399.

4. My guide for this entire development is Vincente Risco, "Creencias Gallegas. La procession de las animas y las premoniciones de muerte," *Revista de dialectología y tradiciones populares* 2 (1946): 380–429. For more on the cross bearer, see 407.

5. Vincente Risco, *La procession de las animas parece indudablemente construida a base de dos modelos: el accompañamiento del Santo Viático y el entierro,* 399.

6. J. Agricola, *Sybenhundertundfünfftzig Teutscher Sprichwörter* (Hagenau: n.p., 1534), n°667. This story is repeated by E. Eyring, *Proverbiorum copia, Etrlich viel Hundert lateinicher und Teutscher Sprichwörter,* 3 volumes (Eisleben: n.p., 1601–1603).

7. E. Mudrak, "Das wütende Heer," 18–20, and the *Handwörterbuch des deutschen Aberglaubens,* s.v. Eckhart.

8. Motif F, 131.1

9. O. Löhmann, "Die Enstehung der Tannhäusersage," *Fabula* 3 (1960): 224–53.

10. M. Crusius, *Annales Suevici* III, 11, 18 (Frankfurt: n.p., 1596), 653; text in K. Meisen, *Die Sagen vom Wütenden Heer und wilden Jäger,* 121.

11. Henry Kornmann, *In hoc monte audiebatur saepissime multus clamor et eiulatus animarum sive spiritum;* H. Kornmann, *De Miraculis morturoum* II, 47, text in K. Meisen, *Die Sagen vom Wütenden Heer und wilden Jäger,* 124.

12. W. Heider, *Orationum Volumen* II, 28 (Iena: n.p., 1630), 1222; text in K. Meisen, *Die Sagen vom Wütenden Heer und wilden Jäger,* 125.

13. Wolfgang Behringer, *Chonrad Stroecklin und die Nachtschar. Eine Gesichte aus der frühen Neuzeit* (Munich: Piper, 1994), 62. Translated into English by H. C. Erik Midelfort as *Shaman of Oberstdorf, Chonrad Stoecklin and the Phantoms of the Night* (Charlottesville: University Press of Virginia, 1998), 23.

14. G. M. Pfefferkorn, *Merkwüdige und auserlesne Geschichte von der berlümten Landgraffschafft Thüringen* (Frankfurt, Gotha: n.p., 1684), 25.

15. J. Prätorius, *Saturnalia, propositio LV* (Leipzig: n.p., 1663), 403–5, *Propositio LVIII*, 405. Prätorius speaks of "the loyal Eckart's spectral army of lemurs" (*des treuen Eckarts exercitus montruosus Lemurum*). We should refer to one of the meanings for *monstrum* here—"ghost, revenant"—to understand the adjective *monstruosus*.

16. Claude Lecouteux, *Au-delà du merveilleux* (Paris: P.U.P.S., 1995), 167–77.

17. The two fundamental studies of Percht are Marianne Rumpf, *Perchten, Populäre Glaubensgestalten zwischen Mythos und Katechese* (Wurtzburg: Königshausen and Neumann, 1991), Quellen and Forschungen zur europ. Ethnologie 12, 10*ff*, 24–27, and 32; and V. Waschnitius, *Percht, Holda und verwandte Gestalten* (Vienna: n.p., 1913), Sitzungsberichte d. kaiserl. Akad. D. Wissenschaften, phil.-hist. class 174.

18. D. Spada, "La chasse sauvage," *Antaios* 12 (1997): 43–63, here 60.

19. See Angela Nardo-Cibele, "Superstizioni Bellunesi e Cadorine," *Archivio per la Tradizione Populare* 4 (1885): 590.

20. The entire text with commentary can be found in Lecouteux and Marcq, *Les esprits et,* 101. The English text was adapted from M. R. James, ed., "Twelve Medieval Ghost Stories," *The English Historical Review* 37 (1922).

21. For more on this entire development, see F. Conte, "Traditions russes et prénoms bolcheviks," *Revue des études slaves* LXV (1993): 439–57 (with bibliography), particularly notes 454–56.

22. J. F. Milon, ed., *Multos de domina Aminda vidimus decreptos et de familia Hellequini,* thesis, University of Caen, 1972, 142–44, here 144.

23. J. Dufournet, *Adam de la Halle à la recherché de lui-même ou le Jeu de la feuillée* (Paris: SEDES, 1974), 139–68.

24. Jacquemart Gielée, *Renard le novel* (Paris: Ed. H. Roussel, 1961), SATF. See Patrice Uhl, "Hellequin et Fortune: le trajet d'un couple emblématique," *Perspectives médiévales* 15 (1989): 85–89.

25. O. Driesen, *Der Ursprung des Harlekin* (Berlin: n.p., 1904), 57, 67.

26. Motif D, 1344.8.1.

27. See P. Ménard, "Une parole rituelle dans la chevauchée fantastique de la Mesnie Hellequin," *Littératures* 9–10 (1984): 6.

28. See Régis Boyer, *Contes populaires islandais* (Reykjavik: Almenna Bokafelagid, 1983), 56–58.

29. R. Cysat, *Collectanea chronicao und denkwürdige Sachen pro cronica Luchermensi et Helvetiae,* ed. J. Schmid (Lucerne: n.p., 1969), text in K. Meisen, *Die Sagen vom Wütenden Heer und wilden Jäger,* 111–13.

30. K. Beitl, "Die Sagen von Nachtvolk, Untersuchung eines alpinen Sagentypus," *Laographia* 4 (1965): 14–21.

31. See M. van den Berg, *De volkssage in de province Antwerpen in de 19de en 20de eeuw,* 3 volumes (Gand: n.p., 1993), vol. 2, 1504–10.

32. A. Büchli, "Wilde Jagd und Nachtvolk," *Schweizerische Volkskunde* 37 (1947),: 65–69, here 69. See also the fine short synthesis by G. Luk, *Rätische Alpensagen. Gestalten und Bilder aus der Sagenwelt Graubündens* (Coire: n.p., 1935), 26–31.

33. See Bächtold-Stäubli, III, 146.

34. Text in Behringer, *Chonrad Stoecklin und die Nachtschar. Eine Geschichte aus der frühen Neuzeit,* 28.

35. Ibid., 17*ff.* (original text); [see 54 in the English translation. —*Trans.*]. See also G. Bonomo, *Caccia alle streghe* (Palermo: Palumbo, 1985), 15–38; 89–108.

36. Lecouteux, *Witches, Werewolves, and Fairies,* 53–55.

37. Behringer, *Chonrad Stroecklin und die Nachtschar. Eine Geschichte aus der frühen Neuzeit,* 59.

38. Ibid., 62, 55–56.

39. L. Muraro, *La Signora del gioco* (Milan: Feltrinelli, 1976), 46–123, here 75; E. Verga, "Intorno a due inediti documenti di stregheria Milanese del secolo XIV," *Rendiconti del R. Instituto Lombardo di Scienze e Lettere* 32 (1899): 165–88; G. Bonomo, *Caccia alle streghe,* 84–87, 255*ff*; A. Panizza, "I processi contro le streghe nel Trentino," *Archivio Trentino* 7 (1888): 205, 239; *Archivio Trentino* 8 (1889): 145.

40. Margherita Vanzina de Tesero, in *Chonrad Stoecklin und die Nachtschar (quello degli incubi e delle paure notturne),* 65.

41. *Tractatus de strigibus* (Rome: n.p., 1584), 141; see also J. Hansen, *Quellen und Untersuchungen zur Geschichte des Hexenwahns und der Hexenverfolgung im Mittelalter* (Bonn: n.p., 1901), 281.

42. *Zimmersche Chronile,* vol. 4, 219.

43. J. Trausch, *Straßburger Chronik* II, 2; text in K. Meisen, *Die Sagen vom Wütenden Heer und wilden Jäger,* 98*ff.*

44. R. Cysat, *Collectanea,* in K. Meisen, *Die Sagen vom Wütenden Heer und wilden Jäger.*

45. K. Meisen, Ibid., 116.

46. Ronsard, *Hymnes des daimons,* ed. A. M. Schmidt (Paris: Henri Dider, 1939), 347.

47. See also Risco, "Creencias Gallegas. La procession de las animas y las premoniciones de muerte," 414.

48. See also H. Bächtold-Stäubli, H. Hoffmann-Krayer, *Handwörterbuch des deutschen Aberglaubens,* 10 volumes (Berlin: Walter de Gruyter, 1927–1942), vol. 1, 177; 630; 1013; vol. 2, 562; 903; vol. 6, 644; 1371; vol. 7, 465; 1264; 1463; vol. 8, 675, 1201; vol. 9, 46.

49. *Da haben alle solche Gespenst undt Boldtergeister nach gelassen undt ein Endt genommen, Strausbourg Chronicle* II, 2, text in K. Meisen, *Die Sagen vom Wütenden Heer und wilden Jäger,* 98ff.

Chapter 12. The Wild Hunt, Masked Men, and Bawdy Fellows

1. Carlo Ginzburg, "Charivari, association juvénile et chasses sauvages," in Jacques Le Goff, Jean-Claude Schmitt, *Le Charivari* (Paris: La Haye, 1981), 105–44.

2. Henry Rey-Flaud, *Le Charivari* (Paris: Payot, 1985), 89–103.

3. M. Delbouille, "Notes de philologie et de folklore: la légende de Herlekin," *Bulletin de langues et littératures wallones* 69 (1947): 105–44.

4. Chaillou de Pestain in Gervais du Bus, *The Roman de Fauvel,* 2 volumes (Paris: Ed. A. Langfors, Firmin Didot, 1914–1919), SATF.

5. Research into the abbeys for youth, specialists of the nightly *magnum tumultum* should be further undertaken as well. See also I. Taddei, *Fêtes, Jeunesse et Pouvoirs. L'Abbaye des Nobles Enfants de Lausanne* (Lausanne: University of Lausanne, 1991), *Cahiers lausannois d'histoire médiévale* 5, 55.

6. C. Marcel-Dubois, "Village Festivals and Ceremonial Commotion or a Music and its Opposite," in *Les Fêtes de la Renaissance,* vol. 3 (Paris: CNRS, 1975), 603–15, here 613.

7. P. Saintyves, *Essais de folklore biblique. Magie, mythes et miracles dans l'Ancien et le Nouveau Testament* (Paris: n.p., 1922), 423–63.

8. Patrice Uhl, "Hellequin et Fortune: le trajet d'un couple emblématique," 88.

9. Ibid.

10. J. H. Grisward, "Les fées, l'aurore et la Fortune," in *Mélanges A. Manly* (Nancy: n.p., 1980), 121–36.

11. N. Freeman Regalado, "Masques réels dans le monde de l'imaginaire, Le rite

et l'écrit dans le charivari du Roman de Fauvel, BNF ms 146," in *Masques et Déguisements dans la littérature mediévale* (Montreal: University of Montreal Press, 1988), 116–26.

12. For the following, I used R. Wolfram's study, "Robin Hood und Hobby Horse," in *Festschrift für R. Much, Wiener prähistorisches Zeitschrift* 19 (1932): 357–74.

13. See Philippe Walter, "Der Bär und der Erzbischof: Masken und Mummenschanz bei Hinkmar von Reims und Adalbero von Laon," in D. Altenberg, J. Jarnot, H. H. Steinhoff, *Feste und Feiern im Mittelalter* (Sigmaringen: Jan Thorbecke, 1991), 376–88.

14. See P. Nilsson, "Studien zur Vorgeschichte des Weihnachtsfestes," *Archiv für Religionswissenschaft* 19 (1916): 50–150.

15. M. Meslin, *La Fête des calendes de janvier dans l'Empire romain* (Brussels: Collection Latomus REL, 1970), 115, 79.

16. W. Mannhardt, *Die Götter der deutschen und nordischen Völker* (Berlin: n.p., 1860), 108–31.

17. F. Liebrecht, *Des Gervasius von Tilbury Otia imperialia* (Hanover: n.p., 1856), 173–211.

18. Lecouteux, *Au-delà du merveilleux*, 167–77.

19. See F. Schneider, "Über Kalendae Ianuariae und Martiae im Mittelalter," *Archiv für Religionswissenschaft* 20 (1920/21): 360–410.

20. See what Mircea Eliade says about the relationship between sexuality and plant life, and the representatives of plants: *Traité d'histoire des religions* (Paris: Payot, 1949, 267–70. Translated into English by Rosemary Sheed as *Patterns of Comparative Religion* (Lincoln: University of Nebraska Press, Bison Books, 1996).

21. O. Driesen, *Der Ursprung des Harlekin, ein kulturgeschichtliches Problem* (Berlin: n.p., 1904), 143–51.

22. Ibid., 72–79.

23. Text in K. Meisen, *Die Sagen vom Wütenden Heer und wilden Jäger*, 124.

24. Ibid., 127.

25. Chrétien de Troyes, *Œuvres complètes* (Paris: Gallimard, Bibl. de la Pléiade, 1994), 408. In the note on this passage (1398), Anne Berthelot commits a serious error when she makes the king of the alders—Erlkönig, whom she transforms into Erla-König—the leader of the Wild Hunt, which was already the result of an error that German poets (including Goethe) made on Olav, the name of the hero of a Scandinavian ballad.

26. Text in K. Meisen, *Die Sagen vom Wütenden Heer und wilden Jäger*, 131.

27. Ibid., 103.

28. Ibid., 122.
29. Jean Chartier, *Chronique de Charles VII, roi de France.*
30. Doris Ruhe, *Gelehrtes Wissen, Aberglauben und pastorale Praxis im französischen spätmittelalter Der Second Lucidaire und seine Rezeption,* 14–17. (Wiesbaden: n.p., 1993), 115.
31. Text in K. Meisen, *Die Sagen vom Wütenden Heer und wilden Jäger,* 80.
32. Ibid., 73.
33. Ibid., 128.
34. Ibid., 33 and 135.
35. Ibid., 139*ff.*
36. Gervais du Bus, *Charivari in quo utuntur larvis in figura daemonum. Fauvel,* 108.
37. See O. Höfler, *Kultische Geheimbünde der Germanen* (Frankfurt: M. Diesterweg, 1934), 101; K. Ranke, "Das wilde Heer," 390.
38. See Gervais du Bus, *Fauvel,* Luck 30.
39. Paris, Bibliothèque nationale, fonds français, 146, folio 34v°.
40. Claude Gaignebet, *Le Carnaval. Essai de mythologie populaire* (Paris: Payot, 1974).

Chapter 13. The Wild Hunt in Scandinavia

1. *Hoskelreia* in the Telemark, Aust-Ager, and Vest-Adger, *Joleskreidi* in the Sogn and the Fjordane, *Jolesveinane* in Valdres and Lussi in the Rogaland. See Christine N. F. Eike, "Oskoreia og ekstaseriter," 237–309, maps, 242 and 247.
2. Some other geographical variants on Imridn are Immerkølludn and Imbreford, see Eike, Ibid., 250.
3. Ibid., 239–41 and 294*ff.*
4. See Lecouteux, *Witches, Werewolves, and Fairies,* 168–76.
5. Olaus Magnus, *Historia de gentis septentrionalibus* XVIII, 45 (Rome: n.p., 1555), 642. This testimony can also be found in *Der vielförmig e Hinzelmann* (Leipzig: n.p., 1704). appendix, 38.
6. Ibid.
7. *I Nat, da du sov, var Jeg med og drak av dit Øl.* Ibid., 295.
8. A. Lecoy de la Marche, *Anecdotes historiques, légendes et prologues tirés du recueil inédit d'Étienne de Bourbon, dominicain du XIIᵉ siècle* (Paris, n.p., 1877, n° 97.
9. Ibid.
10. Ibid.

11. In one of the texts cited by Eike ("Oskoreia og ekstaseriter," 234), a man named Knut Nottovsson arrives riding a stake (*kom ridande på ein staur*).

12. See B. Holbeck, I. Piø, *Fabeldyr og sagnfolk* (Copenhagen: Politikens Forlag, 1967), s.v. *Knarkvognen*. The phenomenon is connected to the Wild Hunt and the nightjar (*caprimulgus*), a kind of lark. It is said they are the souls of the damned condemned to fly over the earth.

13. See the etymological discussion of O. Sandaaker, "Asgard og Oskorei," *Maal og Minne*, 1998, 63–73.

14. F. Ström, "Tidrandes död. Till frägen om makternas demonisering," *Arv 7* (1952): 77–119, especially 98–115.

15. Ibid.

16. Snorri Sturluson, *Sturlunga Saga*.

17. Ström, "Tidrandes död. Till frägen om makternas demonisering," 77–119.

Chapter 14. The Passage of the Wild Hunt

1. While express reference has not been made to it, I have been using: H. Bächtold-Stäubli, *Handwörterbuch des deutschen Aberglaubens*, 10 volumes (Berlin: n.p., 1927–1942). We can find a considerable amount of information when we consult this work regarding with the name of the festival or saint concerned, for example, Lichtmeß (Candlemass), V, 1261–72; Martin, V, 1708–15; Lucia, V, 1442–46, and so forth.

2. *12te natt för Jul: 11 dagar fyre jol; tri dagar fyre jol.* We can find interesting material in E. Birkeli, *Huskult og hinsidghestro* (Oslo: n.p., 1944), 120–23 and 163–65.

3. See Renward Cysat's *Chronica* in K. Meisen, *Die Sagen vom wütenden Heer und wilden Jäger*, Munster: Aschendorffsche, 1935), 116.

4. See also C. Macherel, "Un purgatoire alpin (Loetschental)," *Le Monde alpin et rhodanien* (Grenoble: Centre Alpin et Rhodanien d'Ethnologie, 1988), 87–112.

5. *Mortui e tumuli ad balneum et epulos invitant;* Lascius, *De diis Samagitarum* 43 (Vilnius: n.p., 1969).

6. Bächtold-Stäubli, II, 1234–61, "Fasten; Fastenzeit, Fastnacht," and III, 115–20, "Fronfasten."

7. See also M. Eliade, *Traité d'histoire*, 334.

8. See Emile Jobbé-Duval, *Les Morts malfaisants, larvae, lemurs, d'après le droit et les croyances populaires romains* (Paris: Librairie de la Societé du Recueil Sirey, 1924), 166. For more on the *dies parentales*, see page 2.

9. Michel Jonval, *Les Chansons mythologiques lettones* (Paris: Picard, 1929), n°1163, see also 1164 and 1170.

10. *In mense Februario hibernum credi expellere;* M. Eliade, *Traité d'histoire*, 268–71.

11. See Philippe Joutet, *L'Aurore celtique*, 104.

12. E. Smedes, "De keltische achtergrond van het lied van Heer Hallewijn," *De Giids* (August 1946): 70–94. For more on the corpus, see H. O. Nygard, *The Ballad of Heer Halloween. Its Forms and Variations in Western Europe. A Study of the History and Nature of a Ballad Tradition* (Helsinki: n.p., 1958), FFC 169.

13. It is well worth reading L. Kretzenbacher's excellent study *Santa Lucia und die Lutzelfrau* (Munich: Verlag R. Oldenbourg, 1959), Südosteurop. Arbeiten 53.

14. For more on the feast of the dead in ancient Iran, see E. Mudrak, "Das wütende Heer," 16.

15. See E. Smedes, "De keltische achtergrond," *De Giids*, 71.

16. Philippe Walter, *Christianity: Origins of a Pagan Religion* (Rochester, Vt.: Inner Traditions, 2006), 74.

17. See Claude Gaignebet, *A plus haut sens: l'ésotérisme spirituel et charnel de Rabelais* (Paris: n.p., 1989), 279–304.

Chapter 15. Scholars and the Tradition

1. J. Grimm, *Deutsche Mythologie*, vol. 2, 766–93; vol. 3, 280–84.

2. J. W. Wolf, *Beiträge zur deutschen Mythologie* II (Göttingen: n.p., 1857), 135.

3. L. Weniger, "Feralis exercitus," *Archiv für Religionswissenschaft* 9 (1906): 201–47.

4. Julius Lippert, *Die Religionen der europäische Kulturvölker* (Berlin: n.p., 1881), 154.

5. W. Golther, *Handbüch der germanischen Mythologie* (Leipzig: n.p., 1895), 283–95.

6. L. Laistner, *Das Rätsel der Sphinx. Grundzüge einer Mythengeschichte* (Berlin: n.p., 1889), vol. 2, 224–50.

7. Hans Plischke, *Die Sage vom Wilden Heere im deutschen Volke*, dissertation (Leipzig: 1914).

8. A. Endter, *Die Sage vom wilden Jäger und von der wilden Jägd. Studien über den deutschen Dämonenglauben*, dissertation (Frankfurt: 1933).

9. E. Mudrak, *Das wütende Heer und der wilde Jäger* (Berlin: Walter de Gruyter, 1937), Bausteine zur Geschichte, Völkerkunde und Mythenkunde 6.

Summarized in E. Mudrak, "Die Herkunft vom wütenden Heer und vom wilden Jäger," *Laographia* 4.

10. Geza Roheim, *Les Portes du rêve* (Paris: Payot, 1973), 521–33. This work is liberally scattered with egregious mistranslations: page 524, *upp und darvan* means "let's depart," not "let us climb ever higher"; page 526, Hosenflecker is a person who "soils pants," not one who "mends pants."

11. K. Meisen, *Nikolauskult und Nikolausbrauch im Abendlande* (Dusseldorf: Schwann, 1931), 457.

12. Ibid., 454–62.

13. See also the account sheet of H. M. Flasdieck's studies, "Harlekin, germanischer Mythos in romanischer Wandlung," *Anglia* 61 (1937): 225–340, here 265–82.

14. Ibid.

15. For example, *Dictionnaire étymologique et historique de la langue française* (Paris: Livre de Poche, 8089, 1996), 45, s.v. Arlequin; Chrétien de Troyes, *Œuvres complètes,* (Paris: Gallimard, La Pléiade 408, 1994), 1,398.

16. Otto Höfler, *Kultische Geheimbünde der Germanen,* vol. 1 (Frankfurt: n.p., 1934).

17. Ibid.

18. Flasdieck, "Harlekin," *Anglia* 61, 289–93.

19. H.-P. Hasenfratz, "Der indo-germanische Männerbund. Ammerkungen zur religiösen und sozialen Bedeutung des Jugendalters," *Zeitschrift für Religions- und Geistesgeschichte* 34 (1982): 143–63.

20. See also V. Risco, "La Procesiòn de las ànimas y las premoniciones de muerte," *Revista de Dialectolog'a y Tradiciones Populares* 2 (1946): 380–429, here 423–25.

21. Se also Eike, "Oskoreia og ekstaseriter," 229–309.

22. F. Ranke, "Das wilde Heer und die Kultbünde der Germanen. Eine Auseinandersetzung mit Otto Höfler," reprinted in Friedrich Ranke, *Kleinere Schriften,* eds. H. Rupp and E. Studer (Bern, Munich: n.p., 1971). German Library 12, 380–408.

23. K. Meisen, *Die Sagen vom Wütenden Heer und wilden Jäger,* 53.

24. K. Gärtner and W. J. Hartmann, eds., *Diu urstende,* (Tübingen: n.p., 1989), ATB 99, verses 176–89,

25. K. Meisen, *Die Sagen vom Wütenden Heer und wilden Jäger,* 56*ff.*

26. Ibid., 72.

Chapter 16. The Indo-European Roots of the Wild Hunt

1. See Lecouteux, *The Return of the Dead.*

2. Elisabeth Liebl, *Atlas der schweizerischen Volkskunde,* 761; 772–75; 778*ff.*

3. *Der Türscht jagt; S macht der Türscht jagt.* Text in K. Meisen, *Die Sagen vom Wütenden Heer und wilden Jäger,* 65*ff.*

4. Ibid., 71.

5. Ibid., 89.

6. Ibid., 110, 114, 134.

7. Ibid., 115.

8. Ibid., 119.

9. Renward Cysat, *Der heutige Volksglaube und das alte Heidentum* (Berlin: Programm des Friedrich Werderschen Gymnasuiums, 1850).

10. J. Gonda, *Les Religions de l'Inde* I: *Védisme et Hindouisme anciens* (Paris: Payot, 1962), 80.

11. Régis Boyer, *L'Edda poétique* (Paris: Payot, 1992), 287, strophe 28.

12. S. Wikander, *Der arische Männerbund* (Lund: n.p., 1938), 74.

13. Georges Dumézil, *Les Dieux des Indo-Européens* (Paris: PUF, 1952), 8.

14. J. Gonda, *Les Religions,* vol. 1, 111.

15. Jan de Vries, *Contributions to the Study of Othin, Especially in His Relation to Agricultural Practices in Modern Popular Lore* (Helsingfors: FFC, 1931), FFC 94.

16. Adam of Bremen, *Gesta* IV, 26.

17. H.-P. Hasenfratz, "Der indogermanische Männerbund," 154.

18. See Claude Lecouteux, "Kopflose," in K. Ranke et. al., *Enzyklopädie des Märchens* (Berlin, New York: Walter de Gruyter, 1981), vol. 8, col. 270–73.

19. K. Ranke, "Das wilde Heer und die Kultbünde der Germanen," 386.

20. H.-P. Hasenfratz, "Der indogermanische," *Männerbund,* 152.

21. See L. Freytag, "Das Pferd im germanischen Volksglauben," in *Festschrift zum 50 jährigen Jubiläum des Friedrich-Realgymansiums* (Berlin: n.p., 1900), 1–79, here 47–50.

22. E. Liebl, *Atlas,* 773.

23. Ibid., 779.

24. See J. Kuoni, *Sagen des Kantons Sankt-Gallen* (Saint-Gall: n.p., 1903), 78*ff.,* 250*ff.*

25. Colmar, Unterlinden Museum.

26. For more on the relationship of the horse and the dead, see J. von Negelein, "Das Pferd im Seelenglauben und Totenkult," *Zeitschrift für Volkskunde*

11 (1901): 406–20; *Zeitschrift für Volkskunde* 12 (1902): 14–25, 377–90; L. Malten, "Das Pferd im Totenglauben," *Jahrbuch des deutschen archäologischen Institut* 29 (1914): 179–225.

27. See Sylvie Althaus, *Die gotländischen Bildsteine, ein Programm* (Göppingen: Beck, 1993), G.A.G. 588.

28. E. L. Rochholz, *Schweizersagen aus dem Aargau,* 2 volumes (Aarau: n.p., 1856), vol. 2, 21.

29. I. M. Thiele, *Danmarks folkesagn,* 3 volumes (Copenhagen: n.p., 1843–1860), vol. 1, 138.

30. See also U. Müller, *Sagen aus Uri,* vol. 2, 89 (°602). You will also discover there a revenant that is half man and half horse (°603).

31. M. R. James, ed., "Twelve Medieval Ghost Stories," *English Historical Review* 37 (1922): 413–22, N°1 and 7.

32. L. Malten, "Das Pferd im Totenglauben."

33. Such as the English "horse," the German *Roß,* and the Norwegian *hross.*

34. A. Eskeröd, *Årets äring. Etnologiska studier i skördens och julens tro och sed* (Stockholm: Natur & Cultur, 1947), 115.

35. Lecouteux, *The Return of the Dead,* 189–92.

36. M. Eliade, *Traité d'histoire,* 295*ff.*

37. N. Gryse, *Spegel des antichristlichen Pawestdoms* (Rostock: n.p., 1593); text in K. Meisen, *Die Sagen vom Wütenden Heer und wilden Jäger,* 121.

38. M. Crusius, *Annales Suevici* vol. 3 (Frankfurt: n.p., 1596), chapter 18, 654.

39. J. Prätorius, *Saturnalia* (Leipzig: n.p., 1663), 403.

40. Höfler, *Kultische,* 286.

41. Lecouteux, *Witches, Werewolves, and Fairies,* 68*ff.;* M. Bertolotti, "Le Ossa e la pelle dei buoi: un mito popolare tra agiografica e stregonaria," *Quaderni Storici* 41 (1979): 470–99.

42. E. Mudrak, "Das wütende Heer," 16*ff.*

Chapter 17. Two Hypotheses

1. See K. Liestøl, *Draumkvæde,* 70*ff.*

2. Ibid., 121.

3. J. de Vries, *Altergermanische Religionsgeschichte,* 2 volumes (Berlin: n.p.,1957), 326.

4. Johannes Locenius, "Reisen," *Suebo-Gotland Antiquities,* 126.

5. Ibid., 131*ff.*

6. Ibid., 133*ff.*

7. Johann Peter Schmitt, 1742.

8. de Vries, *Altergermanische Religionsgeschichte,* 102.

9. Flörke, *Freimuthiges Abendblatt,* May 18, 1832.

10. F. G. C. Pogge, *Fremuthiges Abendblatt,* October 25, 1832.

11. V. Risco, "La Procesiòn de las ànimas y las premoniciones de muerte," *Revista de Dialectolog'a y Tradiciones Populares* 2, 423–25.

12. *Zimmerische Chronik,* vol. 4, 119.

13. See also V. Meyer-Matheis, *Die Vorstellung eines Alter Ego in Volkserzählungen,* dissertation, (Friburg-im-Brisgau: 1974), 14.

14. Ibid., appendix, n°25.

15. Ibid., 12–15; appendix, n°19–21, 34.

16. Ibid., 17.

17. P. Ménard, "Une parole rituelle dans la chevauchée fantastique de la Mesnie Hellequin," *Littératures* 9–10 (1984): 2–11, here 7.

18. Eike, "Oskoreia og ekstaseriter," 265–73.

19. Risco, "La Procesión de las animas," *Revista de Dialectolog'a y Tradiciones Populares* 2, 412.

21. Lecouteux, *Witches, Werewolves, and Fairies,* 195–203.

Appendix 1. For Protection Against Spirits of the Night

1. Claude Lecouteux, "Der Bilwiz," *Euphorion* 82 (1988): 238–50.

2. See Luke 18, 43.

3. Psalms 3, 5.

4. Psalms 129, 1.

5. See II Macchabees 6, 11.

6. Luke 2, 29 (Kantisme Simeonis).

7. Luke 1, 68.

Appendix 2. The Wild Hunt in Constance

1. Cysat, *Collectanea Cronica,* vol. E, folio 333a–334a; text cited by K. Meisen, *Die Sagen vom Wütenden Heer und wilden Jäger,* 116–19.

Appendix 3. No One Escapes His Fate

1. *Zimmern Chronicle,* ed. Barack, vol. 4, text in K. Meisen, *Die Sagen vom Wütenden Heer und wilden Jäger,* 109–11.

Appendix 4. The Society of the Bone

1. Risco, "La Procesión de las animas," *Revista de Dialectolog'a y Tradiciones Populares* 2, 423–25.

Appendix 5. The Coach of the Diabolical Huntsman

1. D Hyde, *Gaelic Stories*, trans. Georges Dottin, *Contes gaéliques* (Monaco: Rocher, 1995), 133–37, here 134*ff.*

Appendix 6. The Names of the Wild Hunt and Its Leader

1. See Claude Seignolle, *Les Évangiles du diable* (Paris: Robert Laffont, 1967), 612*ff.;* Paul Sébillot, *Le Folklore de France,* vol. 1, 166–78; Patrice Boussel, *Guide de la Bourgogne et du Lyonnais mystérieux* (Paris: Tchou, 1974), 31*ff.;* Bernard Duhourcau, *Guide des Pyrénees mystérieuses* (Paris: Tchou, 1973), 14*ff.;* René Alleau, *Guide de Fontainebleau mystérieux* (Paris: Tchou, 1967), 153–59, on the great huntsman.

2. Vol. 1, 45*ff.,* names of fantastic hunts; vol. 3, 141, Herbault article; vol. 5, 25, 153*ff.*

3. See index of *Mythologie française* 141 (1986): 11, see "hunt" and references.

4. See F. Sieber, "Dietrich von Bern als Führer der wilden Jagd," *Mitteilungen der schlesischen Gesellschaft für Volkskunde* 31–32 (1931): 85–124.

5. Edition H Oesterly, Berlin, 1872, reprinted Hildesheim, 1980.

6. For all these names, see Risco, "La Procesión de las animas," *Revista de Dialectolog'a y Tradiciones Populares* 2, 389–95.

Bibliography

Studies

Althaus, S. *Die gotländischen Bildsteine, ein Programm.* Göppingen, G.A.G. 588, 1993.

Alver, B. "Dauinggudstenesta, ein europeisk førestellingskrins i norsk tradisjon." *Arv* 6 (1950).

Behringer, Wolfgang. *Chonrad Stoecklin und die Nachtschar. Eine Gechsichte aus der frühen Neuzeit.* Munich: Piper, 1994. Translated by H. C. Erik Midelfort as *Shaman of Oberstdorf, Chonrad Stoecklin and the Phantoms of the Night.* Charlottesville: University Press of Virginia, 1998.

Beitl, K. "Die Sagen vom Nachtvolk. Untersuchung eines alpinen Sagentypus." *Laographia* 4 (1965).

Benoît, L. "Th. Körner et la Chasse sauvage." *Antaios* 12 (1997).

———. " Compère Guilleri: une reminiscence de la Chasse sauvage." *Antaios* 12 (1997).

Birkeli, E. *Huskult og hinsidghestro.* Oslo: Skrifter utgivt av Det Norske Videnbskaps-Akademi, 1944.

Bø, O. *Vår norske jul. Det Norske Samlaget.* Oslo: n.p., 1970.

Bonomo, G. *Caccia alle streghe.* Palermo: Palumbo, 1985.

Bouet, "La Mesnie Hellequin." In *Mélanges Kerlouégan.* Besançon, Paris: Les Belles Lettres, 1994.

Bringsvoerd, T. A. *Phantoms and Fairies from Norwegian Folklore.* Oslo: Tanum-Norli, 1979.

Büchli, Arnold. "Wilde Jagd und Nachtvolk." *Schweizerische Volkskunde* 37 (1947).

Carozzi, C. *Le Voyage de l'âme dans l'au-délà d'après la literature latine (Ve–XIIe siècles),* Rome: Collection de l'École française de Rome 189, 1994.

Celander, H. "Gravso och Gloso," *Arv* 8 (1952).

David, Charles. "Le Grand Veneur ou le Chasseur Noir," *Bulletin de liaison des Associés franciliens de la Société de Mythologie française* 15 (1996).

Deneke, B. *Legende und Volkssage. Untersuchungen zur Erzählung vom Geistergottesdienst,* dissertation. Frankfurt: 1958.

Dinzelbacher, P. *Angst im Mittelalter. Teufels-, Todes und Gotteserfahrung: Mentalitätsgeschichte und Ikonographie.* Paderborn: Schöningh, 1996.

Dreisen, O. *Der Ursprung des Harlekin.* Berlin: n.p., 1996.

Dufournet, J. *Adam de la Halle à la recherche de lui-même ou le Jeu de la feuillée.* Paris: SEDES, 1974.

Eike, Christine N. F. "Oskoreia og ekstaseriter." *Norveg* 23 (1980).

Eliade, Mircea. *Traité d'histoire des religions.* Paris: Payot, 1949. Translated by Rosemary Sheed as *Patterns of Comparative Religion.* Lincoln: University of Nebraska Press (Bison Books), 1996.

Ellekilde, Hans. "Odinjægeren paa Møn." in *Nordiskt Folkminne Studier tillägnade C. W. von Sydow.* Stockholm: n.p., 1928.

Endter, A. *Die Sage vom wilden Jäger und von der wilden Jägd. Studien über den deutschen Dämonenglauben,* dissertation, Frankfurt: 1933.

Eskeröd, A. *Arets äring. Ethnologiska studier I skördens och julens tro och sed.* Stockholm: Nordiska Museet, 1947.

Ferrand, B. L. *Le Grand Veneur ou Chasseur noir de la forêt de Fontainebleau.* Paris: Librairie d'Argences, 1979.

Feilberg, H. F. "Der Kobold in nordischer berlieferung." *Zeitschrift des Vereins für Volkskunde* 8 (1898).

Flasdieck, H. M. "Harlekin, Germanischer Mythos in romanischer Wandlung." *Anglia* 61 (1937).

Gallais, P. *La Fée à la fontaine et à l'arbre: un archétype du conte merveilleux et du récit courtois.* Amsterdam: CERMEIL 1, 1922.

Von Geramb, V. "Die verwunschene Pfarrerköchin." *Blätter für Heimatkunde* 22 (1948).

———. "Zum Sagenmotiv von Hufbeschlag." *Beiträge zur sprachlichen Volksüberlieferung,* Berlin: Akademie Verlag, 1953.

Gérard, C. "Feralis exercitus." *Antaios* 12 (1997).

Ginzburg, Carlo. "Charivari, association juvénile et chasses sauvages." In Jacques Le Goff, Jean- Claude Schmitt. *Le Charivari.* Paris: La Haye, New York: Mouton, 1981.

———. *Les batailles nocturnes.* Paris: Flammarion, 1993. Translated as *The Night*

Battles: Witchcraft and Agrarian Cults in the Sixteenth & Seventeenth Centuries. Baltimore: Johns Hopkins University Press, 1992.

Gonda, J. *Les Religions de l'Inde* 1: *Védisme et Hindouisme anciens.* Paris: Payot, 1962.

Grambo, Ronald. "Balladen om Hakje og bergermannen." *Arv* 28 (1972).

———. "Julen I Middelaldern. Hedenskap og kristendom." *Mittelalter Forum* 1 (1996).

———. *Gjester fra Graveren. Norske spøkelsers liv og virke.* Oslo: Ex Libris, 1991.

Grimm, Jacob. *Deutsche Mythologie,* 3 volumes. Berlin: n.p., 1878. Reprinted Darmstadt: WBG, 1965.

Grisward, J. H. "Les Fées, l'Aurore et la Fortune. Mythologie indo-européenne et *Jeu de la feuillée.*" In *Mélanges A. Lanly.* Nancy: Université de Nancy1980.

Hachet, P. *Les Origines germaniques de la Mesnie Hellequin,* dissertation, Grenoble: 1994.

Harmening, D. *Superstitio.* Berlin: E. Schmidt Verlag, 1979.

Hasenfratz, Hans-Peter. "Der indogermanische Männerbund." *Zeitschrift für Religion und Geistesgeshichte* 34 (1982).

Haudry, Jean. *La religion cosmique des Indo-Européens.* Milan: Arché, 1987.

Hell, Bertrand. *Le sang noir: Chasse et mythe du sauvage en Europe.* Paris: Flammarion, 1994.

Höfler, Otto. *Kultische Geheimbünde der Germanen.* Frankfurt: n.p., 1934.

Jobbé-Duval, Emile. *Les Morts malfaisants, larvae, lemures, d'après le droit et les croyances populaires romains.* Paris: Librairie de la Societé du Recueil Sirey, 1924.

Joisten, Alice, C. Abry. *Etres fantastiques des Alpes.* Paris: Éditions Entente, 1995.

Joisten, Charles, C. Abry ."Du Roi chasseran au Récheran scieur des têtes: un avatar de la Chasse sauvage en Savoie." Ernest Schulle. *Mélanges.* Bern: n.p., 1983.

Jolicoeur, Catherine. *Le Vaisseau Fantôme, légende étiologique.* Quebec: Les Presses de l'Université Laval, 1970.

Jouet, Philippe. *L'Aurore celtique. Fonctions du héros dans la religion cosmique.* Paris: Porte-glaive, 1993.

Karlinger, Felix. *Zauberschlaf und Entrückung. Zur Problematik der Jenseitszeit in der Volkserzählung.* Vienna: n.p., 1936.

Karlinger, F., J. Pögl. *Totentanz und Fronleichnamsspiel: Farsa llamada dança de la muerte von Juan de Pedraza.* Salzburg: Lib. Hispano-Lusa 1, 1992.

Kellner, Beate. *Grimms Mythen. Studien zum Mythosbegriff und seiner Anwendung in Jacob Grimms Deutscher Mythologie.* Frankfurt, N.Y.: n.p., 1994. Mikrokosmos, 41.

Koopmans, J. *Le Théâtre des exclus au Moyen Age: hérétiques, sorcières et marginaux.* Paris: Imago, 1997.

Kretzenbacher, L. *Santa Lucia und die Lutzelfrau.* Munich: Südosterup, Arbeiten 53, 1959.

Krogmann, K. "Harlekins Herkunft." *Volkstum und Kultur der Romanen* 13 (1940).

Laistner, L. *Das Rätsel der Sphinx. Grundzüge einer Mythengeschichte.* Berlin: Wilhelm Hertz, 1889.

Lecouteux, Claude. *Dictionnaire de Mythologie Germanique,* Paris: Eds. Imago, 2006.

———. *Mondes parallèles: l'univers des croyances du Moyen Age.* Paris: Honoré Champion, 2007.

———. *Au-délà du merveilleux.* Paris: P.U.P.S., 1995.

———. *Geschichte der Gespenster und Wiedergänger im Mittelalter.* Cologne and Vienna: Böhlau Verlag, 1987.

———. *Witches, Werewolves, and Fairies: Shapeshifters and Astral Doubles in the Middle Ages.* Rochester, Vt.: Inner Traditions, 2003.

———. "Lamia." *Enzyklopädie des Märchens.* Berlin, New York: Walter de Gruyter, 1995.

———. "Lamia, holzmuowa, holzfrowe, lamîch." *Euphorion* 75 (1981).

———. *The Return of the Dead.* Rochester, Vt.: Inner Traditions, 2009.

———. *Les Nains et les Elfes au Moyen Age.* Paris: Eds. Imago, 1988, 2nd edition, 1997.

———. *Mélusine et le Chevalier au cygne.* Paris: Eds. Imago, 1997.

———. *Démons et Génies du terroir au Moyen Age.* Paris: Eds. Imago, 1995.

———. "Chasse sauvage/Armée furieuse: réflexions sur une légende germanique." *La Mesnie Hellequin.* Paris: Philippe Walter, 1997;

———. "Geiler de Kaisersberg et Das wütende Heer." *Etudes germaniques* 50 (1995).

Lecouteux, C., and Philippe Marcq. *Les esprits et les morts.* Paris: Honoré Champion, 1990. Essais 13.

———. *Berthold de Ratisbonne: péchés et vertus, scènes de la vie du XIIIᵉ siècle.* Paris: Desjonquères, 1992.

Lesourd, D. "Diane et les sorciers. Etude sur les survivances de Diane dans les langues romanes." *Anagrom* (1972).

Liebl, Elisabeth. "Geisterheere und ähnliche Erscheinungen." In Geiger, P., and R. Weiss, *Atlas der schweizerischen Volkskunde,* Kommentar, 2nd part. Basel: Schweizerische Gesellschaft für Volkskunde, 1971.

Liestøl, Knut. *Draumkvæde. A Norwegian Visionary Poem from the Middle Ages.* Oslo: Samlaget, 1946.

Luttrell, C. "Folk Legend as Source for Arthurian Romance: The Wild Hunt." In *Mélanges L. Thorpe.* Glasgow: University of Scotland, 1981.

Malten, L. "Das Pferd im Totenglauben." *Jahrbuch des deutschen archäologischen Institut* 29 (1914).

De Marliave, O. *Petit dictionnaire de mythologie basque et pyrénéenne.* Paris: Entente, 1993.

Meisen, K. *Die Sagen vom wüttenden Heer und wilden Jäger.* Münster: n.p., 1935.

———. *Nikolauskult und Nilolausbrauch im Abendlande.* Dusseldorf: n.p., 1931.

Ménard, Philippe. "Une parole rituelle dans la chevauchée fantastique de la Mesnie Hellequin." *Littératures* 9–10 (1984).

Meslin, Michel. *La Fête des calendes de janvier dans l'Empire romain.* Brussels: Collection Latomus REL, 1970.

Meyer-Matheis, V. *Die Vorstellung eines Alter Ego in Volkserzählungen,* dissertation. Freiburg-im-Brisgau: 1974.

Mourreau, J. J. "La Chasse sauvage, mythe exemplaire." *Nouvelle Ecole* 16 (1972).

Mudrak, Edmund. "Das wütende Heer und der wilde Jäger." *Bausteine zur Geschichte, Völkerkunde und Mythenkunde* 6 (1937).

———. "Die Herkunft vom wütenden Heer und vom Wilden Jäger," *Laographia* 4 (1965).

Müller, Ingeborg. "Der Tod und die Toten." *Deutsches Jahrbuch für Volkskunde* 13 (1967).

Negelein, J. Von, "Das Pferd im Seelenglauben und Totenkult." *Zeitschrift für Volkskunde* 11 (1901).

Nilson, M. P. "Studien zur Vorgeschichte des Weilnachtfestes." *Archiv für Religionswissenschaft* 19 (1916).

Nygard, H. O. *The Ballad of Heer Halloween. Its Forms and Variations in Western Europe. A Study of the History and Nature of a Ballad Tradition.* Helsinki: FFC 169, 1958.

Perez de Castro, J. L. "El Origien de la animas y su presencia en la etnografia del Eo (Asturias)." *Revista* 34 (1978).

Peschel, G. "Freunde im Leben und Tod." In K. Ranke et al. *Enzyklopädie des Märchens,* vol. 5. Berlin: Walter de Gruyter, 1987.

Petry, M. *Herne the Hunter.* Reading: William Smith, 1972.

Petzold, Leander. "Die Botschaft aus der Anderswelt." In *Märchen, Mythos, Sage, Beiträge zur Literatur und Volksdichtung.* Marburg: n.p., 1989.

————. *Der Tote als Gast. Volkssage und Exempel.* Helsinki: FFC 200, 1968.

Plischke, Hans. *Die Sage vom Wilden Heere im deutschen Volke,* dissertation. Leipzig: 1914.

Ranke, Fredrich. "Das wilde Heer und die Kultbünde der Germanen." In F. R. *Kleinere Schriften.* Edited by H. Rupp and E. Studer. Bern, Munich: Library Germanica 12, 1971.

Ranke, Kurt. *Indogermanische Totenverehrung I: Der dreissigste und vierzigste Tag im Totenkult der Germanen.* Helsinki: FFC 140, 1951.

Rey-Flaud, Henry. *Le Charivari. Les rituels fondamentaux de la sexualité.* Paris: Payot, 1985.

Risco, Vincente. "Creencias Gallegas. La procession de las animas y las premoniciones de muerte." *Revista de dialectología y tradiciones populares* 2 (1946).

Rörich, Lutz. "Herr de Tiere." In Kurt Ranke et. al. *Enzyklopädie des Märchens.* Berlin: Walter de Gruyter, 1990.

————. *Erzählungen des späten Mittelalters und ihr Weiterleben in Literatur und Volksdichtung bis zur Gegenwart.* Bern, Munich: Francke Verlag, 1966.

Romero, F. Alonso. "Los Origines del mito de la Santa Campaña de las isles de Ons u Salvatora." *Cuardernos de Estudios Gallegos* 32 (1981).

Roux, J. "Les chasses fantastiques en Limousin." *Revue des traditions populaires* 9 (1894).

Rühlemann, M. *Etymologie des Wortes "Harlekin" und verwandter Wörter,* dissertation. Halle: 1912.

Rumpf, Marianne. *Perchten, Populäre Glaubensgestalten zwischen Mythos und Katechese.* Wurtzburg: Quellen and Forrschungen zur europ. Ethnologie 12, 1991.

Sainéan, L. "La Mesnie Hellequin." *Revue des traditions populaires* 20 (1905).

Sandaaker, O. "Asgard og Oskorei." *Maal og Minne,* 1968.

Schmitt, Jean-Claude. "Temps, folklore et politique au XIIe siècle. A propos de deux récits de Walter Map." In *Le Temps chrétien de la fin d'Antiquité au Moyen Age.* Paris: Colloque du CNRS, no. 604, 1984.

Schneider, F. "Über die Kalendae Ianuariae und Martiae im Mittelalter." *Archiv für Religionswissenschaft* 20 (1920/1921).

Sébillot, Paul. *Le Folklore de France,* four volumes. Paris: Eds. Imago, 1988).

Seiler, J. *Die Armen Seelen in der Volkssage,* dissertation. Munich: 1957.

Sieber, F. "Dietrich von Bern als Führer der wilden Jagd." *Mitteilungen der schlesischen Gesellschaft für Volkskunde* 31–32 (1931).

Smedes, E. "De keltische achtergrond van het lied van Heer Hallewijn." *De Giids* (August 1946).

Spada, D. *La Caccia Selvaggia.* Milan: Barbarossa, 1994.

Stramoy, J. "Les Chasses fantastiques." *Revue des traditions populaires* 13 (1898).

Ström, Folke. "Tidrandes död. Till fragan om makternas demonisering." *Arv* 7 (1952).

Uhl, Patrice. "Hellequin et Fortune: le trajet d'un couple emblématique." *Perspectives médiévales* 15 (1989).

Vries, Jan de. *La Religion des Celtes.* Paris: Payot, 1963.

———. *Contributions to the Study of Othin, Especially in His Relation to Agricultural Practices in Modern Popular Lore.* Helsingfors: FFC 94, 1931.

———. *Altgermanische Religionsgeschichte,* 2 volumes. Berlin: Walter de Gruyter, 1957.

———. "Wodan und die wilde Jagd." *Die Nachbarn* 3 (1962).

Das Wallis vor der Geschichte: 14000 v. Chr.–47 nach Chr. Sitten: Kanton Museum, 1986.

Walter, Philippe. *Christianity: The Origins of a Pagan Religion.* Rochester, Vt.: Inner Traditions, 2006.

———. "Hellequin/Hennequin et le mannequin." In *La Mesnie Hellequin.* Paris: Philippe Walter 1997.

———, ed. *Mythe de la Chasse sauvage dans l'Europe médiévale.* Paris: Honore Champion, 1997. Essais 19.

Waschnitius, V. *Percht, Holda und verwandte Gestalten.* Vienna: Sitzungsberichte d. kaiserl. Akad. D. Wissenschaften, phil.-hist. Class 174, 1913.

Wolfram, R. "Robin Hood und Hobby Horse." *Festschrift für R. Much, Wiener prähistorisches Zeitschrift* 19 (1932).

Text Anthologies

A Collection of Highland Rites and Customes Copied by E. Lhuyd from the Manuscript of the Rev. James Kirwood (1600–1709). Cambridge: Cambridge University Press, 1975.

Bø, O., R. Grambo, H. Hodne, and Ø Hodne. *Norske segner i utval med inleiing og kommentar,* 2nd Ed., n°11–29. Oslo: n.p., 1995.

Du Bois, Louis. *Préjugés et Superstions en Normandie.* Paris: n.p., 1843.

Kuoni, J. *Sagen des Kantons Sankt-Gallen.* Saint-Gall: n.p., 1903.

Luk, G. *Rätische Alpensagen. Gestalten und Bilder aus der Sagenwelt Graubündens.* Coire: n.p., 1935.

Mackensen, L. *Niedersächsische Sagen.* Leipzig–Gohlis: Teil 2, 1925.

Martinet, L. *Le Berry préhistorique.* Paris: n.p., 1878.

Müller, U. *Sagen aus Uri,* vol. 2. Basel: n.p., 1929.

Neckel, G. *Sagen aus dem germanischen Altertum.* Darmstadt: n.p., 1964.

Rochholz, E. L. *Schweizersagen aus dem Aargau,* 2 volumes. Aarau: n.p., 1856.

Von Schönwerth, F. *Aus der Oberpfalz, Sitten und Sagen* 1. Augsburg: n.p., 1857.

Thiele, I. M. *Danmarks folkesagn,* 3 volumes. Copenhagen: n.p., 1843–1860.

Zingerle, I. V. *Innsbruck: Sagen, Märchen, und Gebräuche aus Tirol,* 1859.

Reference Works

Bächtold-Stäubli, H. *Handwörterbuch des deutschen Aberglaubens,* 10 volumes. Berlin: Walter de Gruyter, 1927–1942.

Clover, Carol. *Kulturhistoriskt lexicon für Nordisk Medeltid,* 21 vols. Malmö: n.p., 1982.

Müller, Ingeborg, Lutz Röhrich. "Der Tod und die Toten." *Deutsches Jahrbuch für Volkskunde* 13 (1967).

Petzold, L. *Kleines Lexikon der Dämonen und Elementargeister.* Munich: BsR 427, 1990.

Peuckert, W. E. *Handwörterbuch der Sage.* Göttingen: Vandenhoeck and Ruprecht, 1961–1963. Only three installments have appeared. S.v. Arme Seelen.

Ranke, Kurt, R. Brednich. *Enzyklopädie des Märchens.* Berlin, New York: Walter de Gruyter, 1977. This work is still in progress.

Thompson, S. *Motif-index of Folk Literature, A Classification of Narrative Elements in Folktales, Ballads, Myths, Fables, Medieval Romances, Exempla, Fabliaux, Jest Books, and Local Legends.* Helsinki: FFC 106–09, 1932–1936.

Tubach, Frederic C. *Index Exemplorum: A Handbook of Medieval Religious Tales.* Helsinki: Suomalainen Tiedeakatemia, 1969. FFC 204.

Index

Page numbers in *italics* refer to illustrations.

Books of Related Interest

The Secret History of Vampires
Their Multiple Forms and Hidden Purposes
by Claude Lecouteux

Witches, Werewolves, and Fairies
Shapeshifters and Astral Doubles in the Middle Ages
by Claude Lecouteux

The Return of the Dead
Ghosts, Ancestors, and the Transparent Veil of the Pagan Mind
by Claude Lecouteux

Monsters
A Bestiary of Devils, Demons, Vampires, Werewolves, and Other Magical
Creatures
by Christopher Dell

Barbarian Rites
The Spiritual World of the Vikings and the Germanic Tribes
by Hans-Peter Hasenfratz, Ph.D.

The Pagan Book of Days
A Guide to the Festivals, Traditions, and Sacred Days of the Year
by Nigel Pennick

Pagan Christmas
The Plants, Spirits, and Rituals at the Origins of Yuletide
by Christian Rätsch and Claudia Müller-Ebeling

A Druid's Herbal of Sacred Tree Medicine
by Ellen Evert Hopman

INNER TRADITIONS • BEAR & COMPANY
P.O. Box 388
Rochester, VT 05767
1-800-246-8648
www.InnerTraditions.com

Or contact your local bookseller